Reconstructing Reconstruction

RECONSTRUCTING RECONSTRUCTION

The Supreme Court and the Production of Historical Truth

Pamela Brandwein

DUKE UNIVERSITY PRESS   Durham and London   1999

© 1999 Duke University Press
All rights reserved
Printed in the United States of America on
acid-free paper ⊛   Typeset in Berkeley Medium
by Tseng Information Systems, Inc. Library of
Congress Cataloging-in-Publication Data appear
on the last printed page of this book.

To my parents, Lisa and Larry Brandwein

&

Vera and Ben

Contents

Acknowledgments   ix

1   Introduction   1

2   Slavery as an Interpretive Issue in the 39th Reconstruction
Congress: The Northern Democrats   23

3   Republican Slavery Criticism   42

4   The Supreme Court's Official History   61

5   Dueling Histories: Charles Fairman and William Crosskey
Reconstruct "Original Understanding"   96

6   Recipes for "Acceptable" History   132

7   History as an Institutional Resource: Warren Court Debates
over Legislative Apportionment   155

8   Constitutional Law as a "Culture of Argument": Toward a
Sociology of Constitutional Law   185

9   Conclusion   208

Notes   215

Bibliography   257

Index   267

Acknowledgments

As a sophomore at the University of Michigan, I took a course on civil liberties. William F. Harris was the teacher and this course set me off on the road that has led to this project. Will is a wonderful and really quite extraordinary teacher and, of course, by no means responsible for the content here.

In its previous life this book was my dissertation. There are not many dissertations in sociology that treat questions about civil rights but Arthur L. Stinchcombe offered wisdom, comprehensive criticism, and a willingness to read drafts many times over. Art has been influential in the lives and careers of many graduate students, and I consider myself extraordinarily lucky to count myself among them. Art tells me that I make an "odd" sort of sociologist, but I am better at it than I would have been without him as a teacher. The good words he has offered me over the years have uncommon value.

Kim Scheppele has been reading and commenting on my work since I was an undergraduate and I have reaped enormous benefits. In addition to pointing me in the direction of Art Stinchcombe, she provided a great deal of support as I pursued a set of questions that took me across disciplinary divides. Her criticism has consistently pushed me to the next level, and for that I am deeply grateful. Robert L. Nelson has offered a friendly and critical eye from the early days of this project. I thank him for his questions and encouragement and for his belief that my work should end up in print. I also want to express my gratitude to Arthur McEvoy. His remarks on dissertation chapters were absolutely precise, cutting sharply and cleanly to core matters.

As fortune would have it, earlier versions of several chapters landed on the desks of a number of unwitting people. Sanford Levinson and Howard Gillman read and commented on a previous version of the Fairman-Crosskey chapters, and I am extremely happy to have the opportunity to thank them in print for their remarks. Stanley Aronowitz, Mark Graber, and Ronald Kahn were discussants on panels (at annual meetings of various professional associations) on which I happened to be placed. All three responded with extremely helpful comments and encouraging words.

Special thanks is also due Michael Kent Curtis. I ran across his book quite by accident many years ago and it was this book that set this project in motion. His correspondence, which offered kind words and several helpful remarks on the Fairman-Crosskey material, marked the point at which this project came full circle.

Richard L. Aynes took the time to send me a set of detailed comments and reflections, also on the Fairman-Crosskey material. He took up my work with great care, and I am very appreciative. Michael Grossberg, Royce Hanson, Ted (Edward J.) Harpham, George Farkas, and Richard Scotch offered questions and feedback that benefited me as well.

I would also like to thank the anonymous reviewers at Duke University Press for their extensive reports, and Stanley Fish for his support for the project and his reading suggestions. I do not know if most authors learn a lot from the referees and editors at their publishing house, but I did. Thanks go to Bob Mirandon, too, for his copyediting. His queries and comments improved the clarity of my arguments in numerous instances.

The American Bar Foundation provided me with two years of doctoral support and I would like to express my thanks to them. Without the Doctoral Dissertation Fellowship, this project would have taken even longer to complete, and I would have been left with a steep debt. Every graduate student should be as lucky.

On the dissertation, Jacqueline Battalora offered a stream of questions, fine editorial skill, and a great deal of support. Amy Rosenbaum (nee Rosenzweig) read portions of chapters, gave valuable feedback, and helped me learn to write in English.

On the book, Erin Smith was generous enough to read two drafts of the introduction at the last minute. I have no doubt the rest of the chapters would have benefited from her consideration. She was also very kind in extending support as I experienced the horrors of computer meltdown (a virus in my book files) at the last stages of chapter formating.

Thanks, finally, go to Cafe Express South in Evanston, where I worked for years writing the dissertation, and La Madeleine in Dallas, where I worked for years turning the dissertation into this book. My patronage brought both establishments very little money, but instead of being shown the door I was always made to feel welcome.

1

Introduction

"Easily the most dramatic episode in American history," states W. E. B. DuBois, "was the sudden move to free four million black slaves in an effort to stop a great civil war, to end forty years of bitter controversy, and to appease the moral sense of civilization."[1] This book is about how that "great civil war" developed into a war of words, laws, and narrative histories, and how a victory in the battle of historical description affected constitutional decision-making. The period of Reconstruction following the Civil War saw the beginning of a long and continuing rhetorical contest among Northerners to define the nation's slavery and Reconstruction experience. Since Robert E. Lee's surrender at Appomattox, the halls of Congress, the federal courts, and law schools have been major sites in an ongoing contest to define Reconstruction history. The interpretation of Reconstruction has its own history, and I examine the practice of building and using that history in constitutional law. How did one version of Reconstruction come to overwhelm alternative versions, and what difference has this made?

The competition to interpret Reconstruction history involves issues of race, rights, and national identity. Had there been a single critique of slavery, a shared view about what it was in the slavery system that was "the problem," competing versions of Reconstruction history might never have arisen. In 1866, however, Republican and Northern Democratic congressmen diagnosed the threat of slavery differently. In the Reconstruction Congresses, they presented different versions of the slavery experience to support their views about which political and constitutional reforms were proper and best. For the Northern Democrats, the problem with slavery was the Southern demand for federal enforcement of slave law in the western territories. This demand violated the Democratic doctrine of popular sovereignty, which preserved for local majorities the right to decide the slavery question for themselves. In 1866, Northern Democrats conceded federally imposed formal emancipation as an issue of war. In their view formal emancipation defined the destruction of slavery and marked the resolution of the slavery problem. Republicans saw slavery's threats more broadly. The problems with slavery included slavery's destruction of white men's civil liberties, its stagnating economic effects, and the accretion of illegitimate political power to the aristocratic, slaveholding elite. Republicans argued that formal emancipation and Southern renunciation of the secession right did not mark the "closing off" of the slavery problem.

When the Supreme Court interpreted the Reconstruction Amendments in the 1870s, it endorsed crucial elements of Northern Democratic perspectives on slavery, even though the Democrats voted against these amendments. The Court acknowledged new federal power to prohibit slave law, something Republican in origin, but the Court presented individual ownership of self as the definition of slavery's destruction, a Northern Democratic definition. In addition, the Court's definition of slavery's destruction (formal emancipation only) rested on a Northern Democratic version of the war's issues. The Supreme Court limited its version of these issues to the grounds that Northern Democrats employed to distinguish themselves from Southern slaveholders. The Court's version of the slavery/war experience contained some Republican elements but made no mention of the Republicans' political critique of slavery (that slavery destroyed civil liberties) or the Republicans' "free labor" concerns for labor independence and opportunity. The Court in its version of slavery and Reconstruction history reduced the dimensions of slavery politics.

In the 1950s a famous scholarly debate between Charles Fairman and William Crosskey over the original understanding of the Fourteenth Amendment helped validate and justify the Court's version of the war's issues and the Court's corresponding definition of slavery's destruction. In the 1960s this dominant version of war/slavery history worked to render Warren Court expansions of rights vulnerable to the criticism that they were the products of politics, not law. In other words, this institutional version of Reconstruction history provided "objective" ammunition for critics of Warren Court expansions of rights in the 1960s.

My goal, then, is to examine the creation of historical "truths" about Reconstruction and the ways that these truths are taken up by actors in a variety of social institutions for a variety of purposes. By tracing the production and use of the dominant history of Reconstruction, I provide a rhetorical tool (an account of the production of "credible" Reconstruction history) that would be useful to Warren Court defenders. This book focuses on crucial moments in American legal history: the Reconstruction debates, famous Reconstruction era Supreme Court decisions, and the Fairman-Crosskey debate. The book's chapters are organized chronologically so that the process of this history's production—as built mostly by Northern Democratic congressmen in 1866, reconstituted by the Supreme Court in the 1870s, and validated by Charles Fairman in the 1950s—may be followed. The last substantive chapter examines the impact of this history on Warren Court arguments about legislative apportionment.

My point of departure is the understanding that descriptions of events are contested ground.[2] Official versions of events are now heavily scrutinized in academic scholarship and alternative versions are offered in their place, but the rhetorical contest through which "authoritative" accounts are created has not yet come under investigation. There are few studies of how particular versions of events beat out their competition and gain truth status. Additionally, little research has been done on the social and historical circumstances that give rise to prevailing legal orthodoxies. Because no "scientific" or neutral criteria exist for verifying historical accounts, the process by which historical knowledge gains "truth" status is a subject for sociological analysis. The very existence of competition to describe events suggests the need to understand trajectories of credibility, that is, the conditions and circumstances under which the institutional acceptability of historical accounts is won and lost. Further, how is the status of such an institutional history linked to the life of the institution?

I study the production of historical meaning *as work,* that is, as interpretive work. How is this interpretive work organized? How does it proceed? In what social and institutional settings do competing histories of Reconstruction and the Fourteenth Amendment meet and interact? What are the specific historical junctures at which terms of debate over Reconstruction are established? How are interpretive victories the product of contestable interpretive assumptions and institutional pressures? By addressing these sorts of questions, I map how interpretive practices in the nineteenth century and the 1950s affected the construction of legal arguments by the Warren Court majority and dissenters in the 1960s.

A New Approach to an Old Constitutional Debate

The extensive legal literature on Reconstruction[3] revolves around two questions. What were the real intentions of Republican congressmen regarding specific legislative and constitutional provisions? To what extent is originalist jurisprudence justifiable? So far, study of the *Congressional Globe* (the official record of statements and proceedings in the Reconstruction Congresses) has yielded what William E. Nelson calls an "impasse in scholarship."[4] Legal historians have dug in their heels, disagreeing on the question of whether the congressional Republicans undertook a revolution in federalism or sought to eviscerate the traditional federal system, and whether the Supreme Court subverted Republican objectives. To a large extent, historical disputes over the nature of Reconstruction have been disputes over the legislative objectives of the Republicans, both Moderates and so-called Radicals.[5] (When I refer to Republicans, I am including the Moderates. Occasionally, I say something specific about the Moderates or Radicals. At those times, I identify the groups specifically.) The Northern Democrats, as noted, were the losers in the legislative battles of the 39th Congress.[6]

In 1954, William Crosskey (in)famously put forward the proposition that Republicans held an unorthodox interpretation of the original Constitution. He argued that the Reconstruction debates could not be correctly understood unless the Republicans' constitutional theory was uncovered. In the decades that followed, Jacobus ten Broek, Howard Graham, William Wiecek, and Michael Kent Curtis chronicled the antislavery history of the Republican congressmen. They argued that the antislavery origins of the Republicans provided vital clues in the search for the legislative objectives of the Fourteenth Amendment.[7] In the past decade, many scholars of Reconstruction, such as Lea S. VanderVelde, David A. J. Richards, Akhil Reed Amar, and Bruce Ackerman, have taken interpretive approaches in analyzing the Reconstruction debates. They have further uncovered, and have sought to elevate, the political and constitutional theory of the Republican majority that framed and passed Reconstruction legislation.

I approach the question of Fourteenth Amendment history from a new direction. I take interpretations of Reconstruction history as an object of study. I return to the *Congressional Globe* and the old debates over the "original understanding" of the Fourteenth Amendment to offer a partial record of the legal controversy over how the "facts" of Reconstruction history were established. I show how these "facts," in turn, have shaped the way in which civil rights decisions are defended.

A key point at issue is whether the Fourteenth Amendment originally applied the Bill of Rights to the states.[8] Those who are unfamiliar with constitutional history will be surprised to learn that a Supreme Court decision in 1833 held the Bill of Rights applicable to the national government only; according to this decision, the states were free to abridge the Bill of Rights. A major debate in constitutional history has concerned whether Republicans intended to overrule this decision with the Fourteenth Amendment so that the Bill of Rights would then be protected from state abridgement as well. In the late 1930s the Supreme Court began to apply the Bill of Rights to the states in a piecemeal fashion (the Court did not use legislative history as the vehicle to accomplish this aim), but questions about *original* incorporation remained relevant in rights disputes. What was at stake in the debate over original incorporation was a general history of Reconstruction. In the 1960s, this general history seemed to prove that the Warren Court majority's reading of the Fourteenth Amendment was the product of political preferences.

Scholars have presumed that historical justifications for a vigorous Fourteenth Amendment jurisprudence such as that of the Warren Court depend on evidence that Republicans intended to eviscerate the traditional federal system. It is important to call attention to this presumption. One of my arguments is that the question of whether Republicans intended to eviscerate the traditional federal system is ill suited for investigating Republican intent. (I could also state this argument using concepts favored by originalists: the question of whether Republican legislation was originally understood as eviscerating the traditional federal system is ill suited for investigating original understanding.) Either way, the question is not tooled to take account of the Republicans' multi-dimensional relationship to the federal system. Let me explain.

The term "traditional federal system" is vague in at least two respects. First, the term can refer, for example, to state license to deny Bill of Rights guarantees and to limited federal power. Both characterized the federal system in the antebellum period. Evidence suggests that Republicans saw themselves as changing the former but preserving the latter. It is crucial to understand that Moderate Republicans saw their reforms, including application of the Bill of Rights to the states, as a narrow grant of federal power *consistent* with traditional limitations of federal power. The Fourteenth Amendment was Moderate legislation. It fell short of the goals sought by Radicals, though they voted for it. A key point is that Moderates tended to assume Southern compliance. They did not predict that the new federal oversight provisions they enacted would be frequently triggered. On the Moderates' behalf, we should remember that events had not yet taught otherwise. As they accumulated experience with Southern resistance, they began to understand that their twin commitments—to limited, infrequent use of federal power and to civil and personal rights protections—were in deep tension. So Moderates reluctantly passed more legislation to accomplish their initial goals.

Twentieth-century scholars have equated incorporation with a large expansion of federal power, and this assumption has run investigations aground. Some scholars have concluded from evidence of incorporation that Republicans were comfortable with a large expansion of federal power. Others have concluded from evidence of Republican attachment to limited federal power that Republicans did not apply the Bill of Rights to the states. Both are right by half. The culprit here is the assumed equation between incorporation and big expansion of federal power. Once this equation is broken, that is, once we see that Republicans could hold commitments to both incorporation and limited federal power, we can see that the term "traditional federal system" must be clarified before we can say whether Republicans intended to change it.

This term is vague in a second respect. Traditional means pertaining to or in accord with tradition, and tradition includes practices, behaviors, modes of thought, and precepts. If tradition is defined solely in terms of practice and behavior, or in terms of what is institutionally approved, then Republican reforms will be seen as a repudiation of the traditional. Indeed, Republicans argued that certain aspects of the state-federal distribution of power, for example, the lack of a federal remedy for state denials of antislavery activists' civil liberties, needed to be changed. Republicans justified this change by arguing that the lack of a federal remedy in such instances reflected the corruption of the "true" federal system. According to Republicans, original constitutional principles associated with the Declaration of Independence had not been securely enacted due to slavery and the Slave Power. Thus, Republicans saw their repudiation of federalism as it was practiced as an affirmation of the "true," federal system. Their reclamation of original ideas was traditional in this respect. In fact, Republicans called their legislation both merely corrective and revolutionary. This is understandable in light of their view of federalism as corrupted by slavery. The return to "original" principles was at once traditional and revolutionary. Because Republican reforms could be traditional in this sense, scholars must be careful not to limit their definition of traditional to what is practiced or institutionally approved. For if they do, the Republicans' repudiation-as-affirmation theme will be obscured.

This leads us back to the question, What evidence is necessary for historical justifications for more aggressive federal protection of rights? Such justifications might be based on a showing that Republicans targeted certain features of the antebellum system for change even if they understood these changes as consistent with the notion of limited federal power. Such justifications might emphasize substantive Republican ends—for example, securing free labor opportunity to blacks and Bill of Rights protections to both blacks and whites—and discuss the Republicans' evolving understanding of how much federal oversight was necessary to achieve these ends. The "might" here is significant. For while such arguments are possible, they are not necessary. This is an important point. Historical justifications for less aggressive federal protection might continue to be based on a showing that Republicans were not hearty enthusiasts for broad federal power.

Historical justifications for *any* Fourteenth Amendment jurisprudence will have to emphasize one Republican commitment over the other. What has happened, however, is that institutional history has preserved only one strand of Republican thought. So far, it has been the "limited federal power" element of Republican thought that has been institutionally emphasized, putting "history" on the side of a narrow, less aggressive jurisprudence. This was not mandated by the events of the 1860s. Using Republican history in different ways is possible once institutionally suppressed elements of it are recovered, such as Republican criticism of Southern denials of white men's civil liberties and Republican "free labor" commitments to labor opportunity. The recovery of these aspects would not lead *inevitably* to a more aggressive Fourteenth Amendment jurisprudence. It would, however, open avenues for building plausible historical justifications for federal protections of black rights, avenues that so far have remained blocked.

Such a recovery would also provide historical ammunition for criticizing recent Rehnquist Court reactions to Warren-era decisions. Rehnquist Court decisions, notably, have not relied explicitly on historical justifications. The nonreliance on historical justification might be taken to mean that the institutional history of Reconstruction is not as important as I suggest. Also, at least certain aspects of Republican thought (federal oversight authority over rights) can be seen as triumphing in Rehnquist Court cases prohibiting, for example, set-aside programs. Of course, the Rehnquist Court's definition of discrimination can be challenged.

Rehnquist Court decisions take me beyond the scope of this book. However, some brief comments are in order, given that these decisions might be on the minds of readers. In the concluding chapter, I sketch some preliminary arguments about the relationship between the Rehnquist Court's color-blind standard and the institutional history of Reconstruction. One of those arguments is that suppressed elements of Republican history provide a historical basis for criticizing the Rehnquist Court's color-blind standard. Another is that the very dominance of the institutional history of Reconstruction permits originalists such as Justice Antonin Scalia to take it for granted. He uses it implicitly, bringing in Reconstruction history through the back door while denying it entry through the front.

An Overview

Chapter 2 considers slavery in rhetorical as well as constitutional terms. I treat slavery as an object of interpretive dispute, and I show that slavery criticism provided a major vocabulary for the Reconstruction debates. Slavery criticism—the construction and use of competing versions of the "slavery experience"—was a central means by which Reconstruction congressmen debated the Fourteenth Amendment. Analyses of slavery criticism, however, are largely absent from constitutional scholarship.[9] Arthur Bestor noted more than thirty years ago that constitutional questions became "the narrow channel through which surged the torrent of ideas and interests and anxieties that flooded down from every drenched hillside upon which the storm cloud of slavery discharged its poisoned rain."[10] Reconstruction scholars have continued this focus.

A problem arises, however, regarding constitutional language as *the* major channel through which Reconstruction debate took place. Congressmen's slavery criticisms played a crucial role in setting up alternatives for the Supreme Court in the 1870s. If scholars miss the use of slavery criticism as a major channel for Reconstruction debate, a clear picture of how the rhetorical structure of the debates set the table for the Court will remain elusive.

I show that constitutional language and slavery criticism were intertwined discourses. They are analytically separable, and neither can be reduced to the other. One is a textual dispute over the meaning of the original Constitution. The other is a dispute over the description of events, the classification of antebellum and postbellum events as belonging, or not belonging, to the slavery experience. The North's military victory settled one constitutional question, that is, whether the federal government had the authority to regulate slavery. The new questions—*what did it mean* to destroy slavery and what constitutional reforms were necessary to accomplish this end—brought on the contest to define the slavery experience and the ways in which slavery threatened the Republic.

Today, the Thirteenth Amendment is commonly regarded as a wedge that separates slavery from postslavery. In 1866, however, no consensus had been reached that the Thirteenth Amendment marked the destruction of slavery and the closing off of the slavery period. Formal emancipation was the minimal definition of abolition, but it was not a neutral or objective definition. The racially based nature of Southern slavery made this especially so.[11] Had American slavery not been racially based, it would have been easier for former slaves to "pass" in the never-a-slave group, and so get opportunities at least as good as those received by the least privileged in this group. Postwar efforts to maintain the old order would have been more difficult because the former slaves would have been harder to identify. To the extent that former slave status is harder to identify, formal emancipation is a more objective definition of slavery's destruction. Because slavery was confined to blacks and based on a belief that blacks were subhuman, constitutive elements of slavery—the meanings of blackness and whiteness—could easily survive formal emancipation. These meanings could work to deny blacks the regard granted even to poor whites, namely, acknowledged membership in "the people," and the opportunities that such acknowledgment opened.

Periodization—the division of time into slavery and postslavery periods—was a political act in more than one sense in 1866. Since there were no objective or neutral criteria for dividing the stream of events into these two periods, all such divisions were interpretive acts.[12] Periodization was political in the traditional sense, too. Arguments about the criteria that separated slavery from postslavery were the basic stuff of Reconstruction politics. Harold M. Hyman has noted that "Lincoln's contemporaries were fond of employing the figure of a falling curtain to symbolize separation between events of wartime and problems of Reconstruction. . . . Lincoln also employed a before-and-after terminology in responding to the happy news of Lee's surrender."[13] After the passage of the Thirteenth Amendment, however, Republicans were prompted by events (e.g., Southern Black Codes in 1865–66, which enacted vagrancy laws, apprenticeship laws, criminal penalties for breach of contract, and harsh punishments for blacks[14] in an effort to control black labor) to reject this language. They constructed a continuum of events from the 1830s to 1866 and insisted that the slavery experience extended beyond emancipation to include postwar political violence and takeovers by ex-Confederates of political institutions. Northern Democrats were the ones who continued to use before-and-after language.

The achievement of formal emancipation acted like a depth charge, forcing to the surface and into conflict divergent understandings of "the problem" with slavery. The ambiguities of free soil, along with Southern Democratic rejection of popular sovereignty doctrine, enabled these divergent understandings to coexist in 1861. Free soil was the shorthand term for the policy of nonextension, that is, not extending slavery into the western territories. Free-Soilers argued that slavery degraded white labor. But was it slave law, per se, that sapped white labor's motivation? Or was it the performance of labor by *blacks* that made labor degrading for whites? With nonextension as the stated objective of the antislavery movement, questions of race could be sidestepped. Northerners concerned with slavery's effects on whites could be brought into the antislavery movement, even though they cared little or not at all about the actual slaves. Nonextension was an "appeal to the lowest common denominator of party ideology, allowing Republicans to sidestep the problem of race and the effects of slavery upon the enslaved."[15] Indeed, many Free-Soilers wanted to reserve the western territories for free white labor.

After the achievement of formal emancipation, different understandings of the problem with slavery could no longer be avoided. I examine Reconstruction debate as the next phase of the antebellum contest to define the nature of slavery's threat to the Republic. I track these different slavery criticisms and show how a persuasive definition of the problem with slavery was a political and legal prize. What hung in the balance of the contest to provide a persuasive slavery critique was the authority of various political and constitutional doctrines.

My purpose in chapters 2 and 3 is not to elevate one critique of slavery over the others but to identify the range of these critiques and their associated racial belief systems. This enables me in subsequent chapters to track the various strands of these critiques as they were adopted or discarded by the Supreme Court in the 1870s, justified by Charles Fairman in 1949, and used by Warren Court justices in the 1960s. One of my points is that a Northern Democratic racial belief system was implicitly institutionalized when the Court endorsed Northern Democratic slavery criticism. The very latency of the questions of race contributed to the "impacted" (i.e., hard to manipulate) status, to use Duncan Kennedy's term, of Court precedents on the history of the Reconstruction Amendments.

In recent years, Sanford Levinson and Derrick Bell have treated slavery as an interpretive issue in constitutional law.[16] They have argued that it is a mistake to view slavery as a historical artifact with little or no contemporary relevance. In 1974, Eric Foner remarked that it was "no longer possible to view the peculiar institution as some kind of accident or aberration existing outside the mainstream of national development. Rather, slavery was absolutely central to the American experience." Levinson is troubled by an underappreciation (among the writers of five major constitutional law casebooks and among law students) of "the extent to which the basic decision in 1787 to enter a Union with slaveholders had consequences for every aspect of American constitutional doctrine."[17] Bell argues, too, that the analysis of contemporary legal doctrine is shaped by possession of information about slavery. Bell is critical of constitutional scholars who "explain away recognition and protection of slavery in the original Constitution as a historical anomaly."[18]

This book lends weight to Levinson's and Bell's argument that slavery remains a relevant issue in constitutional law by (1) showing that slavery criticism provided major terms for the Reconstruction debates and (2) showing how this slavery criticism was constitutionally formative.

Chapter 4 examines famous Reconstruction era Supreme Court decisions. The rhetorical structure of the Reconstruction debates, in which opposing slavery criticisms became linked to the amendments, set up alternatives for the Court in the 1870s. I argue that many elements of Northern Democratic history seemed "best" in light of these choices.

In presenting its version of the slavery experience and the war's issues, the Supreme Court mixed strands of Northern Democratic and Republican perspectives. Only certain elements of Republican thought were institutionally preserved. In the *Slaughter-House Cases* of 1873, Justice Samuel F. Miller accepted the Northern Democratic definition of abolition. Miller's rendering of the citizenship clause and the privileges or immunities clause was stabilized by a Northern Democratic slavery criticism. Significantly, Miller limited his representation of the war's issues to the grounds on which Northern Democrats distinguished themselves from Southern Democrats.

For Miller, liberty now included the freedom not to be a legal slave. But liberty remained conceived in mostly traditional terms, that is, in terms of the liberty of popular majorities against a central government. This conception was associated with the Revolutionary experience. As Miller presented it, "the evil which [the Reconstruction Amendments] were designed to remedy"[19] had little to do with Southern abuses of the rights of white antislavery activists before the war, Southern legal treatment of free blacks before the war, or the treatment by former Confederates of white and black Republicans after the war. These Southern actions, especially Southern censorship, had brought harsh criticism from Republicans and had been included in Republican slavery criticism.

While Miller made the link between slavery and Reconstruction in a way that endorsed crucial elements of Northern Democratic perspectives on slavery, Justices Joseph P. Bradley and Noah H. Swayne in their dissenting *Slaughter-House* opinions articulated an alternative version of the slavery and war experiences. As these justices recounted the past, Southern "intolerance of free speech and free discussion" and the treatment by ex-Confederates of free blacks during the antebellum years were part of the problem with slavery. The Fourteenth Amendment was designed to remedy these problems among other things. For the dissenters, the light of experience showed that states could be as much a danger to individual liberty as could the federal government. They expanded the meaning of liberty to include the liberty of individuals against elected majorities.

The Waite Court majority cemented Miller's slavery history. The majority justices' definition of "slavery's incidents" also reflected substantial Northern Democratic content and sharply restricted the potential uses of the Thirteenth Amendment.[20] The majority viewed mobility (e.g., access to public conveyances and public inns) as a social right, not as a right essential to freedom. Mobility, however, was linked to economic opportunity and free labor principles. In 1866, Republicans had condemned Southern vagrancy codes as a civil rights/free labor violation. The Waite Court majority did acknowledge (in dicta) congressional authority under the Thirteenth and Fifteenth Amendments to protect civil rights and political rights, such as voting against racially motivated private assaults. In these opinions the Waite majority partially and temporarily preserved certain elements of Republican perspectives on "the problem" with slavery. The Fuller Court, however, later rejected the Waite Court's approach to racially motivated private deprivations of civil and political rights under the Thirteenth and Fifteenth Amendments, consigning these vestiges of Republican perspectives to the sole dissenting opinions of the elder Justice John M. Harlan. In his opinions, Harlan echoed the versions of slavery history earlier provided by Justices Bradley and Swayne.

In presenting its version of Reconstruction, the Court majority in the 1870s and 1880s drained institutional memory of several aspects of slavery and Reconstruction politics. Had these traces of slavery and Reconstruction politics been institutionally preserved, the "formal equality only" view of Republican intent could be more easily challenged. Further, the Warren Court majority in the 1960s might have been able to use legislative history, a traditional source of law, to support their expansions of rights. This point is key. As it was, "history" looked to be on the side of the Warren Court dissenters, who argued that the majority's decisions were not based in law.

The aspects of slavery and Reconstruction politics drained by the Reconstruction Court included (1) the Republicans' critique of antebellum Southern suppressions of civil liberties, (2) Republican-Northern Democratic debate over the definition of an "established" state right, and (3) Republican-Northern Democratic dispute over the criteria that marked the "destruction" of slavery. Aspects of Republican thought preserved by the Court included the Republican attachment to limited national power and at least greater federal oversight over rights than the Northern Democrats wanted.

Subsequent histories of Reconstruction cemented the Court's erasure of many dimensions of Republican slavery criticism. Dunning School[21] histories of Reconstruction from the early twentieth century represented Republicans in highly negative terms. These histories, like D. W. Griffith's film *Birth of a Nation*, painted Republicans as vengeful and full of hatred. Southern Redeemers and the Ku Klux Klan were portrayed in heroic terms. Progressive histories of Reconstruction[22] also discredited the Republicans, identifying them as agents of Northern capitalists who had no genuine interest in civil liberties generally or black rights in particular. W. E. B. DuBois presented a far more positive view of the Republicans and Reconstruction in *Black Reconstruction in America* (1935). His account, unsurprisingly, appears to have been ignored in legal institutions at the time.[23]

Chapters 4 and 5 examine the Fairman/Crosskey dispute. As noted, the debate between them over the original understanding of the Fourteenth Amendment is famous in the legal literature. Judicial dispute over Reconstruction history had been bubbling to the surface of Supreme Court opinions in the years leading up to their debate.[24] Controversy over this history ignited in 1947 after the appearance of Justice Hugo Black's dissent in *Adamson v. California*.[25] In this famous opinion, Black challenged the accepted view that the Fourteenth Amendment had not originally applied the Bill of Rights to the states. His incorporation thesis was rejected harshly by Justice Felix Frankfurter in a concurring opinion.

In 1949, Fairman argued that Justice Black's incorporation thesis was wrong. The Supreme Court, Fairman asserted, had ruled correctly that the Fourteenth Amendment did not originally apply the Bill of Rights to the states. Crosskey responded to Fairman in 1954. Crosskey argued that Black was correct and the Supreme Court wrong. Each scholar charged the other with "mishandling" the evidence.

Fairman's version of Fourteenth Amendment history was widely accepted at the time and eventually became classic. It still enjoys wide support, but his position has slipped in recent years. While legal scholars at the time roundly rejected the Black-Crosskey incorporation thesis, today it is drawing an increasing number of advocates. Curtis defended the incorporation thesis in the 1980s, and since then support for incorporation has come from Amar, Earl Maltz, Richard Aynes, and Michael Zuckert.

The Fairman/Crosskey dispute is significant because it established the modern terms of debate over the original understanding of the Fourteenth Amendment. Their debate also reinforced the institutional version of slavery/war history, which contained crucial elements of the Northern Democratic perspective. For these reasons, it is important to reconstruct the social and historical juncture at which the debate took place.

My examination of the Fairman/Crosskey dispute shows how their historical reconstructions took place with reference to preexisting interpretive frameworks. I borrow the concept of "frame analysis" from Erving Goffman, and I look at how Fairman's and Crosskey's interpretive frameworks shaped their recoveries of Fourteenth Amendment history. Both of them sorted through the documentary record in structured ways, just as Northern Democrats and Republicans did with respect to slavery history. Fairman's and Crosskey's respective assumptions shaped (1) where they looked for evidence of original understanding, (2) when in history they started looking, and (3) how they assessed what they found.

Fairman was a member of a Harvard-based interpretive community, which included Frankfurter, whose assumptions and standards of relevance were deeply institutionalized, and the earlier success of Fairman's history must be understood with reference to these institutional factors. Fairman's and Crosskey's histories interacted in an institutional setting in which a number of pressures and forces were at work, one of which was Crosskey's tarnished reputation as a historian. After examining the "credibility" of Fairman's history as a complex social and historical product, I argue that his interpretive victory in the 1950s was not a product of the intrinsic merits of his argument.

Chapter 6 discusses the Warren Court legislative apportionment cases. In it, I show how Fairman's success in the 1950s had an indirect impact on Warren Court approaches to disputes over rights. Fairman's non-incorporation thesis reinforced the institutional version of Reconstruction history. This development blocked the Warren Court majority from using the events of the 1860s to legitimate their decisions. Nothing in those events determined this institutional barrier. While the history of the 1860s could have been interpreted in ways that supported both the majority and dissenting arguments in Warren Court cases, the history of Reconstruction turned out to be a virtually exclusive resource for the dissenters.

By the time that Warren Court justices debated the claim, for example, that state apportionment practices fell within federal jurisdiction under the federal courts, the justices' knowledge of Civil War and Reconstruction experience was, like a ship in a bottle,[26] so firmly established that it looked as though it always must have been just as it was. And ships in bottles, of course, look as if they can never get out.

An institutionally credible version of Reconstruction (which was neither necessary nor inevitable) tied the hands of the Warren majority, undercutting their ability to meet certain institutional standards and definitions of coherency. These standards grew from the Newtonian,[27] mechanics-based model of law. The institutional version of Reconstruction provided ammunition for critics of Warren Court decisions, who argued that the decisions were the product of politics. The dissenting justices argued that history supported their position that the Fourteenth Amendment left apportionments in the hands of state legislatures. Some historians went on record to offer their agreement.[28]

The "truth" status of the institutional account of Reconstruction has rigged persuasion by granting judges such as Frankfurter, the younger John Marshall Harlan, and the Warren Court dissenters privileged and unearned access to Fourteenth Amendment history as a source of law and legitimization. This account has worked to render the Warren Court's expansions of rights vulnerable on historical and Newtonian grounds.

It is important to emphasize that the institutional version of Reconstruction is not a trump card able to win a Court majority every time it is thrown. The Warren Court dissenters invoked the institutional account of Reconstruction in criticizing the majority's view of the Fourteenth Amendment. The dissenters, of course, lost. But they were not a powerless minority. It makes sense to talk about the Warren Court dissenters as a powerful minority because they held high institutional ground in appealing to history and precedent as sources of law and legitimization. This lofty perch enabled the dissenters to argue (persuasively to a segment of the legal community) that Warren Court decisions were illegitimate. The institutional account of Reconstruction remains credible in spite of the defeats endured by the Warren dissenters and in spite of the fact that the account is no longer reputable among most academic historians. The durability of this account, then, is indeed in need of explanation. This study focuses on the institutionally privileged history of Reconstruction, but at the same time it throws some light on the social and historical roots of intellectual reaction against the Warren Court.

A Note on Original Understanding

A few words are in order about original understanding, or originalism. For the uninitiated, originalism is an approach to constitutional interpretation. It is associated with the interpretive method called textualism, and with figures such as Robert Bork and Justice Antonin Scalia. The textualist method directs judges to find the meaning of a particular constitutional provision in the words or language of the text. The presumption is that meaning resides in the language of the provision and is therefore independent of the judge and invariant. According to originalists, assessments of the meaning of a provision are not aided by searches into the legislative history of that provision (e.g., legislative debates, drafts of legislation). Reliance on legislative history is not only unnecessary (because meaning lies in the text) but dangerous because pieces of that history could be seized to justify a result favored for political reasons. Proponents of originalism claim that it is the only neutral method of constitutional interpretation, the only antidote to judicial willfulness and arbitrariness.

Proponents also distinguish original understanding from original intent, regarding the latter as a merely subjective assessment of a provision's meaning. Original intent refers to what legislators wanted to accomplish with a particular provision, or what legislators thought the language of the provision meant. Original understanding, which refers to what the words of a provision could reasonably be taken to mean, is regarded as a more objective assessment of that provision.

At first glance, this distinction appears tenable. A gap, for example, might exist between legislators' intent (their aims, objectives) and the reasonable meaning of the language chosen as the vehicle to accomplish these objectives. The legislators might have failed to match their objectives with textual language that reasonably represented these objectives. This distinction could also be defended on the grounds that it is possible for judges to figure out the reasonable understanding of a particular provision while it is impossible for judges to get inside legislators' heads and thus figure out their intentions.

The impossibility of getting inside legislators' heads, however, does not mandate the distinction between original understanding and original intent. This book provides an example of when and how the distinction breaks down.[29] As chapters 4 and 5 show, those who have assessed the original understanding of the Fourteenth Amendment have gone to the Reconstruction debates for clues. They have looked to legislative history for indicators of original meaning, something regarded as necessary due to the open-ended clauses of the amendment. Thus, constructions of legislative history become implicated in assessments of original understanding. This is an important point because it is at odds with claims about how original understanding is supposed to work.

A Sociology of Constitutional Law

Few legal studies treat the sociology of law as a branch of the sociology of knowledge.[30] The problem considered in this book is one in the sociology of knowledge: how crucial elements of an accepted version of Reconstruction could be institutionalized from a minority position (the Northern Democratic and Whig Republican stance immediately after the Civil War) and how this version of Reconstruction history could enable the Warren Court dissenters (also a minority) to hold certain parts of the high ground in the "culture of argument"[31] that joined them with justices in the majority.

I engage with familiar topics in constitutional law, but my questions are sociological in nature. What has been the distribution of opportunities among judges to use the events of the 1860s as a source of law and legitimization? How has this distribution changed over time? What have been the political effects of blocked chances to use these historical events as resources? The institutional account of Reconstruction affects the real world, though indirectly, on various political distributions. Courts need not resolve political issues (they do not typically achieve this outcome, in any case) for the institutionalization of certain versions of history to affect political distributions.

While the legal literature on Reconstruction tends to revolve around questions about the real objectives of the Reconstruction Amendments, this book is different because it investigates how versions of legal history and original understanding have been socially constructed. Indeed, scholarly debate on Reconstruction history is part of my data. By investigating the production and impact of "credible" Reconstruction history, I link constitutional interpretation closely to slavery politics in the Civil War and Reconstruction era and to institutional factors in the New Deal period.

Sociologists study work, which is why this book is partly a study of judicial work. In examining the Court's Reconstruction era cases and Warren Court legislative apportionment cases, I adapt Duncan Kennedy's concepts of "freedom" and "constraint" in judicial decision-making.[32] I also suggest that the institutional account of Reconstruction be best conceived as a legal resource—that is, a source of law and legitimization—within an array of resources.[33] Institutional resources do not exist objectively in the world. They come into existence through social processes. Shifts in institutional and historical contexts also work to enable and constrain access to particular resources. The Warren Court majority, for example, used resources that had become available only during the 1940s and 1950s with the rise of European fascism and the influence of NAACP lawyers. When it is understood that the institutional version of Reconstruction is a powerful resource but not a trump card, a larger sociological problem might be posed: how are histories mobilized by Court justices at different historical junctures, and to what end?

In these pages I bring a sociological approach to the study of narrative construction and competition. The process of narrative construction has both more visible dimensions (material, lived) and less visible dimensions (conceptual, taken-for-granted). I focus on the less visible dimensions—the framing assumptions, the interpretive structure of arguments, the institutionally embedded vocabularies, etc. The institutional version of Reconstruction, for example, has a "virtual" existence, even while it exists simultaneously as an objectified mechanism, a thing that might be consciously mobilized and used to support a particular argument. Justices carry around in their heads taken-for-granted beliefs about the experiences of slavery, the Civil War, and Reconstruction. These beliefs exist as components in the justices' interpretive frameworks, and they shape orientations to action. The institutional version of Reconstruction history is used both explicitly and implicitly in the course of judicial work, both with and without the conscious awareness of judges. A challenge—one that requires further work—is to forge links between the more visible and less visible dimensions of the process of narrative construction.

This process of construction and competition also involves movement within levels of society (e.g., across institutions, such as the Supreme Court, law schools, and history departments) and between levels of society (e.g., from the level of collectives, such as Northern political organizations, to the institutional level of the Supreme Court). Historical meanings circulate both within and across levels of society. Given all of these elements, the goal is to be highly specific about the accessibility and transmission of cultural objects such as competing versions of the past. Where in institutions are dominant and subordinate versions of history accessible or available? If dominant versions of history are resisted, as they often are, at what institutional locations or at what points of contact between levels of society does this resistance occur? Understanding how heterodox versions of past events survive, circulate, and even gain status (such as Crosskey's) requires us to ask these kinds of questions.

By focusing on the processes by which histories are built and resisted, such histories, which have been used in both the reproduction of hierarchies and their erosion, can be made socially and historically specific. The overarching goal is to help develop a sociology of constitutional law.

My methods have been influenced by sociologists in the field of science studies,[34] previously known as the "sociology of scientific knowledge." Researchers in this area examine such things as scientific fact-making, and they invent systematic and dialectical units of analysis for their investigations. Often these researchers are self-conscious about their methods and their orientation to research. Susan Leigh Star, a sociologist, sums up the methodological directives for researchers: "Try to understand the processes of construction and persuasion entailed in producing any narrative, text or artifact. Try to understand these processes over a long period of time. . . . Understand the language and meanings of your respondents, link them with institutional patterns and commitments and, as Everett Hughes said, remember that 'it could have been otherwise.'"[35] The goal, as she states it, is to restore an account of the actual work involved in producing scientific facts and artifacts and the organization of that work.

In the language of science studies, I examine the processes of construction and persuasion involved in producing (and then using) an institutionally accredited account of Reconstruction. Phrased more abstractly, I reinsert into my analysis part of the "production history" of the institutional account of Reconstruction: i.e., as the institutional presentation of Reconstruction was built using crucial elements of Northern Democratic history in 1866, reconstituted by the Supreme Court between 1873 and 1883, validated by academic historians in the early twentieth century, explicitly justified by legal scholar Charles Fairman in 1949, and used by Warren Court justices in the 1960s (implicitly and explicitly by the dissenters, implicitly by the majority).

As a result of the practices of multiple social groups over several generations, an account of Reconstruction history achieved a "closed"[36] status for justices and many legal scholars. This book restores an account of the actual interpretive work involved in the production of arguments about Reconstruction and the organization of that work. My question about how a particular version of Reconstruction gained truth status for Court justices and how this historical "knowledge" affected race policy and political distributions is really a version of Max Weber's question about how subjective meanings become objective realities.

A Note on Theory

In recent years a crisis of belief in truth and the possibility of objectivity has pervaded academic disciplines. Scholars have been vexed by a perceived contradiction between asserting antifoundationalist epistemology (a general account of knowing in which all meanings are identified as provisional and contingent) and making particular claims to knowledge. What, for example, is the status of my claims in regard to the social construction of knowledge about Reconstruction? Are my claims any less determined by the social and institutional frameworks that I inhabit while I undertake my scholarly work?

I am like anybody else in that belief structures shape my sense of relevant and weighty evidence. And like anybody else, I am certain in my sense of relevant and weighty evidence. The source of this certainty is my belief structure, and my ability to be certain is neither helped nor hindered by any epistemology. Stanley Fish has argued that there is no contradiction between antifoundationalist epistemology and specific claims-making.[37] That is so because antifoundationalist theory cannot underwrite research practice (that is, yield a methodology). Indeterminacy and general openness to revision and transformation are not methodological programs that can be enacted. While "openness to revision and transformation may characterize a human history in which firmly drawn boundaries can be shown to have been repeatedly blurred and abandoned, openness to revision and transformation are not methodological programs any individual can determinedly and self-consciously enact."[38] No one is capable of being *generally* reflexive and open. Some set of assumptions, not subject to reflexiveness, is necessary for consciousness and action. Only context-specific openness is possible. The attempt of scholars to align their claims to knowledge with antifoundationalist epistemology, therefore, makes no sense. It is an impossible undertaking.[39]

When someone takes issue with my claims, it is business as usual. My historical analysis will be assessed according to institutional standards governing sociolegal, constitutional, and discourse analysis. And as my analysis of the Fairman/Crosskey debate shows, those standards are contested and can be reconfigured over time. My claims, then, are subject to examination and reexamination in the same way that Fairman's and Crosskey's claims are.

An epistemology, furthermore, is not necessary to buttress my historical analysis. I could declare an allegiance to antifoundationalist or constructionist theory, but such a declaration would make *no difference* to any reader's sense of which account of Reconstruction is more or less true. For example, for those convinced that Crosskey was something of a nut, no general argument or theory that all historical accounts are contingent and provisional would change their minds about the incorporation thesis. What might persuade a scholar who always accepted Fairman's account to reconsider his or her view would be the actual argument that I present, an argument that is *as particular* as the grounds on which Fairman's account rests. Just as an epistemology did not guide my research practice (a belief structure did), my readers are not using an epistemology when they attempt to decide whether Fairman's or Crosskey's history is truer.[40] Articulating or defending an epistemology, then, is beside the point.

My objective is to uncover regularities in the practices of those interpretive communities that have argued about Reconstruction. These regularities, of course, are not invariant or predictive; they are high-order generalizations drawn from a finite corpus of data that hold (if they do hold) for this corpus only.[41] Each time that history brings forth new versions of Reconstruction, it will be necessary to recharacterize the regularities.

When it comes to actual disputes about our knowledge of slavery, the Civil War, and Reconstruction, the debate will not be epistemological. The debate, finally, will be over historical evidence and its significance, such as the dimensions of slavery politics, the structure of references that is discernible in the speeches of Reconstruction congressmen, and the Harvard connection between Frankfurter and Fairman. This is not a return to positivism. It is simply a recognition of truth in the Kuhnian sense, and, as Fish has remarked, this is an occasion for neither cynicism nor despair.

2

Slavery as an Interpretive Issue

in the 39th Reconstruction Congress:

The Northern Democrats

"All knew," said Lincoln in his second inaugural address, that slavery "was, somehow, the cause of the war."[1] But to say that the war was about slavery, or to say that slavery was a threat to the Republic, raises more questions than it answers. This is the case because it was possible to identify different dimensions of the slavery system as "the problem." Was the moral sin of slave ownership the problem? Was the problem Southern demands for federal enforcement of slave law in the territories? Was the problem that the expansion of slavery threatened small capitalist institutions? Or that it threatened free soil for Northern *white* labor? Or that it threatened capital expansion and corporate growth? Or that it caused the impoverishment of the nonslaveholding Southern white population? Did the threats of slavery include repressions of antislavery activists' civil liberties, the murder of antislavery newspaperman Elijah Lovejoy,[2] Henry Hammond's gag rule,[3] the suppression of Hinton Helper's antislavery book, *The Impending Crisis*?[4] Did the problems of slavery include a view of black inferiority that justified the "mudsill"[5] theory of white men's democracy and the second-class treatment of free blacks?[6]

In short, the war could be understood in many ways to be "about" slavery, with each understanding embodying different beliefs about the nature of slavery's threats. In 1866, congressional arguments about the proper basis of Reunion, the federal supervision of states, and federal jurisdiction over individual rights flowed from beliefs about what in slavery was "the problem."

In May 1865, after Congress passed the Thirteenth Amendment,[7] William Lloyd Garrison urged the American Anti-Slavery Society to dissolve in triumph. Garrison declared, "My vocation, as an Abolitionist, thank God, is ended." Frederick Douglass, also at the meeting, insisted that the work of the Anti-Slavery Society was not yet done. Responding to Garrison, Douglass argued that "[s]lavery is not abolished until the black man has the ballot."[8] Douglass's response has the ring of mere rhetoric, a weak attempt to stretch the definition of slavery further than it would go. But to regard it this way would be a mistake.

In discussing the transition from slavery to freedom, historians have usually located interpretive room on the side of "freedom," not on the side of "slavery." While they identify and discuss the contest to define freedom, they tend to treat slavery as something defined objectively by formal slave law.[9] Lea VanderVelde is one historian who does remark on the contest to define what it meant to abolish slavery: "In the minds of the Radicals, abolishing slavery and involuntary servitude was more than merely abolishing the formal legal status of human beings held as property."[10]

In this chapter I consider slavery in rhetorical terms. I examine the interpretive contest over slavery that took place after ratification of the Thirteenth Amendment and leading up to passage of the Fourteenth Amendment. During this period, congressmen debated the Civil Rights Bill of 1866 and the Fourteenth Amendment. They also made assertions about the Thirteenth Amendment. Their "backward" reflections on the Thirteenth Amendment—their assertions about what it meant to pass this amendment and destroy slavery—functioned as forward-looking arguments about the Civil Rights Bill and the Fourteenth Amendment. I focus on these reflections on the Thirteenth Amendment where congressmen expressed their understandings of what it meant to destroy slavery and resolve the war's issues.

Eric Foner's work on the ambiguity of antislavery[11] provides a basis for examining slavery in rhetorical terms. Relying on Foner's studies, I first summarize the different sorts of slavery critiques mounted by Northern political factions in the years before the Civil War. This will be old news to historians. I then spend the bulk of the chapter showing that slavery criticism provided a major vocabulary for Fourteenth Amendment debate.

The Multiple Meanings of Antislavery

Before the Civil War, moral, economic, and political critiques of slavery were made. The evangelical abolitionism associated with William Garri-

son had its roots in Christian benevolence and the revivals of the Second
Great Awakening, which identified moral progress with each individual's
capacity to act as an instrument of God. The evangelicals defined slave
ownership as a mortal sin. The "personal sin of the individual master
against the individual slave"[12] defined the problem. Formal emancipation therefore fixed it. Slavery was not viewed as a class relationship. The
evangelicals, like almost everyone during that era, viewed black men
and women as inferior beings. Most Northerners had doubts about black
capability. Important variations could be found, however, in the racial
belief systems in force at the time. (More on this point below.)

Evangelicism could not make abolition or the nonextension of slavery
into the western territories a majority sentiment. It was political antislavery, that is, the political and economic critiques of slavery, that gained
majority support for nonextension.[13] Political antislavery used "free
labor" as its defining principle. According to the free-labor critique of
slavery, slave labor degraded labor. The dignity of labor was a constant
theme in antebellum Northern culture and politics. "Political antislavery
was not merely a negative doctrine, an attack on Southern slavery and the
society built upon it; it was an affirmation of the superiority of the social
system of the North."[14] Slavery stunted Southern economic development. Slavery sapped the motivation of white Southern laborers.[15] It was
slavery (not the wage system) "which threatened to destroy the independence of the northern worker, his opportunity to escape from the wage
earning class and own a small farm or shop."[16] The western territories
were a safety valve for Northern workers, keeping open the possibility of
social mobility, and the expansion of slavery into the western territories
threatened this outlet. The territories seemed to be the answer to urban
poverty, and for this reason many workingmen supported Free-Soil.

The platform of Free-Soil, Foner emphasizes, was purposely vague to
permit coalition-building. "In order for the political antislavery movement to attract a wide following, it would have to adopt a platform so
broad that both the prejudiced and the advocates of equal rights could
support it."[17] Before the war, Salmon P. Chase observed "an obvious dis-
position among many to place our cause on the lowest possible ground—
to connect it with the least possible advocacy of principle."[18]

Crucial ambiguities existed at the heart of the free labor critique. Was
it slavery's effect on all labor (including black labor) or slavery's effect on
white labor that was of concern? All agreed that slavery degraded white
labor, but was it the slave law, per se, that sapped white labor's motiva-

tion, or was it the performance of labor by *blacks* which made that labor degrading? Sometimes, Republicans said it was the institution (slave law, per se) that degraded labor; other times, they made little distinction between free blacks and slave blacks. While Republicans believed deeply in economic opportunity for labor, they also doubted the capabilities of blacks and Irish immigrants.[19]

Supporters of Free-Soil, especially the Barnburners of New York, sometimes supported laws that barred black entry to the territories. In the 1850s, four Free-Soil states, Indiana, Illinois, Iowa, and Oregon, passed laws prohibiting the entry of blacks. Here, free soil meant free soil for whites. Many in the labor movement hated the abolitionists while condemning slavery and the Slave Power. As Foner notes, "it is important to distinguish the labor movement's response to abolitionism and indeed to black competition from its attitude toward slavery."[20] To condemn slavery and to hate the abolitionists seems like a contradiction to the twentieth-century observer who assumes that concern for the actual slaves was a motivating concern for antislavery supporters. However, it is not a contradiction if one understands that different dimensions of the slavery system could be, and were, identified as "the problem." Slavery could be critiqued in many ways.

Related to the economic critique of slavery was the political critique, not to be confused with Foner's general designation "political antislavery." The Republicans' political critique had several dimensions. First, Republicans condemned the conspiratorial Slave Power, which, they believed, had seized control of the federal government. There was resentment of Southern political power. Slaveholders were hated because they were a privileged class, an aristocracy. Second, Republicans condemned Southern repressions of white men's civil liberties. This civil liberties' critique gained strength after the murder of Elijah Lovejoy in 1837. Foner refers to antebellum Southern repressions of civil liberties as "the most thorough-going repression of free thought, free speech and a free press ever witnessed in an American community."[21]

Northern Democrats opposed the Republican policy of nonextension, which asserted a federal right to prohibit slavery in the territories. (Republicans conceded that Southern slavery was constitutional and could not be reached by federal power.) Northern Democrats initially opposed nonextension because it violated the principle of popular sovereignty, that is, local majoritarianism. Northern Democrats believed that local majorities had the right to decide the slavery question for themselves.

The Northern Democrats eventually broke with the slaveholding Southern Democrats only after the Southerners insisted on the right to federal
protection of slavery in the territories. This insistence also violated the
doctrine of popular sovereignty. The 1860 Democratic national convention, for example, broke up over the South's insistence on a platform
guaranteeing slavery in the territories.[22] The experiences of the Douglas
Democrats in the years before the Civil War "go a long way toward explaining the unanimity of the North's response to the attack on Fort
Sumter."[23]

In 1861 the war's goals were explicitly limited to the nonextension of
slavery into the western territories (free soil). Republicans went to great
lengths to disavow their intention of getting rid of Southern slavery,[24]
though they felt, too, that the containment of slavery would force it to
die out. It was a commonly accepted axiom of political economy before
the war that slavery had to expand in order to survive.[25] Not until after
1863 and much bloodshed did the abolition of Southern slavery become
an explicit Northern goal. Northerners came to hold the view that victory would be illusory without abolition in the South.[26]

With regard to racial belief systems in force at the time, almost all Republicans held blacks to be naturally inferior to whites. Abraham Lincoln
opposed black suffrage and political rights generally and was an ardent
colonizationist. He insisted, though, that emigration be voluntary. Lincoln supported black civil rights (the right to own property, to contract,
to sue and be sued, to testify in court, to be subject to the same criminal
codes as whites) because they were necessary in pursuing an economic
livelihood (free labor). (Northern Democrats used race and "miscegenation" as political weapons against Lincoln and the Republicans,[27] and
Free-Soilers such as the Barnburners continually insisted on a "white
man's government.") The New York Times summed up Lincoln's position
regarding blacks: "He declares his opposition to negro suffrage, and to
everything looking towards placing negroes upon a footing of political
and social equality with the whites;—but he asserts for them a perfect
equality of civil and personal rights under the Constitution."[28]

This use of "personal rights" perhaps refers to the Bill of Rights. The
position of the Moderate Republicans in 1866 appears to be similar, if
not the same, as the Times summary of Lincoln's views. It is important to
keep in mind that support for black civil rights (but not political or social
rights) and support for applying the Bill of Rights to the states could
grow from the economic (free labor) critique of slavery and the political

critique of slavery, that is, the tendency of slavery to destroy civil liberties. In 1866 the Moderates, as with Lincoln before them, rejected political rights for blacks. Moderates reluctantly came to accept the Fifteenth Amendment. Radicals argued that political rights were necessary for enacting free labor principles. In 1866, Rep. William Higby of California argued, "nothing is effected by simply declaring that you extend to them civil rights if in a republican government in which the power rests with the people they cannot, together with others, possess the political power to protect themselves in these rights."[29] With respect to the question of political rights, we can see variation in Republican free labor visions.

Defining Slavery's Destruction

Since there were different understandings of "the problem" with slavery, it makes sense that there were different definitions of slavery's "resolution." Republicans and Northern Democrats competed to define the criteria that separated the slavery and postslavery periods. Every definition of slavery's destruction held a point of view and every definition worked to affect political distributions. Every definition of slavery's destruction worked to construct not only the boundary between federal (Congress and federal courts) and state matters, but also the boundary between public and private matters (e.g., labor contracts, innkeepers' exclusion of black travelers).

The achievement of even the narrowest definition of abolition (the elimination of formal slave law) was, of course, enormously significant. As late as 1861, the absence of federal power to regulate slavery was generally conceded. On the eve of the Civil War, Lincoln was ready to endorse a constitutional amendment, approved by Congress, which explicitly guaranteed Southern slavery against federal interference.[30] The Northern military victory forced a shift in the constitutional problematic. The federal government now had the power to regulate slavery and prohibit slave law. While congressional Northern Democrats such as Andrew Jackson Rogers (a leading congressional Democrat and member of the Joint Committee on Reconstruction) initially opposed the Thirteenth Amendment, they came to accept it as an "issue of war."

As long as the minimal definition of abolition—formal emancipation only—remained unachieved, Northern factions could stay united under the abolition policy. It is not surprising, then, that overt dispute over the criteria that marked slavery's destruction emerged in the wake of formal emancipation. While the nonextension of slavery into the western terri- tories was the lowest common denonimator in 1861, formal emancipa- tion was the lowest common denominator in 1866.

After Lee's surrender, the Reconstruction Congresses became the new battleground of the Civil War. Observers of the war had foretold this shift. In January 1865, William Mason Grosvenor,[31] reflected on the North's military victory at Gettysburg: "[A]nd with the calm review that followed the tremendous achievements of that period there came to every thinking man, North and South, the conviction that in so far as the con- test should be one of arms alone, the North was sure of ultimate success. From that day the apprehensions of the wisest loyalists and the hopes of the shrewdest rebels were alike turned to the political contests at the North, as affording to the rebellion a second chance of the victory which it could no longer hope to attain by triumphs in battle."[32]

The ex-Confederates gained to the extent that the Northern Demo- cratic version of the slavery experience was accepted by the Supreme Court. The Northern Democrats never advocated slavery. They advo- cated popular sovereignty, which left the slavery question to local ma- jorities.[33] The Northern Democrats insisted that these positions were different. Lincoln, of course, pressed Douglas on the issue of slavery's wrongness. He asserted that Douglas's willingness to leave the slavery question to local majorities meant that his rival saw slavery as a legiti- mate choice. To leave the slavery question to local majorities meant that the choices for accepting and prohibiting slave law were equally legiti- mate. This question—what things should be taken out of the arena of local majority choice, that is, what should popular majorities not be per- mitted to do—generated arguments between Republicans and Northern Democrats both before and after the Civil War. In 1861 these arguments mattered less than the split between Stephen Douglas and the Southern Democrats, for it was Southern demands for federal enforcement of slave law in the territories that united Republicans and Douglas Democrats in opposition. In 1866 arguments between Republicans and Northern Democrats over what elected majorities should be allowed to do emerged with greater disruptive force and consequence. The only postwar matter that Northern Democrats were willing to see taken out of local majoritar- ian control was formal slave law. Otherwise, all matters regarding race, such as the choice to legislate differently for blacks and whites (e.g., the Black Codes), were regarded as local.

Northern Democrats expressed opposition to Republican legislation by presenting a version of the slavery experience that appealed to already institutionalized warrants and justifications: a Revolutionary era conception of liberty[34] (i.e., the liberty of popular majorities against central governments) and a theory of race that held blacks unfit for membership in the national collective.

Republicans expressed scorn for the Democrats' assertions that formal emancipation marked the achievement of the war's goals. Republicans identified the Black Codes, post-Appomattox political violence directed at blacks and white Republicans, and ex-Confederate takeovers of political institutions as among the continued threats of slavery. Republicans also identified "prejudice," as they called it, as a constitutive element of Southern slavery society. This element remained, despite the abrogation of slave law. Republicans identified this prejudice as a motivating force behind the Black Codes and Klan violence.

Republican versions of the slavery experience appealed to warrants that were not deeply institutionalized: a "declaratory theory" of rights[35] that expanded the notion of liberty to include the liberty of individuals against popular majorities, and a theory of race that held blacks as fit for membership in "the people," that is, the national collective (even if blacks continued to be regarded as unfit for political or social equality).

To provide an authoritative critique of slavery, the political contest gave way to a legal one. That legal contest is examined in chapter 3, where I focus on the Court's version of the "history of the times" and show how a particular interpretation of slavery history (mostly, but not exclusively, Northern Democratic) supported the Court's interpretation of the Fourteenth Amendment.

The Northern Democrats

William Nelson has offered a summary of Northern Democratic objections to the Fourteenth Amendment that are familiar to Reconstruction scholars.[36] The Northern Democrats argued that the amendment would centralize power and destroy the states. They further contended that the ex-Confederate states were constitutionally entitled to readmission to Congress and that legislation passed in the absence of the ex-Confederate states was illegitimate. Similar to the Antifederalist's[37] critique of the original Constitution, Northern Democrats argued that the Fourteenth Amendment was illegitimate, without precedent, and destructive of state sovereignty. Some charged that Republicans were possessed by a "bloodthirstiness,"[38] a "vindictive spirit . . . , [a] savage sectional hate and an inordinate lust for power."[39]

The Northern Democrats' constitutional arguments were intertwined with a slavery criticism. The classification and description of events (as belonging, or not belonging, to the slavery experience) and the construction of a text (the original Constitution) together form the rhetorical structure of the debates. Indeed, attention to the competing constructions of slavery history is critical for understanding how the rhetorical structure of the Reconstruction debates set up alternatives for the Supreme Court in the 1870s.

"The Problem" with Slavery

Andrew J. Rogers, a leading House Democrat from New Jersey, identified slavery as "the main principle" upon which the war was waged. Rep. Charles E. Phelps of Maryland remarked similarly, "Slavery was the cause and the only cause of the rebellion."[40] Slavery was "the parent of secession."[41] In this respect, Northern Democrats were just like Republicans. The war was about slavery. But it was clear from their speeches that Rogers and Phelps focused on a particular dimension of slavery as "the problem."

In their speeches, Northern Democrats distinguished themselves from the "Southern Democracy."[42] For the Northern Democrats, Southern claims to federal enforcement of slave law in the territories, along with the act of secession, defined and exhausted the problems with slavery. Southern surrender and Southern renunciation of the right of secession marked the return of "republican government" to the South.

Rep. Aaron Harding of Kentucky stated that the South "made war for the purpose of taking their States out of the Union and establishing a separate and independent government over them."[43] Rep. George S. Shanklin of Kentucky stated, "I admit and assert that they erred. . . . They claimed rights which did not belong to them. But, sir, they have now surrendered all those claims."[44] "Slavery, struggling for perpetuity, expansion and power, struck at the existence of the Government."[45] Referring to secession, Rogers identified the "illegality of the action of the Southern people."[46] Speaking in 1864, Rep. Samuel S. Cox of Ohio stated:

We have, in times apast, affiliated with the Democracy South, but I do not understand that the Democratic party North is responsible for what the Democratic party South did when they separated from us, or since, and when they divided our party and helped you to divide the Union. The Democratic party of the North never was a pro-slavery party, as has been libelously charged. . . . A grosser falsehood was never uttered. Even Horace Greeley is ashamed any more to repeat it. He stated the other day our position correctly, when he said that "northern Democracy is not really pro-slavery, but anti-intervention; maintaining, not that slavery is right, but that we of the free States should mind our own business and let alone other people's." Our platforms are but the repetition of this idea of non-interference. The Democracy ever favored local sovereignty as to slavery and every other domestic matter. They would have extended that sovereignty, and not slavery, from the States to the Territories. On that question of extension, of non-intervention, the Democracy North and South unhappily divided. The consequences are upon us.[47]

Southern Democratic renunciation of popular sovereignty principles was "the problem" with slavery. The Thirteenth Amendment, too, in Cox's view, violated popular sovereignty principles. Cox "repell[ed] with honest scorn the imputation that because we disfavor this amendment [Thirteenth,] we favor slavery or rebellion."

What I desire is, not that gentlemen should debate the question of slavery or anti-slavery but of the power we have over it, and of the propriety of its exercise either now or at any time. . . . Not for Jefferson Davis; not for Virginia; but for our own States, our own Government, do we stand on the principle of self-government over State affairs, and against the use of the power of amendment to change that principle. . . . I place my vote against it [Thirteenth Amendment] because the system it would change is a good one, made in wisdom and to be perpetuated for the future happiness of the people. . . . I believe that this amendment is an obstacle to the rehabilitation of the States. . . . I believe [it] would bring about an eternal separation of the States of the Union.[48]

Like other Northern Democrats, A. J. Rogers initially opposed the Thirteenth Amendment when it was passed in 1865,[49] but he came to accept it as "event of the war."[50]

I never was in favor of slavery. No man, sir, ever heard me advocate slavery in the abstract, but I was in favor of standing by the elementary principles embodied in the Constitution. . . . The abolition of slavery was an event of the war, and the result of one of the principles of the war resorted to by the conquering power that being the arbitrament to which the Southern people submitted. And slavery having been abolished under those circumstances, I wish to keep it dead and buried forever, so far as I am concerned. . . . I did not then approve of it [Thirteenth Amendment], but I believe now it was for the best interests of the country; that as an issue of war it should be given up in the reconstruction, after the war had wiped out slavery, to prevent future agitation upon it.[51]

Rep. Samuel J. Randall of Pennsylvania, speaking during debate over the Fourteenth Amendment, equated Southern seccession and Republican reforms. Both were threats to the government and the Constitution because both were rejections of popular sovereignty doctrine: "I am not a defender of rebellion in any particular. I am against anybody who seeks to overthrow the Government or the Constitution; and while I was in favor of putting down the rebellion when it emanated from the South, I am now today in favor of preventing the success and for putting down that party which seeks to change, to annul and to destroy the Constitution and to centralize this Government, and thereby to take away from the people the privileges which that Constitution formed by our forefathers gave to them. . . ."[52]

The Northern Democrats' narrow definition of the problem with slavery, that is, Southern rejection of popular sovereignty and the claim to the right of secession, is also visible in their protests against the exclusion of ex-Confederate states from the 39th Congress. (Southern states withdrew from Congress when they seceded in 1861.) In an exchange with Rep. James F. Wilson of Iowa, who argued that the exclusion of the ex-Confederate states was legitimate, Rogers argued that Southern states had "republican forms of government" just before the onset of the war in 1861 and that the surrender of Lee's armies signaled a return to republican government. Hence, readmission should follow this surrender. Rogers asserted that it was only with secession that republican government was suspended; republican government had been revived "upon the surrender of the rebel armies."[53]

The Northern Democrats' definition of the problem with slavery worked, logically, to place Southern practices regarding blacks and white

Republicans outside the scope of the war's issues. This can be seen in Northern Democratic assertions that slavery could be removed while leaving local sovereignty (minus the local right to enact slave law) intact. Cox argued that Republicans were "striking at constitutional liberty in striking at domestic slavery." "The question," said Cox, "shall be the old order with Democracy to administer it, or continued revolution with destructives to guide it; the old Union with as much of local sovereignty as may be saved from the abrasion of war, or a new abolition and military unity with debt, tyranny and fanaticism as its trinity."

Slavery's "Resolution"

Northern Democrats repeatedly asserted that formal emancipation meant the death of slavery. Formal emancipation marked the "entire subversion of that institution." The rebellion was now "over" and "crushed."[54] Rep. Phelps quoted President Johnson[55] in asserting that slavery was ended. After formal emancipation, slavery was "dead and buried," according to Rogers. The comment of Burwell C. Ritter of Kentucky is representative:

> They [i.e., the Southern states] have done everything that has been required of them in order to [gain] their admission to seats in this Hall, and still we refuse them, notwithstanding they were told time after time by the highest authority that all that was necessary was for them to lay down their arms and submit to the laws. . . . Sir, why have the people in the lately rebellious States abolished slavery, pronounced their secession ordinances void, repudiated their war debts, unless it has been to conform to the requirement of the conquerors, and thereby give assurances, or guarantees if you please, that they will obey the laws of the United States.[56]

Thus, formal emancipation, the renunciation of the secession right, and the repudiation of the war debt defined slavery's resolution. According to Phelps, only "purblind patriots" still "predict the revival or even affirm the actual present existence of slavery."[57]

Northern Democratic definitions of slavery's destruction also can be found in their assertions and definitions of "peace," which came in several varieties of speeches. In all of them, they neatly parsed the slavery and postslavery periods, with formal emancipation marking the divide. Some speakers emphasized that the ex-Confederate region was loyal and harmonious. Rep. William E. Finck of Ohio, for example, remarked on the "profound peace" in the region; Southerners accepted the fact that slavery was a thing of the past.[58] Others, like Shanklin of Kentucky, emphasized the "persecutions and relentless oppression" that Republicans were enforcing on the South. This policy would lead to renewed war, Shanklin argued. Sen. Edgar Cowan of Pennsylvania, a conservative Republican who voted with the Northern Democrats on Reconstruction legislation, even in his sympathetic portrait of Southerners appealed to the "aristocracy" critique of the Slave Power. The Southern people were "abused by their leaders"[59] and were perfectly ready for readmission, he asserted.

Rep. Phelps perceived (correctly) that the former Confederate states would resist the legislation proposed by the Joint Committee of Fifteen.

> The congressional treatment of the eleven States lately in insurrection, according to the plan of the gentleman from Pennsylvania [Thaddeus Stevens], is so well adapted to provoke continued hostility to the Government and goad a maddened population into desperate resistance. . . . [I] believe that all further guarantees, by way of constitutional amendment or otherwise, as conditions precedent to a cautious and discriminating admission of loyal Representatives from States and districts whose inhabitants have been in insurrection, but who now present themselves in an attitude of loyalty and harmony are unnecessary, impolitic, unstatesmanlike and prejudicial to the peace and welfare of the country. . . . The question is simply one of union or disunion. . . . For myself I wish no new war-cry. . . .[60]

Shanklin insisted that all could be made well in the nation only by discharging the Joint Committee on Reconstruction, by abolishing the Freedmen's Bureau, by repealing the civil rights bill, and by admitting all the delegates from the seceded states to their seats in Congress.[61] In a similar fashion, Rep. Samuel J. Randall of Pennsylvania stated: "We can never have a continued peace until the principles embodied by Andrew Johnson in his veto of the Freedmen's Bureau bill, his veto of the civil rights bill and his speech of the 22nd of February last shall guide this country in a restoration of the Union of these States."[62]

By portraying Southerners as reformed and by portraying secession as the act of a now displaced aristocracy, Northern Democrats presented the slavery problem as fixed. In this way, they could lay the blame for postwar conflict at the feet of the Republicans, who now were sowing the seeds of disunion.[63] The Republicans were no better than the antebellum Southern Democrats because both parties renounced popular sovereignty doctrine and "divided the Union."[64]

Representing Political History

Northern Democrats, as is well-known, consistently charged Republicans with centralizing the government and overthrowing a well-established federalism. The Fourteenth Amendment overturned the "chief excellence"[65] of the Republic and the "chief cause of its wonderful success," namely, the balance set up between the states and the federal government. Rep. Cox called local self-government "the very genius of our civil polity."[66]

Less well-known is how Northern Democratic assertions of an established federalism rested on a representation of slavery history. This version suppressed recognition of many events of slavery politics, among them Lovejoy's murder, Hammond's gag rule, and the crisis over Helper's book. To acknowledge these disputes was to recognize the Republicans' political critique of slavery, that is, that slavery required the repression of civil liberties. It was to acknowledge that the antebellum notion of state sovereignty was under attack before the war, even if that attack was coming from outside institutional channels. This attack progressed, even though a consensus recognized that "state sovereignty" protected Southern slavery from federal reach, and even though *Barron v. Baltimore* (1833) held that the Bill of Rights was not applicable to the states.

In suppressing all acknowledgment of the Republicans' political critique of slavery—a critique which indicated that the limits of state authority over individual rights was under dispute—Northern Democrats strategically aligned themselves with Andrew Johnson.

> Andrew Johnson wants the Union as it was. He wants the Union that was made by the father and sages of the times that tried men's souls. He wants the Union which was intended to be the shield of the rights of the States, and the protector of and guardian of the rights of the Federal Government. He wants the proper equilibrium preserved between the three coordinate branches of the Federal Government. And because he will not violate every pledge of faith that the Republican party made to the people in 1864, he is to be branded here as a tyrant and usurper. . . . This Congress, by its acts, through this central directory of fifteen [the Joint Committee on Reconstruction]

is sapping the very lifeblood and weakening the very foundations of this Government. . . . Let us leave the landmarks of this Government as they were when the Government was made.[67]

Rep. John A. Nicholson of Delaware asserted, "all that we have accomplished as a people and as a nation" is owed to the Democratic Party. Rogers pronounced that Democratic doctrines had brought the country "to a state of prosperity unequaled in the annals of history."[68] Rep. Myer Strouse of Pennsylvania stated: "History should be our guide and counsel. . . . *What necessity is there now,* Mr. Speaker, that demands the change which this bill calls for? The history of the United States is the history of the Democratic party; its creed is the Constitution, and its principles have been for seventy-five years the operative cause of our country's rise, progress, strength, and greatness."[69]

Republicans, as we shall see, argued that necessity was clear. They consistently cited events in 1866 as demonstrating their point. But for Rep. Nicholson, these events were not a source of concern and not part of the slavery experience. His worry was that Republican legislation jeopardized the "excellent" balance set up by the Constitution.

That nicely adjusted balance is now, by this amendment [Fourteenth] to be permanently overthrown. The line of demarcation between State and Federal power, which has been already too much obscured by the great latitude of construction given of late to the several grants of power [e.g., to the legislative branch on the question of restoration and to the Joint Committee of Fifteen], is now to be entirely obliterated. The barriers erected by the Constitution to protect the States in absolute control of their municipal affairs are now to be thrown down for the Federal government to enter this wide domain, to roam at will, and bring prostrate at the feet of Federal power the most inestimable and most fondly cherished of all civil or political rights. That instrument, framed with such affectionate solicitude by the great and good men of the Revolution, who were actuated by nothing but devotion to the common good, is now to be changed. . . .[70]

He concluded, "to the states alone do we look for protection in the rights of life, liberty and property." Rogers frequently appealed to the original Constitution in defining slavery's resolution:

I mean to have peace by restoring and referring to the instrumentalities by which the Constitution and the Union were first established by our fathers; and I believe, if these instrumentalities, which were founded in a spirit of compromise, charity, friendship, love and affection, were employed in this House, the bonds which have been torn assunder by four years of bloody conflict will be again cemented together. . . . I desire to see the Union restored, the Union of our fathers. I want peace, prosperity, happiness, greatness, grandeur and glory such as characterized this nation when the Democratic party had control.[71]

In all of these comments the Democrats vaulted over many events of slavery politics. This leap is also evident in the Democrats' repeated claims that Democratic doctrines had brought "peace." Rogers claimed that the "doctrine of state sovereignty . . . led this country in peace and prosperity for seventy-five years.[72] This claim looks outlandish given the recent war. But it could make sense (Rogers could believe it) *if* he regarded the Southern Democratic rejection of the popular sovereignty principle and the claimed secession right as the *only* problems with slavery. The jump over many events of slavery politics, events that involved Southern suppressions of civil liberties, is consistent with the Northern Democratic understanding of slavery's transgressions. This has been my argument, of course, and it is consistent with Rogers's own claim that the Southern states had republican forms of government until the moment of secession.

In the *Slaughter-House Cases* (1873), Justice Samuel Miller limited the problems of slavery largely to those grounds on which the Northern Democrats distinguished themselves from the Southern Democrats. In rendering his interpretation of the citizenship and privileges and immunities clause, Miller also sidestepped events of slavery politics involving Southern suppressions of civil liberties.

Racial Belief System
The Northern Democratic doctrine of popular sovereignty was married to a strong belief in white supremacy and "white man's government." It was a doctrine of white popular sovereignty. (Moderate Republicans also believed in white superiority, but their commitment to black civil rights and individual rights under the Constitution was premised on a view of black capability that was more generous than that of Northern Demo-

crats but still short of the definition of black capability held by at least some Radicals and by Frederick Douglass.)

Northern Democrats reserved to local majorities the right to pass the Black Codes. Rep. Nicholson stated:

> Now, the Negro race in this country constitutes such a class which is easily and well defined; and the peace and welfare of a State, especially where they are found in great numbers, demand that the radical difference between them and the white race should be recognized by legislation; and every State should be allowed to remain free and independent in providing punishments for crime and otherwise regulating their internal affairs, so that they might properly discriminate between them, as their peace and safety might require. For the Negro is not actuated by the same motives as the white man, nor is he deterred from crime except by punishments adapted to the brutal, sensual nature which characterizes him. . . .[73]

Nicholson continued, "The object of government is not to benefit the individual. . . . The individual must yield to those restraints which a community for its own good sees fit to impose."

Maintaining that white majorities could use the legal system to enact their racialized understanding of the "common good," Northern Democrats asserted that blacks were not fit to be part of the collective national identity. Sen. Thomas A. Hendricks of Indiana stated: "I say we are not of the same race; we are so different that we ought not to compose one political community."[74] Rogers, too, asserted that blacks were not part of the "people."[75] In criticizing the Freedmen's Bureau, Rep. George Shanklin addressed the Republicans:

> [Y]ou have freed four million slaves, who were productive laborers, who were contented and happy and well provided for. . . . You have imposed upon the people a debt which I will not attempt to estimate, for the purpose of supporting a pet institution called the Freedmen's Bureau. Perhaps you have gained another object. You have through that bureau manufactured the materials that have filled the galleries of this Hall during the whole session. Crowds of these negroes have hung over us like a black and threatening cloud, while we were crucifying the Constitution of our fathers and trampling under our feet the rights and liberties of the people in passing the Freedmen's Bureau bill.[76]

When Shanklin refers to "the people," he clearly means white people. Rogers stated explicitly on many occasions, including the following, that the government was "made for white men and white women."

> They do not believe, nor can you make them believe—the edict of God Almighty is stamped against it—that there is a social equality between the black race and the white. I have no fault to find with the colored race. I have not the slightest antipathy to them. I wish them well, and if I were in a State where they exist in large numbers I would vote to give them every right enjoyed by white people except the right of a Negro man to marry a white woman and the right to vote. . . . Representatives of the eastern, middle, western and some of the border States come here and attempt in this indirect way to inflict upon the people of the South negro suffrage. God deliver this people from such a wicked, odious, pestilent despotism! God save the people of the South from the degradation by which they would be obliged to go to the polls and vote side by side with the Negro![77]

Rogers stated: "[The war was fought] because we desired to perpetuate the Union which our forefathers established and handed down to us for the protection and defense of the *white men* and *white women* of this land."[78] In this last comment, especially, Rogers's understanding of the problem with slavery is clearly linked to his racial beliefs. They are inseparable. David M. Potter's[79] comments on Stephen Douglas seem applicable to the congressional Northern Democrats in general. According to Potter, "a readiness to subordinate blacks made [Douglas] responsive to the local majoritarianism of whites."[80] Rogers's and the Northern Democrats' defense of local majoritarianism was always implicitly, and often explicitly, a white local majoritarianism.

Aggressive defenses of white local majoritarianism had a flip side in Democratic rhetoric, namely, Democratic "sympathy" for the emancipated slaves. Northern Democrats characterized emancipation as "the most monstrous act of cruelty." The "master was his best and kindest friend and the abolitionist his worst and most cruel enemy."[81] Referring to the Republicans, Nicholson stated: "They are not his true friends who are striving to thrust him up to the same level with the whites." Blacks were "treated with kindness and affection" as slaves.[82]

Rogers's concern with black men marrying white women is worth a brief comment. Northern Democrats had coined the term "miscegenation" during the presidential campaign of 1864 in an effort to delegitimate Lincoln and the Republicans. (Republicans responded to these assertions by either renouncing them or ignoring them.) The Northern Democrats had brought the specter of sex between black men and white women into wartime debates,[83] and they continued this practice in the Reconstruction Congresses.

My main point is that the Democrats' popular sovereignty/polity principles were racialized. The Northern Democratic version of "the problem" with slavery and the Northern Democratic insistence that local majorities retained the full measure of antebellum control over individual rights, with the one exception of instituting formal slave law, rested on a strong strain of white supremacy and the accompanying belief that blacks were not part of "the people." If scholars conceptualize Northern Democratic opposition to the amendments mainly in terms of their interpretation of the original Constitution without acknowledging that their popular sovereignty doctrine was racialized, the use and impact of racial belief systems in the Reconstruction debates will remain implicit and unrecognized.

When the Supreme Court endorsed much of the Northern Democratic version of slavery history, the Court also implicitly institutionalized their race theory. Questions of race became latent in Court decisions, and this very latency contributed to the "impacted" status of Court precedents on the citizenship clause and privileges or immunities clause of the Fourteenth Amendment.

3

Republican Slavery Criticism

Rep. George W. Julian of Indiana, a leading Radical, identified slavery as the "cause of our National troubles." He wanted "the last vestige of slavery scourged out of life."[1] What Julian meant by "the last vestiges of slavery" is unclear. The Northern military victory was generally understood to have repudiated the right to secession and the compact theory that justified it. Some notion of federal supremacy had been established with the Northern victory, though its contours and scope were left uncertain.

Republicans often began their speeches in the wake of the Thirteenth Amendment by "elucidat[ing] the causes and objects of the war," "assess-[ing] the present condition" and the "causes of rebellion," and "survey-[ing] the present situation."[2] What followed were Republican versions of past experiences and present events. Rep. Sidney Perham of Maine stated: "the doctrine of secession should be repudiated and branded with everlasting infamy."[3] But Southern repudiation of the right of secession did not resolve the war's issues.

These speeches by both Moderate and Radical Republicans provide clues about Republican understandings of what it meant to destroy slavery. In these speeches, both Moderates and Radicals grouped postwar events as part of the slavery experience. For them, slavery was still alive in the postwar South. Some of their speeches refer simultaneously to the end of slavery and the continuation of it, despite its formal prohibition. Sen. Henry Wilson of Massachusetts, alluding generally to laws passed in the Southern states after the adoption of the Thirteenth Amendment, stated: "In several of these States new laws are being framed containing provisions wholly inconsistent with the freedom of the freedmen."[4] Prominent Radicals such as Sen. Charles Sumner of Massachusetts constructed and mobilized a distinction between abolishing slavery "in form" and "in substance." Rep. William Windom of Maine referred to the "body" and "spirit" of slavery.[5]

Republicans consistently linked pre- and post-Appomattox events, constructing a continuum of experiences. Outside the halls of Congress, Carl Schurz observed that the "embers of slavery" were still alive.[6] Inside Congress, Republicans dismissed, usually with great derision, the Northern Democrats' portraits of formal emancipation as a clean break with the slavery past. As Republicans gained experience with the depth and extent of Southern recalcitrance, the contexts changed in which they articulated their objectives and applied their constitutional theory. Expressions of legislative intent were a moving target of sorts. In asserting that Northern Democratic programs for restoration would make a mockery of freedom and lose all that the war accomplished, Republicans also appealed to the soldiers' sufferings.[7]

A View of the South

While Northern Democrats and President Andrew Johnson described the Southern states as having an "attitude of loyalty,"[8] many Republicans responded with scorn.[9] Journalists' reports from the South, especially by those who proclaimed that they were initially "Douglas men," were influential in the North.[10] "The war did not squelch out rebellion," declared Moderate Republican Sen. William Pitt Fessenden of Maine, "it simply disarmed it. . . . Treason is as rampant in that region as it was in 1861."[11] Rep. Glenni W. Scofield of Pennsylvania stated: "There is nothing in their past conduct nor present attitude that justifies the use of the word submission."[12] Rep. Ephraim R. Eckley of Ohio commented: "Peace we are told, reigns throughout our borders. I wish I could believe that." He continued:

> That the rebels are conquered, is an admitted fact. That they have any loyalty, any love, for the peace of the country and permanency of the Government, is not manifested by anything they have done. It is true they say they accepted the situation, so does the culprit. They say they laid down their arms. But their arms were forced from them. They say they disbanded their armies, but their armies were captured or scattered by the Union forces. Then what have they done to prove their submission to the law? They have neglected to pay their

portion of taxes; they have expelled loyal citizens from the South; they have treated with brutality the freedmen, and enacted laws disgraceful to a Christian age or a Christian people. Those who engaged in the rebellion are as disloyal today as they were at any time during the war. Will anyone pretend they have changed? [13]

According to both Moderate and Radical Republicans, the ex-Confederates had not changed. The rebellion was not dead.[14] Rep. William Higby of Pennsylvania stated that a "virulent and deep-seated disease still lingers in a latent form to break forth soon again." Sen. Benjamin Wade of Ohio declared that the Northern military victory was not enough. Principles had not yet triumphed.[15]

It is important to remember that Republicans had articulated economic and political critiques of slavery before the war. It is easy for the twentieth-century reader to regard these Republican declarations as mere rhetoric, as strategic tools used in the service of their political interest. Certainly, the Republicans had an interest in staying in power. But, as William Nelson has argued, Northern Democratic charges that Republicans were only narrowly interested in their own political future should be dismissed. Republican criticisms of the Black Codes, ex-Confederate takeovers of political institutions, and political violence were continuous with congressmen's economic and political critiques of slavery. In defending their reform package, Republicans continued their antebellum condemnations of the Slave Power.[16] Rep. Leonard Myers of Pennsylvania stated that the war vindicated the dignity of labor and the "laboring masses of the South." [17]

Jeffrey Tulis has argued that rhetorical practices are reflections and elaborations of underlying doctrines of governance. "[P]olitical rhetoric is reflective of something more fundamental. But that more fundamental phenomenon is intimately bound up with rhetoric itself; it is the idea or set of ideas that legitimates political practice." [18] The set of ideas held by Republicans included an understanding about *what it was* in the antebellum slavery system that was "the problem." Their postwar distinction between the body and spirit of slavery was the means by which they elaborated this understanding and applied it to an ever-changing set of circumstances (continued Southern recalcitrance).

Republicans commented specifically on Southern racial sentiments. These sentiments, they asserted, had not been altered by the military defeat, and they remained a problem. Ex-Confederates, according to Rep.

Roswell Hart of New York, were "bred in a school which has taught them that a black man can have no rights which they are bound to respect." Rep. Perham stated: "They may accept the fact of emancipation, but they still believe that slavery is the best condition for the colored race, and it is but reasonable to suppose that as far as possible this idea would, if they were allowed to govern, be embodied in law, and carried out in their intercourse with the colored people.[19] Rep. Ebon C. Ingersoll of Illinois asserted that the South "will seek again to enslave them, not perhaps by a sale on the auction block as in the olden time, but by vagrant laws and other laws and regulations concerning the freedmen, which subject them to a surveillance and will eventually subject them to a servitude little less degrading and no less galling than the old chains of slavery which they wore so long."[20] I will return to the subject of Republican racial be-liefs, but it is important to flag the Republican identification of postwar, racially motivated acts as being among the continued threats of slavery.

On the Status of the Former Confederate States

Republican assertions about "the problem" with slavery also can be seen in their arguments about the status of the ex-Confederate states. North-ern Democrats and Republicans made many speeches after passage of the Thirteenth Amendment arguing about the status of the states of the former Confederacy (whether they were "in" or "out" of the Union; whether their secession meant that they had, in fact, left the Union; and whether, upon passage of the Thirteenth Amendment, they were en-titled to readmission to Congress). Lincoln called the question of status a "profitless abstraction."[21] Echoing Lincoln, Ingersoll said he regarded this "technical question" with "supreme indifference." "The president [Johnson] and his friends [the Northern Democrats] continually persist in declaring to the people that the issue now is whether or not a State can secede. . . ."[22]

Rep. Scofield remarked on the absence of "precedents" to guide con-gressmen on this question. He stated, "our fathers did not provide for what they could not foresee. There are no precedents on file to guide us. This is the first disunion rebellion."[23] "The real issue" was a *practical* one, "whether those unrepentant rebels shall be represented in Congress, and by their power here defeat the objects of the loyal majority in Con-gress [and] defeat the restoration of the Union upon a loyal and humane basis."[24] The question of the official status of the ex-Confederate states was not an urgent one for Republicans.

Most Republicans disagreed with Rep. Thaddeus Stevens of Pennsylvania that the ex-Confederate states had the status of "conquered provinces,"[25] but the belief that state status was at least "suspended" was a matter of consensus among them. The untrustworthiness of the ex-Confederates was the immediate Republican concern.[26] Moderate and Radical Republicans alike asserted that exclusion was simply a matter of common sense.[27] They frequently took mocking tones in response to Northern Democratic assertions that the Southern states were loyal and ready for readmission. Just as Northern Democratic assertions about the status of ex-Confederate states reveal their versions of "the problem" with slavery, so too do Republican arguments.

Defending Southern exclusion from Congress, Republicans argued that the war had not ended but had *transmuted*. Based on their assessment of the "Southern heart," Republicans warned that the readmission of the ex-Confederate states to Congress would win the South, politically, what it could not win on the battlefield. Their view echoed that of William Grosvenor, who had predicted that the contest on the battlefield would be moved to the political arena, where the South's chances of success were far better. "The old battles for liberty and justice on the one side and for slavery and tyranny on the other are upon us again, and we must fight them out. The clash of arms, it is true has ceased, the physical battle has ended between the North and South, but the old battle of ideas is upon us still."[28] Rep. Perham stated: "Instead of accepting in good faith the results of the war, they openly declare they are only subdued for the time being, and they will now rely on their influence inside the organization of the Government to accomplish what they have failed to do outside by the bullet.[29] Rep. Myers said: "There is another war being waged, and between the same parties and their respective supporters [i.e., the Northern Democrats] who struggled for ascendancy on the battlefield. It is a war of ideas. . . . The true patriot everywhere will watch with profound interest the result of this great moral and intellectual struggle."[30] Others made similar statements.[31] In light of the Republican view that the war had not ended but had transmuted, it makes sense that they saw Southern renunciation of the secession right as a wholly inadequate remedy for the slavery problem.

In the postwar years, Richard Henry Dana popularized the "grasp of war" theory, the doctrine that it was up to the national government to decide precisely when peace had arrived. Legal scholar Michael Benedict has noted that Dana's "grasp of war" doctrine gave legitimacy to Northern leverage over the defeated ex-Confederate states.[32] This is certainly true. This doctrine, however, was more than a strategic political device. It was part of the Republican effort to draw the line between the "slavery period" and the "postslavery period" in a way that secured the Republic from slavery's threats, as the Republicans understood those threats.

The Continued Threats of Slavery

In support of their view that Southern exclusion from Congress was legitimate and that slavery remained a problem despite the Confederate surrender, Republicans cited Southern political violence: "Their policy is to render it so uncomfortable and hazardous for loyal men to live among them as to compel them to leave. Many hundreds of northern men who have made investments and attempted to make themselves homes in these States have been driven away. Others have been murdered in cold blood as a warning to all northern men who should attempt to settle in the South. Officers charged with the execution of the laws have been intimidated by threats of violence and brutally murdered for a faithful discharge of duty."[33] In addition, many Moderate Republicans cited Southern states' abuses of rights.[34] They condemned the Black Codes which contained racial classifications. Civil rights included "being amenable to the same punishments as other citizens." A government "republican in form . . . recognizes the rights of mankind, irrespective of color, within its local jurisdiction.[35] Sen. Lyman Trumbull of Illinois emphasized that political rights, such as voting and holding office, were not included in civil rights. "The granting of civil rights does not, and never did in this country, carry with it . . . political privileges."[36] According to Foner, protection of the freedmen's civil rights followed from the suppression of the rebellion.[37] Free labor principles were embodied in the principle of equality in civil rights.

Sen. William P. Fessenden, a Moderate, also explicitly condemned the suppression of free speech.[38] Rep. Ralph P. Buckland of Ohio seemed to be referring to antebellum Southern suppressions of antislavery activists' civil liberties when he stated: "The people of the loyal states will never again submit to the indignities and outrages, which were perpetrated upon northern people at the South previous to the war." Foner has remarked on the "systematic violations of Bill of Rights guarantees in the South in 1866," arguing that it was "abundantly clear" that Republicans wished to give constitutional sanction to the states' obligation to respect such key provisions as free speech, press, jury, and protections from cruel and unusual punishments. Some portions of the Bill of Rights, Foner notes, were of little moment in 1866.[39]

Radical Republican Sen. Sumner argued that a group of rights was "essential to Emancipation. Without [these guarantees]," stated Sumner, "Emancipation will be only half done. It is our duty to see it wholly done."[40] After formal emancipation was accomplished, Northern Democrats and ex-Confederates made plain their view that formal self-ownership did not carry an automatic package of civil rights and personal rights under the Constitution. It became clear that such a view would be challenged. A multitude of Republican comments suggests that they, indeed, held this view.[41]

Moderate Republican condemnation of the Black Codes is open to multiple interpretations. It is not clear if this condemnation indicated a commitment to a formal equality model of the Fourteenth Amendment (in which states would be prohibited from using racial classifications in their legislation; individual action to deny rights would not be prohibited). If Republican condemnation of the Black Codes is viewed in isolation, that is, separately from events that occurred afterward, formal equality models are more easily attributable to Republicans. But if this condemnation is viewed with reference to the Enforcement Acts of 1870–71, which brought private, racially motivated deprivations of civil, personal, and political rights within the direct reach of the federal government, this attribution becomes more difficult. I do not investigate the debates over the Enforcement Acts of 1870–71 although I think that minimal information about them is sufficient to warrant a pause in attributing a formal equality model to Republicans. After all, the Black Codes caused an uproar in the North. By the end of 1866, most states had repealed the racially specific provisions, thus conforming to the formal equality model. But unequal enforcement of racially neutral language remained a problem. Republicans believed that Fourteenth Amendment rights continued to be denied. They passed the Enforcement Acts of 1870–71 to correct this. This legislation suggests that Republicans held something more than a formal equality model.

Republicans interpreted Lincoln's Unionism in a distinctive way, one that legitimated federal authority and oversight of certain matters that had been in the hands of the states before the war. The Moderates' dilemma, according to Foner, "was that most of the rights they sought to guarantee for blacks had always been state concerns. Federal action to secure these rights raised the specter of an undue 'centralization' of power."[42] As a strategy to legitimate new federal guarantees for these rights, Republicans argued that the notion of states' rights had been perverted in the antebellum decades. They reiterated their political critiques of slavery developed before the war. Various state powers, such as censorship of antislavery mailings and books, had been exercised illegitimately, they charged, and hence they were not legitimately established.

Republicans developed and mobilized a distinction between arbitrary (slave) power and (legitimate) established right in order to bring certain traditionally local matters under federal oversight. (Other traditionally local matters, such as marriage laws, remained "properly" under state control. Republicans, with a few notable exceptions,[43] declined to challenge the "established" status of planters' property rights.) As Frederick Douglass noted, however, no "political idea" was "more deeply rooted in the minds of men of all sections of the country [than] the right of each State to control its own local affairs."[44]

In 1949, Charles Fairman argued that the Fourteenth Amendment did not originally apply the Bill of Rights to the states. He *assumed* that the Court's 1833 decision in *Barron* (which held the Bill of Rights applicable to the federal government only) defined "established" states' rights. William Crosskey favored the incorporation thesis. He argued that Republicans rejected the *Barron* decision.

My point is that Republicans and Northern Democrats contested the criteria for defining "established" states' rights and that this contest was part of the larger dispute over the nature of slavery's threats. An examination of slavery in rhetorical terms, as well as constitutional ones, clearly shows this to be the case. Republicans and Northern Democrats argued about sources of authority for defining states' rights as "established." Northern Democrats relied on institutional sources such as the Supreme Court (and its *Barron* decision), while Republicans looked to noninstitutional sources, such as their own slavery critiques and the "declaratory theory" of rights. A great deal was at stake in providing an authoritative definition of "established" states' rights. If state power over a particular matter was established, then federal oversight was illegitimate; if that state power was not established, then federal oversight could be legitimate.

Northern Democrats had a rhetorical edge when it came to the contest to define "established" states' rights. After the war ended, Republicans faced a problem that Northern Democrats did not confront. The problem was that Republican policies evolved rapidly during and after the war, especially in response to Southern recalcitrance and Johnson's presidential reconstruction. This meant that Republicans were open to the criticism that their postwar policies contradicted their prewar statements and promises.

In 1861, Congress expressed its Unionist stance in the Crittenden Resolution. This joint resolution[45] reflected a unionist stance: "[T]his war is not prosecuted upon our part in any spirit of oppression, nor for any purpose of conquest or subjugation, nor purpose of overthrowing or interfering with the rights or established institutions of those States, but to defend and maintain the supremacy of the Constitution and all laws made in pursuance thereof, and to preserve the Union with all the dignity, equality and rights of the several States unimpaired; that as soon as these objects are accomplished the war ought to cease."

Interpretation of the Crittenden Resolution was contested in the 39th Congress. The Northern Democrats cited the resolution in arguing that Republican legislation contradicted their antebellum statements of purpose.[46] In a typical statement, Rep. Samuel J. Randall of Pennsylvania asserted that the Republicans "never expressed any purpose before the people to do what they have since done."[47]

Republicans countered by appealing to their own political critique of slavery (that slavery destroyed civil liberties). Fessenden referred derisively to the "Dogma of supreme State sovereignty," a dogma created by the selfishness, political power, and monetary interests of the Slave Power. Moderate Rep. John A. Bingham of Ohio mocked stated sovereignty as a political disease.[48] Slavery went "against the political rights of the masses of Southern white men."[49] "For years," Rep. Myers stated, slavery "sapped at the life of the Republic, at last striking at the life of the Republic."[50] By referring back to their political critiques of slavery, Republicans tried to render their prewar policy consistent with their postwar reform program. But their critiques of state sovereignty doctrine lacked institutional recognition.

The Basis of Political Society

For Republicans, the war had thrown the "foundations of public life" open for discussion. Republicans sought to prevent the reestablishment of white oligarchies and black serfdom.[51] The exclusion of ex-Confederates from the 39th Congress was the most basic step toward accomplishing this goal. Changes in the basis of representation and checks on political violence also were needed. Rep. John F. Farnsworth of Illinois tied these concerns together:

> Those gentlemen on the other side of the House . . . think it would be an excellent idea to have the rebels here, to themselves vote upon and fix conditions of reconstruction. A most happy idea! Having failed to destroy the Government by a resort to arms, now only once let them in here under the old apportionment, which makes a rebel of South Carolina as big as two or three loyal men of Illinois, let them in with the blood of slain patriots yet dripping from their fingers, and the doubly damning crime of starving prisoners still blackening their souls, and then talk about amending the Constitution.[52]

Restrictions on representation were the "only safe rule," for "the day of our peril is not yet passed."[53] Unless the Constitution prescribed penalties for states that disenfranchised black men (what Republicans hoped to accomplish with section 2 of the Fourteenth Amendment),[54] these states would gain great advantages in national political strength. Southern states, the Republicans predicted, would deny black men the vote. Under a population-based apportionment scheme, however, black citizens would count in the apportionment for assessing the number of representatives that a state sent to the House of Representatives. Thus, Southern states would gain political power at the national level by using a black population that they were disenfranchising at home.[55] The Republicans who spoke on section 2 of the Fourteenth Amendment expressed support for this section, though many voiced reservations about section 3.[56] To forgo restrictions on Southern representation would admit no difference between the "virtue" of Northern soldiers and the "vice" of the ex-Confederates:

> To restore these States to their normal relations without any restrictions is to make no distinction between virtue and vice. . . . It is claimed that the inhabitants of these States recently in armed rebel-

lion are repentant. Where is the evidence? Do they manifest it by murdering Union men, by electing traitors to offices of trust, or are we to believe it from their arrogance of manner and the assumptions of their press? . . . Look at it. Our soldiers sacrificed home and all of its joys, turned their wives and their children over to the charities of the nation, and then they offered themselves upon the altar of their country. By this patriotic devotion they saved our Government from its enemies. In memory of this heroism, in reward of this love of country, it is proposed to admit their unrepentant enemies into these sacred Halls to enact laws. . . .[57]

Ex-Confederate takeovers of local political offices also produced deep concern. Rep. Sidney Perham read a clipping from a North Carolina newspaper, the *Raleigh Standard,* that reported the town of Wilmington passing into the hands of the original secessionists. Rep. William Lawrence of Ohio stated: "Already the political ax is falling upon the necks of our friends. Heads are falling in my own State."[58] Former Union General Nathaniel P. Banks of Massachusetts, a Moderate House Republican, did not want "enemies of the country in possession of political power in whole or in part in the local governments or in representation here." He argued as explicitly as any Republican that the basis of political society had to change in order to secure the peace. "It is my belief that reorganization of governments in the insurgent States can be secured only by measures which will work a change in the basis of political society. I do not think this can be done by theoretical constitutional or statutory provisions. Anything that leaves the basis of political society in the southern States untouched leaves an enemy in condition to renew the war at his pleasure."[59] Republicans tied reforms in the basis of representation to their slavery critique. Illegitimate political power was part of the problem with slavery, and the political process needed to be protected from future abuse by ex-Confederates who sought to accomplish by legislation what could not be accomplished on the battlefield. Political violence against white and black Republicans was also a threat to the political process.

Race

Republicans referred to the "prejudices" of Southerners and the "troubling influence" of this prejudice.[60] Sen. William P. Fessenden conceded black inferiority but he went on to condemn the Northern Democrats' "race harangues about a white man's govt."[61] Rep. Perham commented that the ex-Confederates "still believe slavery is the best condition for [blacks] and will strive to achieve a condition "as near as slavery as possible"[62] Michael Benedict's view that many Radicals were "racist"[63] is not contradictory. It was possible to believe in white superiority yet be committed to protecting blacks from racially motivated deprivations of civil and personal (and later political) rights.[64]

Republicans frequently labeled Southern Black Codes as an attempt to re-enslave the freedmen. "[T]he South, being relieved from the military power of the Government, will seek to again enslave [the freedmen] not perhaps by a sale on the auction-block as in the olden time, but by vagrant laws and other laws and regulations concerning the freedmen. . . . Here you have a fair sample of the legislation of a state which has 'accepted the situation.' Is such a State fit to be represented now in Congress? Let the loyal people answer!"[65] Rep. Ingersoll quoted portions of Mississippi's Black Codes:

"An act to regulate the relation of master and apprentice, as relates to freedmen, freed Negroes and mulattos." "Article fifty-eight, section eleven, page 248, Revised Code, makes it punishable with death for a Negro to murder, commit rape, burn houses, commit robbery or attempt to commit such crimes." White persons are not punishable with death for most of the offenses mentioned in this section, or for the attempt to commit any one of them. "Article forty-five, page 245, provides that a slave shall receive twenty lashes if he be found away from the place of his employment without a pass. Reenacted for the freedmen. . . ." "Article fifty-one, page 247, makes it punishable for Negroes to congregate at night, or hold schools. Reenacted for the freedmen."[66]

In citing the Black Codes in their speeches, Rep. Thomas D. Eliot and Sen. Sumner of Massachusetts articulated the view that a federal "duty to protect" was inherent in formal emancipation. "The knot which politicians could not untie during eighty years of peace, the sword of Mr. Lincoln cut at one blow. The power to liberate, which is now confessed, involved the duty to protect. . . . Wherever we turn in our legislative path, we encounter questions of freedmen and freedmen's rights. No peace will come that will 'stay' until the Government that decreed freedom shall vindicate and enforce its rights by appropriate legislation."[67]

Four million slaves have been declared to be freemen; and by whom and by what power? By the national Government; and let me say that, as the national Government gave that freedom, it belongs to the national Government to secure it. The national Government cannot leave those men whom it has made free to the guardianship of custody or tender mercies of any other government [i.e., state government]. It is bound to take them into its own keeping, to surround them all by its own protecting power, and invest them with all the rights and conditions which in the exercise of its best judgment shall seem necessary to that end.[68]

Eliot read aloud reports of brutal violence sent by the generals who were assigned to the Freedmen's Bureau in Texas, Mississippi, Georgia, South Carolina, North Carolina, and Louisiana: "Manifestly, [intervention] is needed; for if the startling facts that come to us from the recent rebel States of fiendish oppression and brutal outrage were wholly undisclosed, we yet should know that masters who had rioted in the lusts of slavery would not let their bondsmen go in peace; or if they did, we still should know that a race prostrate for generations beneath the heel of tyrannous power could not have their freedom made effectual without our legislative aid."[69] As already noted, I do not examine debate over the Enforcement Act of 1870 and the Ku Klux Klan Act of 1871. But Moderate Republican condemnation of political violence in 1866 and their votes for the Enforcement Acts of 1870–71 suggest that they viewed Klan violence as among the continued threats of slavery and a threat to the political process. Radical Republicans, who were the first to condemn racially motivated political violence, did not alter the national climate but they understood the nature and drift of its direction.[70]

Republican critiques of the Black Codes can be understood as a preference for formal equality (against which the Supreme Court's rejection of racial legislative classifications—for example, in *Strauder*—can appear consistent, as can a color-blind jurisprudence). However, Republican critiques of the codes also can be read as a condemnation of Southern attempts to use the legal system to enact a racial caste structure. This could go beyond racial legislative classifications to reach Jim Crow. Republican critiques of political violence and the Black Codes also can be read as a condemnation of blocked job opportunities, especially racially motivated ones. This reading of Republican critiques of the codes can support the argument that the "emptier" formalism of the Supreme Court was not the formalism of the Republicans. My point is that alternative readings of Republican arguments about the Black Codes are possible.

The Original Constitution

Republican constitutional theory has attracted a lot of attention from scholars who argue that Republicans originally applied the Bill of Rights to the states. In this regard, my point is to note the intertwined nature of constitutional language and slavery criticism and the significance of the slavery idiom in communicating legislative objectives.

Rep. John A. Bingham, principal draftsman of section 1 of the Fourteenth Amendment and a Republican Moderate, made multiple references to the antebellum Constitution.[71] In Bingham's comments, slavery appears in both rhetorical and constitutional terms. On one occasion, Bingham stated:

> The necessity for the first section of this amendment to the Constitution, Mr. Speaker, is one of the lessons that have been taught to your committee and taught to all the people of this country by the history of the past four years of terrific conflict—that history in which God is, and in which He teaches the profoundest lessons to men and nations. There was a want hitherto, and there remains a want now, in the Constitution of our country, which the proposed amendment will supply. What is that? It is the power in the people, the whole people of the United States, by express authority of the Constitution to do that by congressional enactment which hitherto they have not had the power to do, and have never even attempted to do; that is, to protect by national law the privileges and immunities of all the citizens of the Republic and the inborn rights of every person within its jurisdiction whenever the same shall be abridged or denied by the unconstitutional acts of any State.[72]

This passage is quoted by both sides in the debate over whether the Fourteenth Amendment originally protected the Bill of Rights against state infringement. Fairman, who denied that the Fourteenth Amendment meant to apply the Bill of Rights to the states, asserted that references to the "lessons" of the war were an "inapt" way to express such an objective.

An important dimension of Republican speeches was the criticism leveled at the Founding Fathers, the original Constitution, and the "old" federalism. Rep. Thaddeus Stevens represented the Civil War as springing from "the vicious principles incorporated into the institutions of our country." Stevens stated: "Our fathers had been compelled to postpone the principles of their great Declaration and wait for their full establishment till a more propitious time. That time ought to be present now. But the public mind has been educated in error for a century. How difficult in a day to unlearn it. In rebuilding, it is necessary to clear away the rotten and defective portions of the old foundations, and to sink deep and found the repaired edifice upon the firm foundation of eternal justice."[73] Discussing section 1 of the Fourteenth Amendment, Stevens identified a "defect" in the Constitution. "I can hardly believe that any person can be found who will not admit that every one of these provisions is just. They are all asserted in some form or other, in our Declaration or organic laws. But the Constitution limits only the action of Congress, and is not a limitation on the States. This amendment supplies that defect and allows Congress to correct the unjust legislation of the States. . . ."[74]

Republicans, it is important to note, held varying views of the original Constitution. Whereas Stevens seemed to think that the original Constitution never limited the states (and hence was correctly interpreted by the *Barron* Court), Bingham believed that the original Constitution did impose limitation on the states but that those limitations were not enforceable. (Chapter 4 cites statements from Justices Bradley and Swayne in their *Slaughter-House* dissenting opinions, which appear to acknowledge this nonenforcement doctrine.) Bingham and Stevens agreed, however, that state infringements of Bill of Rights guarantees had to be prevented in the future. The variety of Republican critiques of the original Constitution, all spurred by Republican assessments of slavery's abuses, went unpreserved in the Supreme Court's account of slavery history.

In 1866, Republicans got warrants for their legislation and "multigenerational synthesis" from postwar Southern resistance, especially, but also from their own slavery critiques and the "declaratory theory" of individual rights. Republican slavery criticism appealed to warrants that were under construction in the decades before the Civil War. These warrants, which included a notion of individual liberty against popular majorities and a theory of race that held blacks as suited for civil equality and perhaps political equality, even while regarding them as unsuited for social equality, were not yet institutionally validated. The idea that popular majorities could be threats to individual liberty was still new, and most Northerners held negative views about black capability. It was only for a few short years that the fate of the freedmen was associated with the Northern victory.

Northern outrage at Southern recalcitrance was the muscle behind the Republicans' restoration program. Republicans had principles, but these principles had little institutional recognition. Popular support for Republican initiatives was real though short-lived. In 1865, Northern Democrats began what Hyman calls an "astonishing renaissance."[75]

Framing Questions About Republican Intent

A traditionally asked question among constitutional scholars is whether the Republicans intended to fundamentally transform or eviscerate the traditional federal system. This question can take another form: namely, did Republicans intend to protect freemen's rights at the expense of traditional limits of federalism? Participants usually enter the fray by answering this question in the negative or affirmative. I enter it by arguing against the question.

As I argued in the introduction, the designation "traditional federal system" is vague, for it is not clear to what it refers. Depending on its referent, the answer to the question of whether Republicans intended to transform it (or whether Republican legislation was originally understood as transforming it) will change. If the "traditional federal system" refers to state authority over civil rights (the nineteenth-century definition of civil rights) and the Bill of Rights, as *practiced* before the war and as *defined by the Court* in *Barron,* then Republicans expressed the goal of changing it. But if the "traditional federal system" refers to a *general notion of limited government,* then Republicans wanted to keep this system. Republicans were not hearty enthusiasts for national power, and they understood the incorporation of the Bill of Rights as a narrow and limited grant of national power. Significantly, they imagined that new federal oversight provided for "fundamental" rights would be triggered infrequently. Evidence suggests that Republicans were somewhat naive with respect to gauging Southern resistance. Of course, they did not have the experience that we have today. It is in the twentieth century, for example, that the equation between incorporation and "broad and undefined" national power has become more widespread.

If scholars ask, "Did Republicans intend to transform the traditional federal system," without understanding that "traditional federal system" can refer to different things, then inquiry into Republican objectives immediately will be put offtrack. If an equation between "incorporation" and "broad national power" shapes inquiry into Republican objectives, then evidence that Republicans held a narrow, corrective vision (evidence that exists) will lead some scholars to conclude that Republicans wanted to maintain the traditional system, not incorporate the Bill of Rights, and not enact aggressive federal protection of black civil rights. And evidence that Republicans wanted to overturn *Barron,* enact a free labor vision, and guarantee black access to civil rights even against race-based denials of those rights by private individuals like landowners (evidence that exists) will lead other scholars to conclude that Republicans supported broad national power. Both groups would be half-right (they have found important evidence) and half-wrong (they have drawn too simplistic a conclusion from this evidence). Both groups would be suppressing evidence that according to twentieth-century lights (but not the Republican lights in 1866) looks contradictory.

The notion of "revolution" in federalism is also vague. Is getting the promise of the Declaration of Independence back on track after ninety years revolutionary? Some Republicans talked about their legislation as revolutionary; others said it was "merely" corrective. Remember Lincoln's repudiation-as-affirmation theme. Republican objectives were revolutionary and conservative at the same time. My point is that the same action (say, applying the Bill of Rights to the states or guaranteeing black access to civil rights) can be alternately described in the high-flown rhetoric of revolution or in the low-key "merely corrective" conservative register. The problem is that twentieth-century scholars have not always been attentive to local Republican vocabularies that were in use during the debates or to the Republican (but not twentieth-century) equation between federal oversight of "fundamental" rights and a narrow federal role. Finally, the question of whether the Supreme Court betrayed Republican objectives is poorly structured. As chapter 4 shows, both "yes" and "no" would be inadequate. A better answer is "partially."

*   *   *

Maurice Halbwachs's work on collective memory[76] provides a useful way of conceptualizing these debates. His work also provides a good transition to chapter 4. In the passage below, Halbwachs speaks of society transforming its religion, but what he says is applicable to the Republicans' attempt to transform society and government:

> [W]hen a society transforms its religion, it advances somewhat into unknown territory. At the beginning it does not foresee the consequences of the new principles that it asserts. Social forces, among others, prevail and displace the group's center of gravity. But in order for this center to remain in equilibrium, readaptation is required so that the various tendencies of all the institutions constituting the common way of life are adjusted to each other. Society is aware that the new religion is not an absolute beginning. The society wishes to adopt these larger and deeper beliefs without entirely rupturing the framework of notions in which it has matured up until this point. That is why at the same time that society projects into its past conceptions that were recently elaborated, it is also intent on incorporating into the new religion elements of old cults that are assimilable into a new framework. Society must persuade its members that they already carry these beliefs within themselves at least partially, or even that they will recover beliefs, which had been rejected some time ago. But this is possible only if society does not confront all of the past, if it at least preserves the forms of the past. Even at the moment it is evolving, society returns to its past. It enframes the new elements that it pushes to the forefront in a totality of remembrances, traditions and familiar ideas.[77]

If "doctrines of governance" is substituted for "religion," and if "Republicans" is substituted for "society" (thus implicitly introducing competition into Halbwachs's Durkheimian rendering), what we have is a sociological formulation of Bruce Ackerman's notion of multigenerational synthesis. Ackerman defines multigenerational synthesis as different blendings of past tradition and experience with present-day visions and goals.[78]

To paraphrase Halbwachs, Republicans had to persuade Northerners that they already carried Republican beliefs within themselves at least partially, or that Republican legislation was a recovery of beliefs, which had been rejected some time ago. (Lincoln's repudiation-as-affirmation trope,[79] that is, the repudiation of slavery as an affirmation of original polity principles, comes to mind here.) Persuading people in this way was possible only if Northern society did not confront all of the past. And Northern Democrats built a slavery criticism that spotlighted deeply institutionalized components of the past: a Revolutionary era conception of liberty (i.e., the liberty of popular majorities against central governments); a theory of race that held blacks unfit for membership in the national collective; and Court precedent such as *Barron v. Baltimore* (the 1833 case holding the Bill of Rights applicable to the federal government only; again, the decision left the states free to abridge Bill of Rights guarantees).

The Republican-Northern Democratic contest to provide an authoritative multigenerational synthesis set the stage for the Supreme Court. William Riker, a political scientist, has studied the processes by which political ideas are transmitted and approved. In his studies of political rhetoric he has found that it is critical to understand how alternatives are set up. "People win politically," Riker states, "by more than rhetorical attraction. Typically they win because they have set up the situation in such a way that other people will want to join them — or will feel forced by circumstances to join them. . . ."[80] With Fourteenth Amendment debate carried on in the terms of slavery criticism, and with the Northern Democrats' version of "the problem" with slavery tied to deeply institutionalized warrants, a set of alternatives was set up to favor the Northern Democrats. The new elements that the Supreme Court endorsed in its postwar decisions were packaged in "a totality of remembrances, traditions and familiar ideas" that borrowed heavily from Northern Democratic slavery criticism.

4

The Supreme Court's Official History

The "one pervading purpose" of the Reconstruction Amendments, declared Justice Samuel Miller famously in the *Slaughter-House Cases,* "found in them all, lying at the foundation of each, and without which none of them would have been even suggested," was "the freedom of the slave race, the security and firm establishment of that freedom, and the protection of the newly-made freeman and citizen from the oppressions of those who had formerly exercised unlimited dominion over him."[1] This passage has been quoted many times, often by those who charge that Miller and the Supreme Court betrayed Republican objectives and subverted the original understanding.

The *Slaughter-House Cases* was the first major Reconstruction era Supreme Court decision. Involving white butchers, not Klansmen, the case dealt with state legislative power and federal judicial authority. However, it also held implications for federal (congressional and judicial) protections of black rights. Commentators agree that the *Slaughter-House Cases* turned the privileges or immunities clause of the Fourteenth Amendment into a "dead letter."[2] They disagree about whether this was a good thing. Those who believe the Republicans used the clause as the vehicle to apply the Bill of Rights to the states condemn the Court's interpretation of the clause. The Reconstruction Court, however, has not been without its defenders. "What is remarkable," states Michael Benedict, "is the degree to which the Court sustained national authority to protect rights rather than the degree to which they restricted it."[3]

My focus is not the doctrinal outcomes (i.e., the Court's interpretations of the amendments), but the Court's version of the "history of the times" that undergirded its doctrine. How did the Court make the link between slavery and Reconstruction? How did a version of slavery history justify the Court's interpretation of the Fourteenth Amendment? What slavery criticism became institutionalized in constitutional law by the close of the nineteenth century?

The Court's version of slavery/war history was a reconstituted mix of Republican and Northern Democratic history. Northern Democratic fingerprints, however, covered the Court's portrayal of slavery politics and the war's issues. Slavery history had many dimensions, and the Court was highly selective about the ones that it acknowledged. Political debate over John C. Calhoun's state sovereignty doctrine culminated in dispute over the right of secession—and in war—but slavery politics also involved heated disputes over Southern censorship and the founding of the Republican Party on free-labor principles.

The Court limited its representation of the war's issues to the grounds on which Northern Democrats distinguished themselves from Southern Democrats. (Northern Democrats, as mentioned, rejected Southern claims that the federal government had a duty to enforce slave law in the territories, and they rejected the claim that secession was a right.) For the Court, these were the war's issues. It became necessary to abolish slavery, explained both the Northern Democrats and the Court. The Court's definition of slavery's "destruction" reflected a Northern Democratic perspective.

The Court did acknowledge the existence of slavery's "incidents and burdens," and it defined those incidents by using a combination of Republican and Democratic views. The Black Codes were included in its definition of slavery's incidents and so partly stemmed from Republican thinking. But in the *Civil Rights Cases* (1883)[4] the denial to blacks of access to public transportation and accommodations was not viewed as an "incident." The Court's identification of mobility (access to public conveyances, public inns) as a social right not essential to freedom was a Democratic position, for in condemning the Black Codes, Republicans had talked about mobility as a civil right, necessary for freedom and economic opportunity.[5]

The Court's eloquent (Republican) expression of concern for the freedmen in *Slaughter-House* is also important, even if this expressed concern at the time amounted to little practical protection for black safety and rights. Some scholars have argued that this language, resuscitated in the twentieth century by the Warren Court, was merely a "strategic obfuscation."[6]

The Court's version of slavery/war history supported its doctrines of nonincorporation and state action. The nonincorporation doctrine held that the Fourteenth Amendment's privileges or immunities clause did not secure Bill of Rights freedoms against state infringement and denial. In other words, when states acted to deny speech, assembly, press, jury trial rights, etc., the Fourteenth Amendment offered no federal remedy. The state action doctrine held that the Fourteenth Amendment guaranteed the "equal protection of the laws" and "due process of law" against state deprivation.[7] Private individuals' actions were not covered. Overt racial classification in state laws, such as those that prescribed different penalties for blacks and whites who had committed the same crime and those that explicitly excluded blacks from jury lists, were prohibited. But the actions of private individuals that denied equal protection and due process (e.g., Klan violence), as well as the failure of states to secure them (e.g., state refusal to prosecute Klan violence), could not be claimed as Fourteenth Amendment violations. Prohibition by the Court of overt exclusions posed a neglible obstacle for whites who desired black subordination and exclusion. As Wiecek notes, "it took little imagination for southern whites to devise techniques of black exclusion that were implicit and based on a universal understanding of how things work in a segregated society."[8]

While slavery's politics and history have many dimensions, the Court related a flattened-out version of the past. The impact of the Court's history was subtle, though significant. With the endorsement of Northern Democratic critiques of Southern Democrats (instead of Republican critiques of Southern Democrats) and the submerging of many dimensions of slavery politics (e.g., disputes over Southern censorship), institutional memory was drained of traces that the Warren Court majority might have mobilized to support federal protections of citizenship in cases where states had a history of abuses.

The "History of the Times"

In the *Slaughter-House Cases,* Justice Samuel Miller stated that the Reconstruction Amendments disclose a "unity of purpose, when taken in connection with the history of the times. . . . Fortunately that history is fresh within the memory of us all, and its leading features, as they bear upon the matter before us, free from doubt."[9] That purpose was the "freedom of the slave race, the security and firm establishment of that freedom."[10]

The "history of the times" did *not* include a clash between two expanding systems with different theories of labor,[11] *nor* did it include the Congressional Gag Rule, *nor* antebellum Southern suppressions of civil liberties, *nor* congressional conflict in 1866 over the definition of legitimately established states' rights. Bitter, multidimensional disputes took place over slavery, but the Court suppressed all but a few dimensions of them.

Miller reduced the points of conflict — the war's issues — to those identified by the Northern Democrats in their criticisms of the Southern Democrats. He acknowledged that the structure of federalism was in some way implicated in the war, and he acknowledged that the Northern military victory accomplished an expansion of federal power. However, in presenting questions about the state/federal relation involved in the war, Miller *limited* them to whether a state had a right to secede. For Miller, liberty now included the freedom not to be a legal slave, to own oneself under federal protection. Liberty, in Miller's view, was considered in mostly traditional terms of popular majorities against a central government. This conception was associated with the Revolutionary experience. When Miller presented the purpose of the amendments as the "freedom" and "protection" of former slaves, freedom was defined as self-ownership.

Miller's Civil War narrative focused on the Southern effort "to separate from the Federal government, and to resist its authority." In recounting the history of the dispute over the state/federal relation, this narrative focus on the act of secession clearly appears.

> In the early history of the organization of government, its statesmen seem to have divided on the line which should separate the powers of the National government from those of the State governments, and though this line has never been very well defined in public opinion, such a division has continued from that day to this. . . . The adoption of the first eleven amendments to the Constitution so soon after the original instrument was accepted, shows a prevailing sense of danger at that time from the Federal power. And it cannot be denied that such a jealousy continued to exist with many patriotic men *until the breaking out of the late civil war. It was then discovered that the true danger to the perpetuity of the Union was in the capacity of the State organizations to combine and concentrate all the powers of the State, and of continuous States, for a determined resistance to the General Government. . . .*[12]

Miller installed a certain definition of slavery's lessons. By identifying secession as the moment when "the true danger" was discovered, he took a view of the war put forward by the Northern Democrats and Andrew Johnson. His references to slavery and his understanding of what it meant for slavery to "perish" also revealed their viewpoint.

> The institution of African slavery, as it existed in about half the States of the Union, and the contests pervading the public mind for many years, between those who desired its curtailment and ultimate extinction, and those who desired additional safeguards for its security and perpetuation, culminated in the effort, on the part of most of the States in which slavery existed, to separate from the Federal government, and to resist its authority. This constituted the war of the rebellion, and whatever auxiliary causes may have contributed to bring about this war, undoubtedly the overshadowing and efficient cause was African slavery. . . . In that struggle, slavery, as a legalized social relation, perished. It perished as a necessity of the bitterness and force of the conflict.[13]

Miller suppressed views of the dangers of slavery that were formed by Republicans in the decades before secession. Republicans, of course, agreed that states could be a danger to the Union in their claiming of federal protections for slavery in the territories[14] and in claiming a right to secession. But as Miller represented the war, these claims *represented a full view* of the dangers that states posed to the Union. The "history of the times" did not witness disputes over the definition of "established" states' rights, nor did it witness the opening of dialogue about what it meant to belong to "the people," that is, the national collective.

The Court's representation of the purpose of the Reconstruction Amendments (protection of the freedmen) held a great irony, namely, that it was those who came to be known as Radical Republicans who had expressed this concern, which had been decidedly unpopular even on the eve of the war. As historians such as Eric Foner have made clear, the vast majority of Northerners who supported the war did so with little concern for the slaves. Northerners fought for the eradication of slavery in the territories, and later in the South, but this aim was by no means synonymous with "fighting for the freedom and protection of black citizens." While concerns for the security and protection of black citizenship rights were ridiculed before the war, and while the treatment of black citizens was linked for only the briefest of times to the meaning of the Northern victory, the Court endorsed these terms. But in this endorsement, it grafted onto them narrow legal meanings. That is, the Court broke the link between the Radicals' language and their substantive concerns.

Northern Democratic versions of slavery history undergirded Miller's interpretation of the citizenship clause and the privileges or immunities clause. The citizenship clause, which was the first clause of the first section of the Fourteenth Amendment, read: "All persons born or naturalized in the United States, and subject to the jurisdiction thereof, are citizens of the United States and of the State wherein they reside." Miller stated: "No such definition was previously found in the Constitution, nor had any attempt been made to define it by an act of Congress. It had occasioned much discussion in the courts, by the executive departments, and in the public journals." [15] "The first observation we have to make on this clause," Miller continued, "is that it puts at rest both the questions, which we stated to have been the subject of differences of opinion." [16]

The first question that the citizenship clause put at rest, stated Miller, was whether black men and women could be citizens of a state or of the United States. The answer was that they could be citizens of both state and nation. Miller said that the clause "overturns the Dred Scott decision" [17] by making all persons born within the United States citizens of the United States. The second question to be resolved dealt with the definition of citizenship, that is, "what should constitute citizenship of the United States, and also citizenship of a State." According to Miller, "the distinction between citizenship of the United States and citizenship of a State is clearly recognized and established." Both forms of citizenship were "distinct from each other." [18] The "privileges and immunities" of a U.S. citizen that the Fourteenth Amendment placed under the protection of the federal Constitution included the right to petition Congress, the right of access to federal buildings, etc. "Those [privileges and immunities] belonging to the citizen of the State . . . must rest for their security and protection where they have heretofore rested [i.e., with the states]." [19] The basic protections of person and property, including all Bill of Rights guarantees, were privileges and immunities belonging to citizens of states. (This meant that if states defaulted in their duty to protect these rights, no federal remedy was available to them. This was essentially the same holding as the *Barron* decision in 1833.) These rights, then, remained under the authority of state laws and state constitutions, some of which were better at protecting them than others. [20]

Miller's famous claim that a settled distinction obtained between state and national citizenship has been widely criticized. Foner notes that Miller's distinction "should have been seriously doubted by anyone who read the Congressional debates of the 1860s."[21] My intention is not to reiterate Foner's argument but to point to Miller's use of Northern Democratic slavery criticism to support his interpretation of the citizenship and privileges or immunities clauses.

Miller's representation of *Dred Scott* also embodies a Northern Democratic/Johnsonian perspective. Miller overturned *Dred Scott* in a minimalist way.[22] In so doing, he suppressed several dimensions of political and legal dispute over the decision, especially over the definition of, and guarantees for, the "common rights of manhood."

Miller employed Northern Democratic slavery history to support his reading. In portraying the distinction between state citizenship and national citizenship as long settled, he stated that the "main features of the general system" were clearly identifiable: "[W]e do not see in those amendments any purpose to destroy the main features of the general system."[23] He claimed that "powers *heretofore universally conceded*"[24] to the states included jurisdiction over Bill of Rights guarantees. These were remarkable assertions. Republican political critiques of slavery precisely targeted state jurisdiction over those guarantees. Republican and Northern Democrats disputed the definition of "established" states' rights. Miller, then, left unacknowledged Republican warnings about leaving power in the hands of states that had misused it, just as he passed over Republican concerns about corruption in the political process. In presenting a distinction between state and national citizenship as long resolved— hence, beyond the scope of legitimate contention—he refused to acknowledge that disputes over the structure of federalism went beyond the question of federal authority over formal slave law. He refused to acknowledge that disputes over the limits of state authority over personal rights also characterized slavery politics and were implicated in the Civil War.

Southern acts of censorship had stimulated Republican reformulations of liberty and the problems of democracy. But this reformulation for the most part was going on without court approval. Miller seemed to refer to this situation with the comment: "Whatever fluctuations may be seen in the history of public opinion on [the state/federal relation] during the period of our national existence, we think it will be found that this court, so far as its functions required, has always held with a steady and even hand the balance between State and Federal power."[25] While the Supreme Court in *Barron v. Baltimore* declared that Bill of Rights protections were not secured from state infringement, Republicans refused to cede final interpretive authority to the *Barron* Court. But only the "steady and even hand" of the Court was relevant for Miller.

The "History of the Times": The Dissenters' Version

The dissenting justices in *Slaughter-House* presented a different version of the slavery experience and the Civil War. For Justices Joseph Bradley and Noah Swayne, the "light of experience" showed that states, as much as the federal government, could be a danger to individual liberty. Significantly, states could be dangerous to the Republic in many ways besides secession. According to Bradley and Swayne, the slavery experience witnessed an expansion of the meaning of liberty to include the liberty of individuals against popular majorities. As these two justices recounted the past (in lower federal court cases, and in dissent in the *Slaughter-House Cases*), Southern "intolerance of free speech and free discussion" and ex-Confederate treatment of free blacks during the antebellum years were part of the problem with slavery, and so part of the problem that the Fourteenth Amendment was designed to remedy. The amendment, they claimed, addressed this issue by invigorating the notion of national citizenship.

The Court's dissenting opinions differed in important ways. Justice Stephen J. Field's opinion (joined by Bradley, Swayne, and Salmon P. Chase) emphasized free-labor principles and unfettered small-scale capitalism. The state-granted monopoly on slaughterhouses was class legislation (which fettered small-scale capitalism and free labor), and Field's opinion supported federal judicial resistance to class legislation. Field's opinion is quoted most often for its assessment of the Court majority's interpretation of the Fourteenth Amendment. If the amendment did no more than what the majority suggested, it was a "vain and idle enactment."

> The amendment does not attempt to confer any new privileges or immunities upon citizens or to enumerate or define those already existing. It assumes that there are such privileges and immunities, which belong of right to citizens as such, and ordains that they shall not be abridged by State legislation. If this inhibition has no reference

to privileges and immunities as were before its adoption specially designated in the Constitution or necessarily implied as belonging to citizens of the United States, it was a vain and idle enactment, which accomplished nothing, and most unnecessarily excited Congress and the people on its passage. . . . But if the amendment refers to the natural and inalienable rights which belong to all citizens, the inhibition has a profound significance and consequence.[26]

Field, of course, dissented in *Strauder*, in which the Court struck down the statutory exclusion of black men from jury lists. Legislative racial classifications were clearly not a problem for him.

Drawing on principles of free labor and making much use of the term "freeman," Field suggested that a freeman be defined by more than self-ownership.[27] Field was a Lincoln appointee and a War Democrat. According to Richard Aynes, he was "maybe a Unionist but not a Republican and certainly not a Radical Republican."[28] According to Akhil Reed Amar, Field worked on a model for incorporation that included some aspects of the pre-1866 Constitution.[29] While he might have favored a refined model of incorporation, he did not appear to give great weight to black political exclusion.

Justice Bradley, in addition to joining Field's opinion, wrote separately that the Fourteenth Amendment made national citizenship "primary" and state citizenship "secondary."[30] But the "spirit of lawlessness, mob violence and sectional hate" had not been "completely repressed as to give full practical effect"[31] to citizenship rights. In addition to this description of the postwar South (certainly more Republican than Northern Democratic), Bradley offered his version of the conditions of affairs that produced the Fourteenth Amendment, a version markedly different from Samuel F. Miller's.[32] In his narrative, Bradley, like many Republican congressmen, combined references to the legal-formal definition of slavery (slave law) with references to slavery's "spirit":

> The mischief to be remedied was not merely slavery and its incidents and consequences; but that spirit of insubordination and disloyalty to the National government which had troubled the country for so many years in some of the States, and that intolerance of free speech and free discussion which often rendered life and property insecure, and led to much unequal legislation. The amendment was an attempt to give voice to the strong National yearning for that time and that condition of things, in which American citizenship should be a sure

guaranty of safety, and in which every citizen of the United States might stand erect on every portion of its soil, in the full enjoyment of every right and privilege belonging to a freeman, without fear of violence or molestation.[33]

Bradley's references to Southern "intolerance of free speech and free discussion," and his general view of political history, distinguished his version from Miller's. Indeed, Bradley stated that Miller's view of citizenship "evinces a very narrow and insufficient estimate of constitutional history."[34]

Bradley also endorsed a version of the John Bingham's nonenforcement doctrine associated with article 4, section 2, of the Constitution. This view was that citizens had a body of fundamental rights, but that the national government did not have the power or authority under the original Constitution to enforce or protect these rights. In drawing a (Republican) distinction between "force" and "right," Bradley argued that "force" did not establish a state right.

> The right of a State to regulate the conduct of its citizens is undoubtedly a very broad and extensive one, and not to be lightly restricted. But there are certain fundamental rights which this right of regulation cannot infringe. . . . I speak now of the rights of citizens of any free government. . . . In this free country, the people of which inherited certain traditional rights and privileges from their ancestors, citizenship means something. It has certain privileges and immunities attached to it which the government, whether restricted by express or implied limitations, cannot take away or impair. *It may do so temporarily by force, but it cannot do so by right.*[35]

Bradley's reference to the nonenforcement doctrine stands in sharp contrast to Miller's choice to ignore it. Bradley sounded very much like Bingham when he said:

> Can the Federal courts administer relief to citizens of the United States whose privileges and immunities have been abridged by a State? Of this I entertain no doubt. Prior to the fourteenth amendment this could not be done, except in a few instances [a reference, probably to the fugitive slave cases], for the want of the requisite authority. . . . In my judgment, it was the intention of the people of this country in adopting that amendment to provide National secu-

rity against violation by the States of the fundamental rights of the citizen. . . .[36]

Bradley referred to the "fundamental rights" of citizens, and he used the terms "privileges and immunities" and "fundamental rights" as synonyms. To find an authoritative declaration of these fundamental privileges and immunities, he looked to the rights specified in the Constitution. The Bill of Rights, of course, was among them. "Admitting . . . that formerly the States were not prohibited from infringing any of [these] privileges and immunities . . . that cannot be said now, since the adoption of the fourteenth amendment."[37]

In *U.S. v. Hall*,[38] Judge William Woods, under Bradley's guidance, had stated clearly that the Bill of Rights spelled out the privileges and immunities of U.S. citizens: "[T]he right of freedom of speech, and the other rights enumerated in the first eight articles of amendment to the constitution of the United States, are the privileges and immunities of citizens of the United States. . . ."[39] In 1874, Bradley reaffirmed this position. "The Fourteenth Amendment declares that no state shall by law abridge the privileges or immunities of citizens of the United States. Grant that this prohibition now prevents the states from interfering with the right to assemble, as being one of such privileges and immunities. . . ."[40]

Bradley's views on the Fourteenth Amendment, of course, shifted.[41] His definition of slavery's "incidents" in the *Civil Rights Cases* was more Northern Democratic than Republican. He labeled black access to public accommodations as a social right (not a civil right associated with the free-labor principle of economic opportunity), therefore leaving innkeepers free to deny accommodations to blacks because of their color.

Justice Swayne agreed with Bradley's view that Southern secession did not exhaust the list of slavery's dangers. State abuses of individual rights during the antebellum period were part of the conditions of affairs that produced the amendments. "These amendments are all consequences of the late civil war. The prejudices and apprehension as to the central government that prevailed when the Constitution was adopted were dispelled by the light of experience. The public mind became satisfied that there was less danger of tyranny in the head than of anarchy and tyranny in the members." Swayne continued: "By the Constitution, as it stood before the war, ample protection was given against oppression by the Union, but little was given against wrong and oppression by the States.

That want was intended to be supplied by this amendment."[42] A suspicion of state control over citizenship was now more immediate than older suspicions of centralized power. The amendments were "a new departure. . . . They trench directly upon the power of the States."[43]

Swayne had written similarly about political history in his opinion in *U.S. v. Rhodes* (1867), which upheld the constitutionality of the Civil Rights Act of 1866 under the Thirteenth Amendment. He gave a version of "the problems" with slavery in this opinion, and his thinking was significantly different from Miller's in *Slaughter-House,* especially in discussing many dimensions of slavery politics that Miller had ignored.

Swayne began with the Founding period, during which people saw "many perils of evil in the center, but none elsewhere. They feared tyranny in the head, not anarchy in the members."[44] He went on to consider "the state of things which existed before and at the time the amendment was adopted, the mischiefs complained or apprehended, and the remedy intended to be provided for existing and anticipated evils."[45] He began an extended narrative on slave codes:

> In Georgia, by an act of 1829, no person is permitted to teach a slave, a negro, or a free person of color to read or write. So in Virginia, by a statute of 1830, meetings of free negroes to learn reading or writing are unlawful, and subject them to corporal punishment; and it is unlawful for white persons to assemble with free negroes or slaves to teach them to read or write. The prohibitory act of the legislature of Alabama, passed at the session of 1831–2, relative to the instruction to be given to the slaves or free colored population, or exhortation, or preaching to them, or any mischievous influence attempted to be exerted over them, is sufficiently penal. Laws of similar import are presumed to exist in the other slaveholding states, but in Louisiana the law on the subject is armed with ten-fold severity. It not only forbids any person teaching slaves to read or write, but it declares that any person using language in any public discourse from the bar, bench, stage, or pulpit, or any other place, or in any private conversation, or making use of any sign or actions having a tendency to produce discontent among the free colored population or insubordination among the slaves, or who shall be knowingly instrumental in bringing into the state any paper, book or pamphlet having a like tendency, shall, on conviction, be punishable with imprisonment or death, at the discretion of the court. Slaves were imperfectly, if at all,

protected from the grossest outrages by the whites. Justice was not for them. The charities and rights of the domestic relations had no legal existence for them.

Swayne then linked the slave codes to the treatment of free blacks. In other words, he joined the treatment of slaves and free blacks. "The shadow of evil fell upon the free blacks. They had but few civil and no political rights in the slave states. Many of the badges of the bondman's degradation were fastened upon them. Their condition, like his, though not so bad, was helpless and hopeless. This is borne out by the passages we have given from Kent's Commentaries. Further research would darken the picture. The states had always claimed and exercised the exclusive right to fix the status of all persons living within their jurisdiction."

For Swayne, the kinds of treatment endured by free blacks during the antebellum period were dimensions of the slavery problem. In emphasizing this point, Swayne's history was Republican. He went on to discuss the conditions after formal emancipation and the resurgence of the "worst effects of slavery":

> On January 1, 1863, President Lincoln issued his proclamation of emancipation. Missouri and Maryland abolished slavery by their own voluntary action. Throughout the war the African race had evinced entire sympathy with the Union cause. At the close of the Rebellion, two hundred thousand had become soldiers in the Union armies. The race had strong claims upon the justice and generosity of the nation. Weighty considerations of policy, humanity, and right were superadded. Slavery, in fact, still subsisted in thirteen states. Its simple abolition, leaving these laws and this exclusive power of the states over the emancipated in force, would have been a phantom of delusion. The hostility of the dominant class would have been animated with new ardor. Legislative oppression would have been increased in severity. Under the guise of police and other regulations slavery would have been in effect restored, perhaps in a worse form, and the gift of freedom would have been a curse instead of a blessing to those intended to be benefited. They would have had no longer the protection which the instinct of property leads its possessor to give in whatever form the property exists. It was to guard against such evils that the second clause of the [Thirteenth] amendment was framed.[46]

In his opinion, Swayne also offered a characterization of the Republicans. "Those who insisted upon the adoption of this amendment were animated by no spirit of vengeance. They sought security against the recurrence of a sectional conflict. They felt that much was due to the African race for the part it had borne during the war. They were also impelled by a sense of right and by a strong sense of justice to an unoffending and long-suffering people."[47] This portrait of the Republicans was clearly more "Republican" than "Northern Democratic." In histories of Reconstruction written in the early decades of the twentieth century, Republicans would be shown as motivated by vengeance and hatred. These negative portrayals were dominant when Felix Frankfurter and Charles Fairman were educated. (Frankfurter and Fairman, as is well known, were two major spokesmen for the doctrine that the Fourteenth Amendment did not originally apply the Bill of Rights to the states.) Swayne's view of the Fourteenth Amendment seemed to go against his own political proclivities.[48] Political affiliation did not lead to outcome.

Building a Sociology of Judicial Work

Justice Miller's version of the slavery experience worked to limit future judicial approaches to the problems of democracy in particular ways. The Court majority submerged several dimensions of Republican slavery critiques, draining institutional memory of traces that might have been mobilized in the twentieth century using traditional sources of law (i.e., legislative history) to support federal protections of individual rights where states had a history of abuses. All Supreme Court decisions, of course, limit judicial approaches to the problems of democracy that can be widely contested. The sociological question is, How does this happen?

The novelty of the situation (tabula rasa with respect to a version of civil war history), plus the institutional practice of stare decisis, gave great power to the *Slaughter-House* majority with respect to defining the slavery experience. Miller's version of slavery/war history became *the* version, even though plausible views of slavery's "dangers" and the war experience, such as those provided by the *Slaughter-House* dissenters, were equally available. In 1900 the Court looked backward to the "known conditions of affairs"[49] that produced the Fourteenth Amendment. Miller's history was definitive. Over time, Miller's version of the war's issues and his critique of "the problem" with slavery took on an objective quality.

The Court's Reconstruction era decisions were on the "growing fringe"[50] of institutions (corporate institutions, postbellum political institutions in which black men and women were designated as citizens) that reflected the Court majority's choices of which needs these new institutions should serve. Postwar federalism[51] was half-formed in the early 1870s. Addressing law students on the subject of what was important for them to learn, Karl Llewellyn said sixty years ago:

> [I]mportant . . . for your study and your understanding are those . . . disputes which typify whole groups of interest-clashes commonly occurring. Here the rule laid down will be a rule whose application people may foresee; a rule whose application, even if they do not foresee it, threatens them. . . . Most commonly, you will find cases of this sort upon the growing fringe of institutions. . . . The court will pass upon some feature of a half-formed institution. Such cases, once they are decided, shape, limit, block its further growth. If, as is likely, the court in the future stands by the decision it has once made, that decision shapes not only the further growth of the law, but the further action of the community. So the decision may have been handed down two centuries ago and still be one which has made and left its mark upon the social organization of today.[52]

Llewellyn continued:

> This is the one side, the power of courts over society. The other [is] the power of society over the courts. It is society and not the courts which gives rise to, which shapes in the first instance the emerging institution; which kicks the courts into action. It is only from observation of society that the courts can pick their notions of what needs the new institution serves, what needs it baffles. Partly courts look directly at society. Partly they look at the deposit of their own work made in the past on similar occasions, that is, at the existing "ways" of law.

Llewellyn's comments are relevant here. As the Court looked to society and the "deposit of their own work" to pick their notions of what needs postwar federalism served, the Court ruled on features of the half-formed relation between the states and the national government. This decision shaped the further growth of this relation, especially as it pertained to federal (congressional and court) authority over citizenship rights.

The constraints that operated on lower-level federal judges from 1866 until 1871 were different from those that operated on Supreme Court justices after 1873. Compared with lower court federal judges in the 1860s who disliked Reconstruction legislation, Supreme Court justices who shared their view faced fewer constraints. In the late 1860s, district court judges were unable to challenge the nationalizing story about the Thirteenth Amendment and the Civil Rights Act of 1866. These judges devised indirect methods for circumventing it. District judges hostile to the Republican program dismissed cases, released prisoners, and failed to hold court regularly.[53] This tactic testified to the strength during the very early years of Reconstruction of the view that national citizenship had been invigorated.

Justices Bradley and Swayne, in multiple opinions, expressed a version of the slavery experience that more closely approximated the views expressed by Republicans in the 39th Congress. Their persuasive abilities were limited, however, by the messages of "ancients," by shifting popular desire to "heal the nation," and by the accumulation of precedent supporting both Miller's civil war history and his nonincorporation thesis. The early Bradley and Swayne history apparently could not be reconciled with the institutional "standards" and notions of legal "coherence" that guided the other justices.

Northern Democratic history was more extensible—that is, more capable of being extended—than Republican versions of slavery history, though this extensibility was *not* inherent but a quality determined by several factors: (1) The antebellum tradition of state-centered federalism. (G. Edward White[54] has discussed the "antebellum assumptions" about federalism held by justices in the Reconstruction period.) (2) The uncertain scope of the Republicans' "new departure," i.e., the uncertain scope of the new authority of the national government (the Congress and the federal courts) over individual rights, especially given their political and economic slavery critiques, which were not clearly contained. (On the matter of economic and business regulations, of course, late-nineteenth-century justices were less fearful of broad federal power.) And (3) a Northern Democratic theory of race extending back to Stephen Douglas, who expressed this theory but was not the source of it. The features of Northern Democratic history interacted with institutional features, or in Llewellyn's words, the "deposit of [the court's] work," to produce the extensibility of Northern Democratic history.

The Supreme Court's decisions in the 1870s implicitly reversed a lower federal court decision, *U.S. v. Hall*. The Court also reined in the lower court's definition of the parties "affected" by a case brought under the Civil Rights Act of 1866. (See *U.S. v. Rhodes*[55] [1867] and *U.S. v. Blyew*[56] [1875]). A shifting institutional context is part of an explanation for these departures. Federal judges between 1867 and 1871 worked under one set of conditions, i.e., under certain degrees of freedom and constraint. Supreme Court justices from 1873 until 1883, however, experienced different degrees of freedoms and constraint.

Let us suppose at this point that Justice Miller had an initial sense of the right outcome in the *Slaughter-House Cases,* namely, that the butchers not be granted a federally protected right to pursue a profession against state-granted monopolies. In his analysis of judicial decision-making, Duncan Kennedy suggests that judges have "initial senses" of the "right" outcome. This sense is not purely subjective or arbitrary. It is formed by a deep familiarity with past decisions and an extensive knowledge of institutional traditions and practices. Let us suppose, too, that Miller wanted to back up his preference with an argument to the effect that to grant the right would "not be in accord with the Constitution."

Miller would want to constitutionalize his position for a number of reasons.[57] First, when he took his job as a Supreme Court justice, he promised that he would "decide according to law." He needed at least a good legal argument to support his actions. Second, he would want his position to be upheld in the future. Reversals by later Courts would diminish his reputation. Third, he would want to shape the outcomes of future cases and influence popular consciousness about what kinds of action were legitimate. His legal reasoning in this case would affect his ability to act in other cases.

"Legal reasoning," says Kennedy, "is a kind of work with a purpose, and here the purpose is to make the case come out the way [a judge's] sense of justice tells [him/her] it ought to, in spite of what seems at first to be the resistance or opposition of "the law."[58] How legal arguments look in the end will depend, Kennedy explains, "in a fundamental way on the legal materials—rules, cases, policies, social stereotypes, historical images. . . ." This dependence, however, is "a far cry from the inevitable determination of the outcome in advance by the legal materials themselves."[59]

Studying legal decision-making means studying both the legal materials and the culture of judges, though these are not sharply distinguishable. A critical question, always, is the amount of interpretive work involved in different kinds of "field manipulations" at particular points in time. Legal fields, Kennedy explains, are a collection of general rules and precedents and legal materials generally. He analogizes these materials to bricks: "One of the ways in which we experience law . . . is as a medium in which one pursues a project, rather than as something that tells us what we have to do. When we approach it this way, law constrains as a physical medium constrains—you can't do absolutely anything you want with a pile of bricks, and what you can do depends on how many you have, as well as on other circumstances. In this sense, that you are building something out of a given set of bricks constrains you, controls you, deprives you of freedom."[60]

Later, Kennedy amends this analogy. The legal field is not a physical medium but "a set of declarations by other people about how ethically serious people ought to respond to situations of conflict."[61] This set of messages carries normative force when judges have an identification with the "ancients." "They are members of the same community working on the same problems. They are old; they are many. They are steeped in a tradition of serious ethical inquiry whose power I have felt on countless occasions, a tradition that seems to be a partially valid great accomplishment of the often cruddy civilization of which I am a tiny part."[62] Kennedy notes the power of conditioning by participation in a legal universe. Judges simply do not have intuitions about legal responses that are independent of their knowledge of what judges and other actors in the legal system have done in past situations.

Justice Miller's restrictive view of the Fourteenth Amendment was not manufactured out of thin air. His separate and compound view of national and state citizenship and his expansive view of state citizenship had its roots in James Madison's view of the compound character of state and national systems set up by the Constitution in 1787. Madison stated in the Federalist No. 45 that national matters were "few and defined." State matters were "numerous and indefinite." For Miller and the Republicans, "few and defined" meant different things. Miller's key move was to represent this view as uninterrupted from the Founding through Reconstruction.[63]

Once Miller's version of citizenship was in place, a change occurred in the degrees of freedom and constraint under which judges worked. In U.S. v. Cruikshank,[64] Chief Justice Morrison Waite repeated Miller's history. Waite told a version of the Founding of the Constitution in which a balance of power was set up between the states and the national government. "The power which one possesses, the other does not. They are established for different purposes and have separate jurisdictions. Together they make one whole."[65] Waite stated that duties originally assigned to the states "remain there."[66]

In discussing the First Amendment right to assembly and the Second Amendment right to bear arms, Waite appealed to the antebellum decisions *Barron v. Baltimore* (1833) and *Gibbons v. Ogden* (1824): "The government of the United States when established found [the right to assembly] in existence, with the obligation on the part of the States to afford it protection. As no direct power over it was granted to Congress, it remains, according to the ruling in *Gibbons,* subject to State jurisdiction." For the protection in the enjoyment of the right to peaceably assemble and to bear arms "the people must look to the States. The power for that purpose was originally placed there and it has never been surrendered to the United States."[67]

Waite's reliance on *Barron v. Baltimore* is noteworthy. Twentieth-century historians have claimed that historical materials support the conclusion that the Fourteenth Amendment was intended to overturn *Barron.* John Bingham, author of the Fourteenth Amendment, made references to *Barron* in the debates on the amendment. In chapter 5, I will return to disputes over the status of *Barron* in 1868 and divergent interpretations of Bingham's remarks. For now, I note only that Waite presented *Barron* as good law in 1873, and he presented this view as if it were historically undisputed and a matter of consensus.

Miller's history in *Slaughter-House* and the view of national citizenship it supported made it relatively easy for the Court in *Cruikshank* to dismiss indictments against Klansmen brought under the authority of the Fourteenth Amendment. Michael Benedict (1978) has argued that this case is an example where the Court upheld Republican intent. In support of this claim, Benedict cites the justices' support, *in dicta,* of congressional authority under the Thirteenth Amendment to directly protect rights against offenses motivated by race. The practical effect of *Cruikshank,* however, was to set Klansmen free who had committed brutal violence. This was the result, Benedict emphasized, of "inappropriate" legislation (i.e., the Enforcement Act had not included the "racial motive" limitation). Also, most of the counts against the Klansmen lacked the racial motive charge.

A number of the counts, however, did contain that charge. The fifth and eighth, for example, charged a race-based motivation to deprive the parties of their "rights, privileges, immunities and protection granted and secured to them respectively as citizens of the United States, and as citizens of Louisiana." These counts were dismissed, however. Why? According to Bradley and Waite, they lacked precision. Bradley called them "vague."[68] Waite said, "There is no specification of any particular right." These counts "lack[ed] the certainty and precision required of the established rules of criminal pleading."[69] Waite spent three full pages discussing the need to have specific indictments "so as to furnish the accused with a description of the charges as will enable him to make his defense." The accused, Waite emphasized, had a right to have a specification of the charge against him.

Waite's ability to tuck this case under a rule that guaranteed "the rights of the accused" was significant. His ability to use this rule depended on the description of citizenship given in the *Slaughter-House Cases*. Miller's *Slaughter-House* decision did not require the decision in *Cruikshank*, but Waite's ability to dismiss the indictments that charged racial motive depended on Miller's nonincorporation doctrine, which rested on a mostly Northern Democratic version of slavery history. Had Waite been forced to confront precedent that contained a Bradley and Swayne version of slavery/war history, which asserted incorporation of the Bill of Rights through the privileges or immunities clause and recognized Republican concern with racially motivated denials of civil and personal rights, Waite could not so easily have dismissed these counts as "vague." Privileges and immunities included the right to assemble peaceably and the right to bear arms, and these rights were clearly claimed in the counts. Waite, however, was able to assert that the indictments did not call for powers granted by the Fourteenth Amendment.

Of course, there is no institutional obligation to take account of past dissenters. It is interesting to note that Bradley's circuit court opinion in *Cruikshank* stated: "The Fourteenth Amendment declares that no state shall by law abridge the privileges or immunities of citizens of the United States. Grant that this prohibition now prevents the states from interfering with the right to assemble, as being one of such privileges and immunities. . . ."[70] Waite ignored this opinion.

In *Cruikshank*, the Court's *in dicta* comments were a rejection of certain aspects of Democratic interpretations of the Reconstruction Amendments.[71] (The Democrats argued that the Thirteenth Amendment did no more than abolish formal slave law, that Congress could do nothing if a state violated the Thirteenth or Fifteenth Amendments, and that the Fourteenth Amendment referred to the action of states only in their corporate capacities, which meant that offending state laws were immediately null and void but that no criminal or civil action could be brought against state officers who carried out those laws.) The case, then, reflected a combination of Republican and Democratic content. Later Court cases strengthened the Northern Democratic interpretation of the Thirteenth Amendment. (The Melville Fuller Court denied congressional power to protect rights under the Thirteenth and Fifteenth Amendments.[72] In a series of cases in the 1890s and early 1900s that challenged new Southern constitutions which disenfranchised blacks, the Fuller Court denied relief.)

Narrow Interpretations Made Easier: The Political and Institutional Context

After *Slaughter-House,* Supreme Court justices were working in a legal field that was firm in some respects and less firm in others. This institutional field was characterized by (1) Court precedent that presented the content of national citizenship as essentially unchanged by the Civil War; (2) declining Republican political strength; and (3) minimal sanctions for being inclined to weigh state jurisdiction more heavily than the democratic participation of black citizens. Also important was the traditional fear of central power and its associated conceptualization of central power as the "danger" to democracy. In addition, there was the institutionally defined interest in causing as little disruption as possible in legal fields. Personal experience and conviction, of course, exist within these institutional fields.

A fear of centralized power could have produced the view that Republicans were simply wrong if they believed that the Congress and the federal courts' role, even if it were expanded to include primary authority over the Bill of Rights, could be contained. The institutional practice of leaving citizenship under the control of states (except regarding the Fugitive Slave Law), and a deeply embedded view that central power was the main threat to democracy, would have made it difficult for justices to conceive new postwar ways of balancing black citizenship and an expanded national citizenship with state integrity.

But it is also likely that Northern Democratic views of blackness and whiteness gave most justices little incentive to invest in building alternative strategies to the nonincorporation doctrine that might have protected both black/national citizenship and state integrity. Had the justices in the majority solidly respected the capabilities of the former slaves, they likely would have been more deeply invested in finding ways of balancing local democracy with federal (congressional and judicial) supervisory power over "fundamental" rights. The initial forays and later retreats by Justices Bradley and William B. Woods and their later endorsements of the state action doctrine also might have had something to do with their susceptibility to weakening their initial commitment to black citizenship. The Fuller Court's reversal of Waite Court comments regarding congressional authority under the Thirteenth and Fifteenth Amendment undoubtedly were affected by the heightened racism of the late nineteenth century. But as Duncan Kennedy observes, the failure to "move" a field of law does not mean the field is intrinsically immovable.

The Grant administration's retreat from civil rights enforcement helped shape the contours of the legal field in the 1870s. President Grant's retreat was a response to changing Northern opinion and played a role in shaping the political life of the South. The administration's policy also had an effect, the extent of which is difficult to determine, in minimizing the amount of interpretive work required for the Supreme Court to void the application of the 1870 Enforcement Act in *Cruikshank*.

It was during the early years of the 1870s that Grant administration policy changed. In contrast to the situation in 1871, when Grant's attorney general, Amos Akerman, argued that prosecution of Klan crimes fostered peace and that appeasement of the Klan bred greater violence (an argument made by Republicans in the 39th Congress), Grant's new attorney general, George H. Williams, in 1872 argued the reverse, claiming that federal legislation and law enforcement bred crime and instigated lawlessness.

The administration now took on the perspective of Northern Democrats, who had argued this position in 1866. Evidence from Georgia and North Carolina suggested that federal prosecutions curtailed violence. Attorney General Williams, however, instructed legal officers to take on only exceptional cases. Federal legal officers who continued to bring prosecutions under the Enforcement Acts were criticized and censured by superiors.[73] The Grant administration's new posture was to leave the Southern states to themselves. Many Republicans were making the same move. Few resisted this backsliding. Black citizens often were without means to secure their physical safety, much less raise a public voice.

By June 1873 the enforcement of civil rights had become a political liability for the Grant administration. Northerners by the early 1870s increasingly accepted Democratic portraits of Republicans as "despotic" and "corrupt." The Northern white populace began to view federal protection of civil rights as a partisan issue intended to buttress flagging Republican strength, and they began to withdraw support for army occupation in the South.[74] The close association of Reconstruction with the rights of blacks eroded support for federal spending. Republican congressmen along with the Grant administration began to want less responsibility for the former slaves on the part of the national government.

With the administration's arguments before the Court in *Cruikshank*, the Republican account of legislative history was converging with that of the Northern Democrats, which was argued by Klan lawyers. The administration made no attempt to preserve the view that the Thirteenth and Fourteenth Amendments invigorated a notion of national citizenship. They proposed no view of the amendments that supported national authority to enforce those civil rights deemed "fundamental."[75] I am making no claims about whether the administration's views were honestly held; my point is that the federal government failed to put alternative views before court views, which were available and which were previously argued by Republican administrations. This failure to use a greater range of options narrowed the Grant administration's points of disagreement with opposing counsel. The government's argument in *Cruikshank* showed that Moderate and Radical Republicans were losing the fight to define the Republican Party's official stance on Reconstruction.

The early to mid-1870s produced altered cultural conditions. At this juncture, the Northern populace was rejecting the Republican Reconstruction agenda. The Northern coalition that fought the Civil War continued dissolving into its component elements, with divergent definitions of "independent" labor being adopted by contending Northern social classes. The symbology of "Republicanism" began to shift in substantial ways. The Republican Party turned into the party of business. The Republican suspicion and fear of monopolies lost ground to the Whig Republican desire to align itself with the business class. In a relatively short time the degree of consensus in 1866 for Radical and Moderate Republican aims eroded significantly.

In 1866, party affiliations had been symbols of clashing ideologies. By the mid-1870s the distance between the parties on questions of citizenship (but not necessarily other questions) narrowed considerably. It would be wrong to presume that Grant administration officials in 1875 traded in the same symbolic currency as the Republicans of the 39th Congress simply because they shared the "Republican" party affiliation or because Grant was a hero to abolitionists at the time of his election.

Northern legislators, according to Eric Foner, formed an understanding with their Southern counterparts that Northern economic development would not threaten planter control of the rural black labor force.[76] Foner calls the Northern view a "let-them-take-care-of-themselves" kind of attitude. Northerners wanted to wash their hands of the "problem." The significance of emergent industry is worth mentioning, for it indicates the many classes of social actors that combined to dismantle Republican programs. Both the Northern industrial class and most Northern white workingmen were none too friendly to black labor. White workers, with few exceptions, perceived black labor as a threat to job stability and wages, and they saw Reconstruction legislation as giving special attention to blacks. Those whites threw their support to the Democrats.[77]

With the Northern shift away from civil rights enforcement and the growing strength of Northern Democratic ideology on questions of citizenship (though not on questions of economic regulation), a Republican redefinition of self occurred. Those who stood by abolitionist principles faded quickly from influence, and black participation in political debates of the national collective was put outside the reach of federal courts (not that being within reach of the federal courts would have helped blacks very much during this period; the situation of Native Americans, after all, was within the reach of the federal courts.

The national governments of the late nineteenth century were Republican. A Northern Democratic version of political history could be institutionalized during this period for these reasons: because civil rights enforcement had become unpopular, because of corruption in Republican legislatures, because racism grew more virulent in the North during the 1880s and 1890s, because Northern Democratic history defended the autonomy of Southern states ruled by Democrats, and because Northern states were jealous of the Southerners' control over citizenship. The rise of Whig Republicanism facilitated the institutionalization of a Northern Democratic history of Reconstruction, to the extent that this history pertained to the resolution of citizenship disputes.

Another significant factor comes into play, namely, the responsiveness of the Supreme Court's historical accounts to certain dimensions of Republican thought that were suspicious of sweeping federal power. Nationalist strands of Republican thought were accompanied by deep attachments to state power. The existence of these multiple strands of Republican thought made it possible for the Court to retain the "limited national power" concept while substituting its own definition of what such limited power meant. This substitution allowed the Court to suppress Republican concerns about ex-Confederates and the Republican reconceptualization of national citizenship. Thus, the Court's account of Reconstruction was rooted in mostly Northern Democratic definitions of the "end" of slavery, but it retained strands of Republican thinking. An understanding of how this account could be institutionalized during the Republican regime of the late nineteenth century requires attention to the historical convergence of all these factors.

Conceivably, Northern Democratic history (which insisted that a state-based federalism had not been fundamentally restructured by the war) could have been used to support state legislative regulation of business. It is noteworthy that when the Court used the Fourteenth Amendment to invalidate state regulations of business and assert federal judicial authority, Northern Democratic Reconstruction history was nowhere to be seen in the Court's opinions. The Court's situational use of state-centered policies was accompanied by a situational use of the Northern Democrats' historical view. State control over citizenship was "established" in the antebellum years, according to the Court, but state control over business and labor was not. (Historians date industrialization to the 1830s. In the South, of course, slave law placed the regulation of labor in the hands of slaveowners. In the North, states regulated labor and business.)

The Court of the late nineteenth century was not alone in using a state-centered approach in citizenship matters and a nation-centered approach in affairs of business and labor regulation. Fairman displayed a similar pattern, although the substance of his economic nationalism (he favored New Deal regulations) greatly differed from the substance of the Court's economic nationalism in the late nineteenth century.

The Court Defines "Badges of Slavery"

The case *Strauder v. West Virginia*[78] involved state legislation that explicitly excluded black men from jury lists. This legislation, like the Black

Codes of 1865–66, had a racial classification "on its face," in legal parlance. The Fourteenth Amendment, Justice Strong stated,

> declares that the law in the States shall be the same for the black as for the white. . . . The words of the amendment, it is true, are prohibitory, but they contain a necessary implication of a positive immunity, or right, most valuable to the colored race . . . exemption from legal discriminations, implying inferiority in civil society, lessening the security of their enjoyment of the rights which others enjoy, and discriminations which are steps toward reducing them to the condition of a subject race. That the West Virginia statute respecting juries . . . is such a discrimination ought not to be doubted.

While the language here is broad, it was the statutory singling out of black men that mattered. The Court acknowledged that states may prescribe the qualifications of its jurors, and in so doing they can make discriminations based on gender, freeholding, citizenship, age, or education. But "the very fact that colored people are singled out and expressly denied by statute all right to participate in the administration of the law, as jurors, because of their color . . . is practically a brand upon them." The impact of *Strauder,* despite its broad language, was limited. State legislatures could not make formal, racial classifications in law, like those in the Black Codes. Segregation laws, however, did not involve these sorts of classifications. Such laws, of course, were upheld in *Plessy v. Ferguson* (1986). Court definitions of "the brands" of slavery were limited to statutes like the Black Codes. The facial exclusion of black men from jury lists was "practically a brand" upon blacks, but segregation laws were not.

In *Civil Rights Cases* (1883), Justice Bradley, writing for the Court, expressly denied that race-based denial of access to public accommodations was a brand of slavery. This case involved the Civil Rights Act of 1875 and congressional power to pass the act under section 5 of the Fourteenth Amendment. The act provided that "all persons . . . regardless of any previous condition of servitude" were to be provided access to all public accommodations, including inns, railroads, theaters, "and other places of public amusement." The Court denied congressional power to pass this act. Bradley stated: "It would be running the slavery argument into the ground to make it apply to every act of discrimination which a person may see fit to make as to the guests he will entertain, or as to the people he will take into his coach or cab or car, or admit to his concert or theatre, or deal with in other matters of intercourse or business. . . .

When a man has emerged from slavery . . . there must be some stage in the progress of his elevation when he takes the rank of a mere citizen and ceases to be the special favorite of the laws."[79]

Justice John M. Harlan, dissenting in *Civil Rights Cases,* presented a version of the "mischiefs to be remedied"[80] by the Thirteenth Amendment. This amendment "did something more than prohibit slavery as an institution, resting upon distinctions of race, and upheld by positive law. . . . Was it the purpose of the nation simply to destroy the institution, and then remit the race, theretofore held in bondage, to the several States for such protection, in their civil rights, necessarily growing out of freedom, as those States, in their discretion, might choose to provide?"[81] For Harlan, access to public accommodations, because of their public or quasi-public nature, was a civil right, not a social right. Such access was part of the essence of freedom. (He clearly defined freedom differently from Justice Miller.) Race-based denials of access to public accommodations were among the "burdens and disabilities which constitute badges of slavery and servitude."[82] Harlan also challenged the Court's state action interpretation of the Fourteenth Amendment. Harlan argued: "The assumption that this amendment consists wholly of prohibitions upon State laws and State proceedings in hostility to its provisions, is unauthorized by its language."[83] He went on to defend the Fourteenth Amendment as a source of authority for the Civil Rights Act of 1875.

Harlan dissented in a series of cases on matters relating to the Reconstruction Amendments and individual rights.[84] In *Hurtado v. California,* Harlan attempted to "move" the field of precedent by arguing against Miller's definition of national citizenship. Dissenting in *Maxwell v. Dow,* he argued that the rights of national citizenship were those protected against federal interference. They included Bill of Rights guarantees. Harlan argued that the Fourteenth Amendment imposed upon the states the same restrictions that had been imposed upon the general government.[85] This view would translate that the Fourteenth Amendment applied the Bill of Rights to the states.

It was possible to imagine that such an application of the Bill of Rights was a narrow and limited grant of power. Of course, there might be different understandings of "few and defined." Even congressional authority to directly protect rights (under the Thirteenth Amendment)[86] when offenses were racially motivated could be viewed as a narrow and defined power, especially *before* experiences piled up that suggested otherwise. It is in the context of accumulated experience with entrenched racial thinking that twentieth-century observers attribute the "broad and expansive" view of federal power to Republicans.

Whether the Republicans and Harlan turned out to be wrong in their belief about the narrow role of federal protection of "fundamental rights" is a real question. However, it is not the question that has been typically discussed. So far, few have wrestled with the possibility that Republicans wanted limited federal power *and* substantive protections for a core group of fundamental rights, including the Bill of Rights. If the Republicans held both of these objectives for their amendments and believed these objectives to be consistent, this position creates great uncertainty when it comes to applying Republican thought and legislative aims (i.e., the application of "original understanding"). "Original understanding" would be constituted by two objectives, which by the twentieth century had become clearly incommensurable.

The wider political context of the 1880s and 1890s is worth a brief mention, though I make no claims about causal relations between context and Court decision. During these two decades, districts were being gerrymandered throughout the South to reduce Republican voting strength. So-called redeemers[87] and Southern legislatures were determined to accomplish legally what they had been working toward by fraud, violence, and intimidation: the effective exclusion of black citizens from public life. The Mississippi constitution of 1890, for example, included provisions for a poll tax, proof of good character, labyrinthine procedures for voter registration, and property ownership—provisions admittedly designed to disenfranchise blacks and probably also Populist whites. The Supreme Court accepted the Mississippi plan in an 1898 case. Said a delegate to the 1901–2 Virginia constitutional convention: "We have come here . . . for the purpose of finding some constitutional method of ridding ourselves of [black suffrage] forever; and we have the approval of the Supreme Court of the United States in making that effort."[88]

Black lawmakers now found it difficult to exert political influence, especially in states with large black populations. In the Deep South, electoral fraud and political violence varied according to the number of black voters. In counties with black majorities and in states with large black populations (e.g., Alabama was 50/50), ballot fraud was rampant, and the threat of KKK violence weighed heavily. In Texas and Arkansas, with large white majorities and where black voters posed little threat, blacks continued to vote freely after Redemption.[89] "Redeemer" legislatures also moved to take control of all-important local offices, transferring the power to select county commissioners to the legislature. They either repealed or ignored civil rights legislation.

By the turn of the century, Justice Miller's reading of the privileges and immunities clause and the citizenship clause had reached an "impacted" state.[90] A substantial number of cases were distributed in a regular pattern, which dispelled doubt that the Bill of Rights had not been applied to the states. With this line of cases in place, Miller's separation of state and national citizenship and his view that the rights of national citizenship were not enlarged by the Fourteenth Amendment looked hard to manipulate, or, in a word, unbudgeable.

In *Maxwell v. Dow* (1900) the plaintiff argued that Fifth Amendment rights were ones of national citizenship and so were guaranteed against state abridgment by the Fourteenth Amendment. Justice Rufus W. Peckham, writing for the majority in *Maxwell,* cited *Slaughter-House* at length and stated that the 1873 case "remains one of the leading cases upon the subject of that portion of the Fourteenth Amendment of which it treats."[91] Citing a line of precedent beginning with *Slaughter-House,* the Court denied that the Fifth Amendment had been applied to the states. Peckham quoted Chief Justice Waite in *In re Kemmler:* "The Fourteenth Amendment did not radically change the whole theory of the relations of the state and Federal governments to each other. . . . Protection to life, liberty and property rests primarily with the States. . . ."[92] Peckham quoted Miller in *Slaughter-House* on the dangers that would result if the fundamental rights of citizenship "heretofore belonging exclusively to the States" were brought within the power of the federal government. Such a transfer "would constitute this court a perpetual censor upon all legislation of the States. . . ."[93]

Battling to Conceive the Problems of Democracy

As chapter 2 discussed, the Northern Democrats held a conception of liberty associated with the Founding period. This view concerned the liberty of popular majorities against central governments (monarchies, as in England). Thus, attached to it was a particular conception of the problem of democracy, which dealt with empowering popular majorities against the government. The Republicans expanded this idea to reconceive the problems of democracy, not only the liberty of popular majorities against governments, but also the liberty of individuals against popular majorities. States could be as much a threat to liberty as could the central government.

James Madison had identified both conceptions of liberty (majority rights and majority tyranny) in Federalist No. 51,[94] though the Founding period, "majority tyranny," tended to be associated with the redistribution of wealth.[95] The unpropertied were the majority that threatened the minority's property. Federalists supported judicial review based on the idea that a Supreme Court could overrule legislatures that might vote to redistribute wealth.

Property rights remained important to Republicans, white and black alike, during the Reconstruction era. Liberty still meant opportunity for land ownership, and many, including Frederick Douglass, were still hopeful believers in the wage labor system. (Antislavery Republicans opposed monopolies and big business.) Liberty required protecting small farmers and artisans from the expansion of big business. Indeed, the threat of redistribution loomed greater once black men could vote and once Populism began to gain strength. Industry (steel mills, shipbuilding) had begun to take root in the 1830s and 1840s, and the growth of the railroads in the 1870s increased the displacement of small farmers and artisans.[96]

When the Court privileged Northern Democratic slavery and Reconstruction history, it privileged the conception of liberty associated with the Founding. The Court suppressed the conception of liberty that Republicans had developed from their experience with slavery. Justices Stephen Field, Bradley, and Swayne articulated a Republican version of the slavery experience and used the Republican's reformulation of the problems of democracy.

Put another way, the Court's Reconstruction era decisions privileged one plot line in the story of the American Republic. Like the Northern Democrats' view of the original Constitution, the Court's view of Reconstruction privileged the local democracy plot (rooted in the Founding era) at the expense of the national democracy plot (that popular majorities also could be potential oppressors) rooted in the slavery era.

In general, the Court's account of Reconstruction permitted tradition to appear in deceptively simple terms. The *Slaughter-House* dissenters expressed new currents in American political thought developed out of the slavery experience, as Republicans defined that experience. As Swayne expressed it, the Reconstruction Amendments embodied this new strain of political thinking: "The prejudices and apprehensions as to the central government which prevailed when the Constitution was adopted were dispelled by the light of experience. The public mind became satisfied that there was less danger of tyranny in the head than of anarchy and tyranny in the members. . . . By the Constitution as it stood before the war, ample protection was given against the Union, but little was given against the wrong and oppression of States. That want was intended to be supplied by [the Fourteenth] amendment." While the Republican articulation of a "national democracy" was given voice by the *Slaughter-House* minority, the case's majority presented political tradition as a singular and unified source of authority. Chapter 5 shows that legal scholar Fairman also privileged the tradition of state control over individual rights.

With the institutional privileging of Northern Democratic slavery history, which elevated concepts of liberty associated with the Founding period, twentieth-century Court justices received an institutional account of Reconstruction that enabled them when resolving citizenship dilemmas to place a relatively light burden of proof on state legislatures, even when patterns in official abuses of discretion occurred. Perhaps the subordinated status of the Bradley and Swayne view of slavery history will change. Usually, losing arguments are buried, but a few notable exceptions (Harlan's dissent in *Plessy*, Holmes's dissent in *Lochner*) have been noteworthy.

The Supreme Court's account of Reconstruction legislation also papered over Republicans' suspicion of sweeping national power, even as they instituted correctives that placed a core of rights under the supervision of the federal government. The Court's imposition of a unified account of Reconstruction legislation submerged the uncertainty produced by the duality of Republican thought.

Supreme Court cases from 1873 until 1883 closed down inquiry among many generations of justices into what it meant to be included in the national collective. The meaning of national citizenship and the basis of public life were not reopened as legitimate judicial questions, except in minority opinions (like Justice Harlan's in *Hurtado, Plessy v. Ferguson,* and *Maxwell v. Dow*) and unsuccessful suits, until Warren Court majorities attempted to do so in the 1960s. By that decade, however, Miller's reading of the citizenship and privileges and immunities clauses, and the institutional version of Reconstruction in general, had shown great durability. (This created problems for the Warren Court majority in the 1960s.)

The Supreme Court's Reconstruction history suppressed the Republican reformulation of the problems of democracy. While many Republicans in the 39th Congress argued that the Thirteenth and Fourteenth Amendments did not expand federal jurisdiction over "political rights"[97] (narrowly defined, as they were, in the nineteenth-century hierarchy of rights for such things as voting, officeholding, and jury service), Republicans still thought of these amendments as protecting the political process; for example, Bill of Rights guarantees such as the rights of assembly and speech secured political participation; security from political violence protected the political process. Protecting black political participation in the national collective, at least against white legislative majorities and possibly against white mobs, was factored into the Republicans' understanding of the problems and challenges of American democracy, as it likewise was for Bradley and Swayne.

In the Court's Reconstruction era decisions, black experiences of subordination by white popular majorities, with the exception of legislation similar to the Black Codes, was put outside the boundaries of legal relevance. The exclusion of blacks from public accommodations and the use of segregation laws to subordinate blacks were excluded from the conceptualization of the problems and challenges of U.S. democracy. This amounted to a process of marginalization in law. The economic subordination of poor whites also was outside the boundaries of legal relevance. The Supreme Court's account of Reconstruction history, in general, served to obscure the political dynamics generated by race and class in which Republican legal reform was shaped.

Had the Republican view of political history succeeded institutionally, institutional directives would have existed to pay attention to abuses by popular majorities and to problems of equal access to the political process. Of course, the definition of equal access would be open to contest. Southern censorship of antislavery mailings was one form of blocked access, as were the sort of racially motivated offenses against rights involved in *Cruikshank*. But the institutional preservation of the principle of equal access would have built *some sort* of egalitarianism into the Fourteenth Amendment, even if the contours of that nationalism and egalitarianism were open to debate. (Legal conservatives in the twentieth century hotly deny that an egalitarianism was written into the Constitution.)[98]

The Mutual Entrenchment of Northern Democratic History,
State-Centered Approaches to Citizenship Dilemmas,
and a Theory of Race

In the *Slaughter-House Cases,* Justice Miller's declarations that the Fourteenth Amendment did not apply the Bill of Rights to the states and did not reconceptualize national citizenship sustained his choice to rely on antebellum strategies for resolving citizenship dilemmas. Miller's state-centered minimalist approach to citizenship dilemmas and a Northern Democratic version of Reconstruction history, which implicitly imported a white popular sovereignty doctrine into Court precedent, were mutually reinforcing. Over time, these components became mutually entrenched.

This entrenchment of Miller's stance meant that anyone who attempted to uproot his view of Fourteenth Amendment history *also* had to supply alternative strategies for resolving citizenship dilemmas. It *further* meant that anyone who attempted to supply alternatives to state-centered resolution strategies had to challenge his Fourteenth Amendment history.

William Crosskey's challenge to Miller is examined in chapters 5 and 6. I then look at Warren Court disputes over the "proper" judicial approach to legislative apportionment. As will be seen, Crosskey challenged Miller's account of the Fourteenth Amendment *without* supplying an alternative to state-centered strategies for resolving citizenship disputes. The Warren majority tried to supply nationalist resolutions to citizenship dilemmas *without* challenging Miller's account. Neither Crosskey nor the Warren majority persuaded their critics, in part, because *each project necessitated the other.* The Warren majority's attempt to nationalize an egalitarian citizenship required that the symbolic elements which had been entrenched with the traditional, state-centered conception of citizenship be explicitly confronted. Otherwise, these elements would work to deny coherence and authority to the new, national, egalitarian citizenship (which is what happened). In short, Crosskey's failure to persuade audiences about incorporation and the Warren Court majority's inability to convince critics that the Fourteenth Amendment authorized a national and egalitarian citizenship were linked.

*   *   *

A state-centered minimalist approach to postwar citizenship dilemmas appeared more legally coherent in the 1870s, given the legal standards in existence at the time (which, of course, were contingent and historically shaped), than it did later. Given the materials and standards that comprised the legal field in which justices in the 1870s worked, a mostly Northern Democratic representation of the war's issues appeared "best" to them. In rejecting most requests for constitutional remedies, but in accepting a small number of others,[99] the Supreme Court modeled a certain kind of post–Civil War thinking about federal enforcement of civil rights.

Questions of race were implicitly brought into Court opinions and not explicitly stated. The implicit presence of a race theory extending back to Stephen Douglas meant that such theory was difficult to perceive. The fact that its presence was only implicit also meant that the Warren Court majority in the 1960s could not simply reject it by observing that racial ideologies had changed. Future Supreme Court justices would first have to establish its presence in order to expunge it.

By the turn of the century, the Supreme Court's reconstitution of a mostly Northern Democratic history was institutionalized. This is evident in judicial citations to cases from 1873 through 1883 when questions are raised about the legislative history of the Reconstruction Amendments; the dwindling of overt judicial dispute over the legislative history of those amendments (i.e., judicial declarations that disputes over legislative history are "settled"); the uncritical presentation of the Court's account of the Civil War in constitutional law textbooks; judicial inattention to the antebellum constitutional disputes over federalism that led up to the Civil War; and the absence of judicial challenges to the account of the Thirteenth Amendment that portrays it as intended only to abolish formal laws which protected the right to own property in other human beings. (To the extent that any of these things is eroded or reversed, the institutional version of the political history of the 1860s is weakened.)

In 1900, in *Maxwell v. Dow*, the Court looked backward to the "known conditions of affairs"[100] that produced the Fourteenth Amendment. Miller's history was definitive. It was not until the 1940s that debate over the history of Fourteenth Amendment again bubbled to the surface of Court opinions. The point of contention in the 1940s was not only the nationalization of citizenship, but the question of whether Republicans were the good guys.[101]

The institutional preservation of Republican slavery criticism would have opened the possibility that legislative history, a traditional source of law, might have been used to justify rights expansions in the twentieth century. As it happened, legislative history has been used to justify opposition to the expansion of rights.

5

Dueling Histories: Charles Fairman

and William Crosskey Reconstruct

"Original Understanding"

Writing legal history puts one in the midst of historiographical puzzles. In the post-New Deal period, Charles Fairman and William Crosskey set out to investigate the "original understanding" of the Fourteenth Amendment.[1] With their conceptual bags packed, they researched the question of whether the amendment originally applied the Bill of Rights to the states. What sorts of materials were relevant to this search? What did evidence of "original incorporation of the Bill of Rights" look like? How did they know it when they saw it? What point marked the beginning of the search? The absence of objective, "scientific" criteria for verifying historical accounts meant that they had to use some other criteria for distinguishing acceptable readings from unacceptable ones. What were these criteria? And would these criteria be consciously defended?

This chapter takes Fairman's and Crosskey's reconstructions of Fourteenth Amendment history as a subject of sociological investigation. I borrow from Erving Goffman the notion of frame analysis, and I examine how opposing (but overlapping) sets of interpretive assumptions shaped Fairman's and Crosskey's competing recoveries of Fourteenth Amendment history. A version of the nation's slavery and Reconstruction experience was institutionalized during the course of scholarly debate over incorporation, especially as a consequence of the Fairman-Crosskey debate.

That debate has generated a substantial literature. Traditional contributors to the discussion make a case for either Fairman's or Crosskey's version. My examination is different. While most contributors build a case for the superiority of one version over the other, my objective is to highlight certain aspects of the socially constructed nature of this debate. To do so, I examine how Fairman and Crosskey built their histories.

Chapter 6 then looks into the institutional acceptability of Fairman's history as a complex social and institutional product. Chapters 5 and 6, together, reconstruct the social and historical juncture at which the modern terms of debate over "original understanding" were established. I reinsert part of the history of this legal problem.

I should emphasize that I do *not* offer a causal analysis of the impact of the Court's institutional history of Reconstruction on Fairman's and Crosskey's work. Neither do I investigate the roots of their interpretive frames (that is, I do not go into the factors and forces that shaped their respective commitments and assumptions). Certainly, such explorations would be part of a more expansive frame analysis but my study is limited to the operations of Fairman's and Crosskey's assumptions and the interaction of their histories in the institutional settings of the 1950s.

As noted in the introduction, descriptions of events have become recognized as contested ground. Legal narrative and legal storytelling have become common themes in sociolegal scholarship. But while legal scholars now routinely emphasize the constructed nature of legal discourse, few investigations remain of the social and historical circumstances that give rise to prevailing orthodoxies. The conflict between Fairman and Crosskey marked the emergence of a classic,[2] or orthodox, view of the Fourteenth Amendment and Reconstruction generally. Fairman's history remains credible, but it no longer is as dominant as it once was. It has been drawing increasing criticism.[3]

My analysis of the debate bears on an understanding of the constitutional history of race relations and legal constructions of race policy. While the debate was not about race policy, it had tacit racial dimensions. As the terms of debate over the original understanding of the Fourteenth Amendment were set, a conceptual apparatus abstracted from the particular power relations of Reconstruction and the post-New Deal period was put into place. This conceptual apparatus had important consequences, which I only mention here. (They will be returned to later on.) The apparatus linked the production of institutionally "credible" representations of Fourteenth Amendment history to political distributions that were harmful to blacks. While this apparatus did not prevent the Warren Court majority from emerging, it enabled critics of Warren Court decisions to gain credibility for their charge that the Court's decisions were the product of "politics, not law." Judicial and scholarly criticism of the antisubordination decisions of the Warren Court are partly rooted in a structure of thinking about the Fourteenth Amendment.

Fairman's history, which argued that the Fourteenth Amendment did not apply the Bill of Rights to the states, explicitly justified and rationalized the knowledge of the Fourteenth Amendment already developed by the Supreme Court during the Reconstruction era.[4] However, his history was far more detailed in its consideration of historical evidence than were the Supreme Court opinions. Crosskey argued that Fairman "mishandled" the evidence and that the Fourteenth Amendment had, in fact, applied the Bill of Rights to the states.

Fairman's article was extremely influential and held sway in the 1950s. While Crosskey's history was widely rejected at the time, harshly condemned by a large majority of the legal audience, which included judges, lawyers, and constitutional scholars, its very existence was evidence that a dispute over the Court's version of the Fourteenth Amendment was possible.

A Frame Analysis of the Fairman-Crosskey Debate

The basic objective of this chapter is to show the interpretive work involved in building descriptions of Fourteenth Amendment history. For both the builders of official versions of events and the builders of distrusted or rejected versions, the process of construction is ordered, though by different mechanisms. Picking out what is authoritative in history is never haphazard and Fairman and Crosskey both sorted through history in structured ways. My question is: What is the relation between what Fairman and Crosskey brought to their subject and what they saw?

Interpretive frameworks are webs of assumptions, interpretive conventions and symbols that work together and interact. More than twenty years ago, Goffman described frames as the basic elements that organize accounts of "what is happening." Frames also organize orientations to action. In this instance, the action is gaining access to the past, or reconstructing history. Frames are made available at cultural and institutional levels. That means, of course, that legal scholars like Fairman and Crosskey were constrained in terms of their access to interpretive tools. A menu of interpretive tools is available, as the competition between the two of them attests, though the choices are limited.

The notion of frames has already been picked up in some law and society scholarship,[5] and black feminist legal scholars have emphasized the interaction of multiple legal categories—for example, gender and race.[6] In constitutional scholarship, Cass Sunstein has argued that access to facts is always mediated by "human frameworks."[7] "Frames," though, have not yet been widely used as a unit of analysis.[8] Felix Cohen emphasized in 1935 that we need to know how judges think if we are to understand the actual processes by which legal outcomes are reached.[9] I use the concept of frames to investigate the socially contingent and structured nature of Fairman's and Crosskey's thinking.

Interpretive frames structure the many practices, or operations, that are involved in historical reconstructions. For example, a situation must be defined, a story must begin,[10] and "relevances" must be established. The elements that made up Fairman's and Crosskey's interpretive frames worked to structure *where* they looked for evidence of "original understanding," *when* in history they began looking, and *how* they knew when they had found it. In short, the play of symbolic structures that made up each of their frames organized different definitions of "appropriate" investigative techniques and "faithful" readings.

The general problem lies in understanding the relation between their assumptions, their methods, and the object of their inquiry (original understanding). Fairman's and Crosskey's frameworks structured different investigative methods (which can be thought of as "nets") for catching the object of pursuit (original understanding). Each net might be perceived as having a particular weave. Each net "caught" some phenomena and correspondingly "lost" others.[11] For both men, I show what their nets caught and what slipped through. It was possible to view the evidence as consistent and univocal in favor of incorporation but Fairman's assumptions led him to perceive contradictions and imprecision and to discount plausible alternatives.

The divergence between Fairman's and Crosskey's frameworks is more easily observable than the convergence or overlap. Frames provide an analytic tool for discussing both what is disputed (the questions of legitimacy that are raised) as well as what is undisputed or assumed (the questions that cannot even be thought). Thus, the divergence between their frameworks signaled the disputed status of particular questions, while the overlap, that is, the sharing of particular assumptions and conventions, marked the taken-for-granted parameters of debate. Fairman and Crosskey argued within institutional parameters, which they both took as natural or self-evident. Neither of them recognized that these parameters might have been differently drawn.

By standing outside these competing investigations of original understanding, it becomes easier to see a (previously unexamined) sense in which such investigations are tricky business. As critics of originalism have already pointed out, many "understanders" of legislation can be found: Republican and Northern Democratic congressmen, state ratifiers, citizens, as well as factions within each of these groups with different motivations for the same action. Multiple groups of understanders present the problem of choosing which group's understanding will prevail. Another problem lies in determining the level of generality at which understanding should be conceptualized. And, of course, difficulties arise in applying original understanding (even if it is conceptualized at the level of principle) to new situations.[12] But a still more fundamental problem exists. It is not clear ahead of time how one might recognize "original incorporation of the Bill of Rights," if, indeed, one saw it.

What markers indicated original incorporation? Fairman's and Crosskey's interpretive frameworks generated different answers to this question. Said differently, their starting assumptions generated different practices for measuring and assessing what they found in the historical record. In a sense, their frames shaped how bits and pieces of historical material would be "filed."[13] Organizing the meaning of historical material, and understanding what markers flagged the existence or nonexistence of intent to incorporate the Bill of Rights, these are two different ways of saying the same thing. Either way, the operations of frameworks organized their (confident) understandings of the historical material. In this sense, the operations of frames configured the object of pursuit (original understanding). The institutional success of Fairman's history meant that his assumptions, more than Crosskey's, had a stronger hand in establishing an institutional method for identifying the markers, or signposts, of original understanding. Today, Michael Curtis, Akhil Reed Amar, and Richard Aynes continue to challenge these institutional markers.[14]

In addition to examining how Fairman's and Crosskey's frames worked to organize historical meaning, I explore the factors that shaped the institutional acceptability of their historical representations. An examination of how frames work to organize meaning does not, by itself, answer questions about symbolic power and persuasiveness. Therefore, in chapter 6, I link my investigation of Fairman's and Crosskey's frames to the investigation of institutional pressures of various sorts.[15] By locating the production of constitutional history within social and institutional settings, it becomes easier to connect the analysis of legal discourse with the analysis of institutions. I identify the factors and dynamics that rendered Fairman's historical narrative more credible to institutional audiences. The reviews of Crosskey's 1953 book, *Politics and the Constitution,* did great damage to his scholarly reputation. This was one important factor, but not the only one, that explains his defeat in the 1950s.

In examining the production and reception of Fairman's and Crosskey's histories, I ask questions drawn from science studies, especially from the work of Steve Woolgar.[16] What counts as legitimate avoidance of that which might otherwise be regarded as insurmountable philosophical difficulties? What tactics and devices are successful in minimizing the possibility of critical intervention by others? What argumentative strategies enable those who recover history to accomplish, sustain, and reinforce the rationality of their interpretations in the face of the ever-present possibility of "better" alternative interpretations? Under what circumstances and conditions do certain definitions of significance hold sway? How are contrary views systematically diminished? By contrasting Fairman's history to Crosskey's, I am able to identify *what it is* in these histories that rendered them more or less institutionally acceptable or legitimate at the historical juncture of the 1950s. In short, chapters 6 and 7 take up the problem of understanding Fairman's "victory."

The success of Fairman's history was not a result of its intrinsic merit; Fairman did *not* provide more strongly documented assertions. (That is, the documentary record did not determine his victory.) The acceptability and persuasiveness of his account resulted from the widely held nature of his assumptions and Crosskey's tarnished reputation. Chapter 6 examines the interaction between Fairman's and Crosskey's histories that took place in social and institutional settings. Fairman's nonincorporation story of the Fourteenth Amendment was an object constituted within institutional and social networks.

A full examination of the relationship between Fairman's and Crosskey's frames (and the histories that their frames generated) and social and political arrangements is beyond the scope of this book. A complete analysis of frames would include (but not be limited to) examinations of (1) the social and historical processes by which frames are produced, that is, the roots of frames in social and political processes; (2) how frames both enable and constrain the construction of legal/historical meaning; (3) how the meanings structured by frames are received and evaluated by institutionally situated audiences; (4) how frames, as a unit of analysis, connect various levels of the social totality, that is, cultural, institutional, collective, and individual; and (5) the varying amounts of symbolic power stored in frames. Powerful frames are those that are able to impose principles of meaning (i.e., the standards by which meaning is constructed) for many institutional players, especially those located in prestigious institutions. To the extent that dominant (normative) symbolic structures are weakened, the ability of those structures to organize notions of acceptable or legitimate legal history is eroded.

Investigations of frames intersect with investigations of agency. What is the interplay of constraint and maneuverability for the actors who use particular frameworks to accomplish particular ends? This question concerns the possibility of change. Frames might be applied in situations where the results are unforeseeable. My discussion cannot cover all of these bases, but it is important to identify some pieces of the analysis that are not explored here.

The Spark: Justice Black's Opinion in Adamson v. California

In the 1940s, judicial debate over Fourteenth Amendment history re-emerged.[17] Decades had passed since Justice John M. Harlan had issued his dissenting opinions in the 1880s and 1890s. In 1947, Justice Hugo Black's famous dissenting opinion in *Adamson v. California*[18] ignited controversy.

Justice Black, in arguing that the Fourteenth Amendment had applied the Bill of Rights to the states, put forward an incorporation thesis that challenged the accepted view; that is, he asserted that the Fourteenth Amendment had *not* originally incorporated the Bill of Rights. Black claimed that section 1 of the Fourteenth Amendment made the first eight amendments secure against state infringement.[19] His examination of the historical evidence produced this conclusion:

> My study of the historical events that culminated in the Fourteenth Amendment, and the expressions of those who sponsored and favored, as well as those who opposed its submission and passage, persuades me that one of the chief objects that the provisions of the Amendment's first section, separately, and as a whole, were intended to accomplish was to make the Bill of Rights applicable to the states. With full knowledge of the import of the *Barron* decision,

the framers and backers of the Fourteenth Amendment proclaimed its purpose to be to overturn the constitutional rule that case had announced.[20]

At the time when Black was writing, only a select few of the Bill of Rights (certain provisions of the First, Fifth, and Sixth Amendments) had been incorporated, that is, applied to the states. This incorporation had been accomplished through Justice Benjamin Cardozo's interpretation of the due process clause in *Palko v. Connecticut*.[21] Legislative history was *not* the vehicle by which this limited incorporation was accomplished. (Justice Black did not like the use of the due process clause as the vehicle to accomplish incorporation. He thought Cardozo's phrase "ordered liberty" was too open-ended and permitted justices too much latitude. Black resisted judicial discretion, and he favored a mechanical incorporation of the Bill of Rights because he thought this approach provided clearer boundaries for justices. Whether he was correct in this assessment is a whole other question. Scholars who favor the incorporation thesis are concerned less with clear boundaries for justices than with greater national protection for citizenship.)

Fairman wrote his history of the Fourteenth Amendment in response to Justice Black. In a 139-page law review article, Fairman charged that Black was wrong. To put it more exactly, he excoriated Black. He argued that the historical materials did not support Black's full incorporation thesis, and, in turn, he supported Justice Felix Frankfurter's view on incorporation, which Frankfurter presented in a concurring opinion in *Adamson*.[22]

In 1954, Crosskey responded to Fairman's historical readings point by point.[23] In his own lengthy law review article, Crosskey asserted that Justice Black's full incorporation thesis was in fact warranted by the historical evidence. Fairman, in Crosskey's view, had "mishandled" the evidence. While Crosskey's reconstructions were far more detailed than Black's, Crosskey's work earned him no more regard.

Fairman's history offered an explicit defense and explanation of the Court's nonincorporation thesis. That thesis, and its account of Reconstruction generally, had never before been explicitly justified. As previous chapters have discussed, this account held that the Civil War's issues did *not* include Southern censorship and denials of white men's civil liberties. Justice Miller limited his representation of the war's issues to Southern demands for federal enforcement of slave law in the territories and Southern secession. The distinction between state and national citizenship rights was settled according to the Court in the 1870s, and Reconstruction did not see a reformulation of the notion of national citizenship.

Harold Hyman[24] has observed that Fairman's analysis has "shaped much of the constitutional field." Citations to Fairman's history can be found in the U.S. Reports, in the pages of law reviews, and in the books of constitutional scholars.[25] His published analysis was the nineteenth most-cited law review article between World War II and 1985.[26] Justice Frankfurter described Fairman's evidence as "conclusive."[27] Alexander Bickel regarded Black's and Crosskey's assertions as "conclusively disproved."[28] Justice Harlan, a member of the Warren Court dissenters, cited Fairman's history on more than one occasion.[29] Said Harlan, "overwhelming historical evidence marshaled by Professor Fairman demonstrates . . . conclusively that the framers did not apply the Bill of Rights to the States." Michael Perry referred to the nonincorporation thesis as "amply documented and widely accepted."[30] Historian Michael Kammen[31] referred to Justice Black's incorporation thesis as a "constitutional fiction" and cited Fairman's conclusion that Black did not "have history on his side." A number of writers[32] also have adopted Fairman's negative assessment of the abilities of John Bingham, framer of the Fourteenth Amendment. Raoul Berger, as Michael Curtis[33] notes, expressed an extreme manifestation of this view in calling for a "rollback"[34] of Court decisions that have applied Bill of Rights guarantees to the states. Crosskey apparently did not produce an acceptable legal reading for Court justices or for most law professors. The unbelievable nature of Crosskey's history, in Fairman's view, was apparent from the tone that Fairman (1954) took in his response to him.

The question of the original understanding of the Fourteenth Amendment was certainly not settled by their exchange. The Fairman/Crosskey dispute, however, served to socialize[35] future participants in the debate over the history of the Fourteenth Amendment. With the exchanges, battle lines were drawn, topics of debate delineated. The modern terms of legal debate on the incorporation question, and the nature of Reconstruction in general, were established.

The competition itself played an important role in constructing the credibility of Fairman's history and in establishing it as a source of ligitimization in legal decision-making. A central theme in sociolegal scholarship is how the legitimacy of law is maintained. My examination of the dispute suggests that the study of Court legitimization must be closely tied to the study of interpretive work and the social conditions and institutional circumstances under which this work is accomplished and evaluated.

The basic imperative of my book is to explore the limitations of knowledge claims about Fourteenth Amendment history. In this chapter, I bring historiography and epistemology together to make visible the ordered character of Fairman's and Crosskey's competing historical reconstructions. The understanding that history is a site of struggle leads to sociological questions about the dimensions of the dispute and its impact in socializing future participants in debate over Fourteenth Amendment history.

The story, of course, is not over. Fairman's history might remain durable for many more years, but its status will change. This is so because his history is institutional and because "no institution is so universally in force and so perdurable that the meanings it enables will be normal forever."[36] The general point is that the credibility of Fairman's history is linked to the life of the institution. The very concept "original understanding," which both Fairman and Crosskey admitted without question, has come under increasing scrutiny.[37] Understanding the careers of these dueling histories means grasping the processes by which historical meanings, and legal problems generally, are constructed, modified, and revised. Finally, then, how did the interpretive work of Fairman and Crosskey proceed?

Fairman's and Crosskey's Frames

Sets of taken-for-granted, conceptual elements worked together to organize Fairman's and Crosskey's sense-making practices. Their frames constrained their pathways to perception. Both of them read the statements in the *Congressional Globe* within presupplied contexts, which is why they each could cite certain meanings as "obvious."[38] The lists of symbolic elements below should not be taken as a ranked ordering because such structuring obscures their interactive dynamic. Think of the elements as a web, or as netting.

The major categories of thought that made up Fairman's framework were (1) a commitment to local democracy and state autonomy on matters of citizenship;[39] (2) universalization of 1940s orthodoxy; (3) a model of institutional actors as "nonstrategic"; (4) a view of durability (in which the durability of state practices automatically signaled a "rational" distribution of state/federal power); and (5) a version of Civil War history taken from the Dunning School, written during the first two decades of the twentieth century.

Fairman's other publications provide supporting evidence for my claims that these were his actual categories of thought. In 1939, his well-known book on Justice Samuel F. Miller appeared.[40] In 1953, he published a law review article, "The Supreme Court and the Constitutional Limitations on State Governmental Authority,"[41] which responded to Crosskey's first sketch of the incorporation thesis in *Politics and the Constitution*. In 1954,[42] he published a relatively brief response to Crosskey's detailed version of the incorporation thesis. In 1971 and 1987, he published a two-volume set, *Reconstruction and Reunion, 1864–1888*, which appeared in the series, *A History of the Supreme Court of the United States*.[43] While my analysis centers on Fairman's 1949 article, I refer (in footnotes, usually) to material in these other sources that supports my analysis.

Fairman's categories of thought produced what Sanford Levinson has called a "catholic" or Court-centered approach to constitutional meaning on the question of incorporation. Fairman's frame limited his ability to imagine that any competent lawyer could view the *Barron* decision as anything other than the "right" view of the original Constitution. He also viewed the *Slaughter-House* and *Cruikshank* decisions as authoritative on the incorporation question. Put differently, he had a limited ability to imagine what the concerns of Republican congressmen could possibly be. His assumptions led him at a series of points in his analysis to ignore evidence that was arguably relevant and to discount plausible alternative conclusions.

The elements that made up Crosskey's framework included (1) a nationalist vision of the original Constitution, (2) an identification of Republican congressmen with the antislavery movement, (3) an assumption that Republican congressmen would act with a view toward abolitionist goals, (4) a social history approach to the *Congressional Globe,* and (5) a model of institutional actors as strategic actors. This set of assumptions led him to take a more "protestant" approach to constitutional meaning on the question of incorporation, an approach that bypassed hierarchical (Court) readings.

It is possible that Crosskey's commitment to a Congress-centered view of the original Constitution (however much this view was condemned) played a role in opening his historical imagination to nontraditional perspectives on the Fourteenth Amendment. After all, Crosskey himself believed that the original Constitution provided for extensive congressional power, and that the original Constitution applied the Bill of Rights to the states. Crosskey himself rejected the *Barron* decision as "incorrectly decided" and "without any warrant at all."[44] These beliefs certainly opened his mind to the possibility that Republicans, too, might reject the *Barron* decision and want to overturn it.

Different possible explanations have been put forward to account for what led Crosskey to consider the antislavery political/constitutional thought of the Republicans. (Crosskey states that the meaning of the privileges or immunities clause was "clear in itself or clear when read in the light of the prior law."[45] Other scholars supporting the incorporation thesis say the meaning of the clause is clear when Republican statements are placed in historical context.)[46] What led Crosskey to the unorthodox constitutional theory of the Republicans is a difficult question. A combination of factors, including his own nationalist vision of the original Constitution, was likely at work. What is clear is Crosskey's view that the key to understanding the debates was the Republicans' rejection of the Supreme Court as the ultimate authority on the Constitution.

Crosskey's framing assumptions led him to catch in his net broad Republican references to the "rights that attach to citizenship in all free governments." These were significant and meaningful references for him, whereas for Fairman such broad statements were empty verbiage. What was lost, or missed, by Crosskey's frame included the variation among Republicans regarding their views of the original Constitution and the implications of this variation for identifying and applying a notion of original understanding. Just as Fairman's imagination and perception were limited by his frame, so too were Crosskey's, although in a different way. Crosskey's framing assumptions produced gaps in his analysis, which made it easier for an (already skeptical) audience to reject his conclusions.

The workings of these opposing frames (what they capture and what they miss) can be seen most clearly, perhaps, by examining particular issues of dispute between the two opponents. What follows is a side-by-side comparison of them on three points of dispute: *Barron v. Baltimore* (1833); institutional action from the Reconstruction era (which includes Court decisions from the 1870s); and political tradition. While it is analytically useful to structure my presentation of Fairman's and Crosskey's histories in this way, one danger is that their reconstructions will not be seen as wholes. To ward off this possible pitfall and to reiterate my point about how framing assumptions work in concert, the sections of this chapter that follow this comparison reintegrate Fairman's and Crosskey's positions on the three points of dispute.

The Matter of Barron v. Baltimore[47]

Fairman's Perspective
Sanford Levinson, as mentioned, identifies what he calls catholic and protestant strains in constitutional thought. Catholic approaches look to sources outside the text (e.g., Court interpretations and tradition) as guides to constitutional meaning. In contrast, protestant approaches to the Constitution give authority to the constitutional text and insist on individual access to that text. Protestants claim that constitutional meaning resides inside the text and not in tradition or practice, a belief that enables them to bypass Court (hierarchical) interpretations.[48]

Fairman's approach to constitutional meaning on the incorporation question was catholic in that he ascribed authority to Court interpretations and institutionally orthodox readings. This predilection was evident in the way that he made sense of Republican references to "the law" generally and to the case of *Barron v. Baltimore* in particular.

In *Barron,* the Supreme Court for the first time faced the argument that a state government had violated one of the provisions of the Bill of Rights (specifically, a clause of the Fifth Amendment). Chief Justice John Marshall, writing for a unanimous Court, held that the Bill of Rights was applicable to the federal government, but not to the states. In other words, the Court ruled that the federal government could not violate Bill of Rights guarantees, but that state violations of the Bill of Rights were constitutionally permissible. The *Barron* decision was reaffirmed repeatedly in the decades before the Civil War, with the dominant view being that the Bill of Rights protected individuals only against the national government. A few "*Barron* contrarians" did exist, and their conclusion that the Bill of Rights also applied to the states was grounded in common law tradition.[49]

The main purpose of Fairman's 1953 article (which responded to Crosskey's 1953 book) was to defend the authority of *Barron* and the Court's reasons for holding that the original Constitution did not apply the Bill of Rights to the states. Fairman catalogued evidence in support of his view that *Barron* correctly interpreted the original Constitution.[50] Fairman's views on *Barron* reappeared in his 1954 article (which responded to Crosskey's 1954 article). In his 1949 article and his 1971 history of Reconstruction, Fairman stated repeatedly that "the law had been clearly established in *Barron v. Baltimore* to the effect that the first eight Amendments did not bind the states."[51]

A significant question for the two men was how to interpret Republican references to *Barron* that were accompanied by statements that the Fourteenth Amendment "took no right from a state that ever belonged to it." Crosskey asserted that such references and statements signaled an intention to overturn *Barron* and an unorthodox constitutionalism. Fairman asserted that such references and statements illustrated Republican incompetence and confusion.

My argument is that Fairman was locked into his view of *Barron* as the *only* authoritative source of law on the incorporation question. This limited outlook led him to discount evidence that the Republicans might have wanted to overturn the decision and might have believed in a "truer" constitutionalism that had been perverted by slavery. Simply, Fairman could not imagine any grounds on which Republicans could challenge or condemn *Barron*.

Such a challenge, however, could happen in at least four ways. (1) It could be argued that the original Constitution did not incorporate the Bill of Rights, but that this omission was a concession to slavery which polluted the document and went against "true" republican principles contained in the Declaration of Independence. (2) That the original Constitution applied the Bill of Rights to the states through the privileges and immunities clause of article 4, section 2, but did *not* provide an enforcement mechanism. (Thus, no federal remedy was at hand for state violations of the Bill of Rights.) (3) That the original Constitution applied the Bill of Rights to the states through the privileges and immunities clause of article 4, section 2, and *did* supply an enforcement mechanism, but that political forces and the Supreme Court worked to subvert this constitutional requirement by imposing a narrow interpretation (what became the standard interpretation) on the clause. (Thus, no federal remedy existed for violations of article 4, section 2, in practice, but one did remain under the "true" constitutional construction.)[52] (4) Finally, the question of whether the original Constitution applied the Bill of Rights to the states could be left unaddressed, and it could be argued that, in any case, incorporation was a wise thing to do after the Civil War. While these positions would produce different assessments of the technical correctness of *Barron,* they all would agree that *Barron* was part of the constitutional landscape and needed to be removed from it, that is, overturned. The Fourteenth Amendment would be necessary to bring about any of these four positions.

Fairman, in general, did not perceive many dimensions of slavery politics. It is uncertain if he knew about, or if he ever took seriously, the hypothesis that Republicans were harshly critical of antebellum Southern infringements of antislavery activists' civil liberties. Republicans spoke on how slavery led to state repression of the rights of speech, press, petition, assembly, due process, and jury trial.[53] As late as 1971, Fairman did not see or concede the existence of such criticism. "The Bill of Rights protected the individual only against the National Government, and complaints on any such ground *had been exceedingly rare.*"[54] Fairman's comment, in 1971, that the original Constitution "had sufficed," denies the existence of Republican diagnoses of "the problems" with slavery.

Fairman's comment that the original Constitution had sufficed came after Jacobus ten Broek and Howard Graham had published findings on the antislavery origins of the Fourteenth Amendment and after Arthur Bestor had conceptualized the Civil War as a constitutional crisis. If anything was clear, it was that the original Constitution had not sufficed. But the academic history of the Civil War and Reconstruction periods probably did not circulate among law school faculties in the 1960s as it does today. No standards of institutional credibility in 1971 required Fairman to address ten Broek, Graham, and Bestor. And in 1949 no mainstream body of scholarship presented evidence that Republicans condemned Southern repression of antislavery activists' rights of speech, press, assembly, etc.

In 1949, Fairman interpreted the meaning of Republican speeches through a filter which assumed that *Barron* was unassailable for any reason. John Bingham, a moderate Republican and author of the Fourteenth Amendment, referred to *Barron v. Baltimore* directly on several occasions,[55] once during an exchange that he had with a fellow congressman. This legislator thought the federal government already possessed the power to adequately protect citizenship rights. He challenged Bingham to produce evidence that the Fourteenth Amendment was actually needed. Bingham responded:

A gentleman on the other side interrupted me and wanted to know if I could cite a decision showing that the power of the Federal Government to enforce in the United States courts the bill of rights had been denied. I answered that I was prepared to introduce such decisions; and that is exactly what makes plain the necessity of adopting this amendment. Mr. Speaker, On this subject I refer the House and the country to a decision of the Supreme Court, to be found in 7 Peters, 247, in the case of *Barron vs. The Mayor and City Council of Baltimore,* involving the question whether the fifth article of the amendments to the Constitution are [*sic*] binding upon the State of Maryland and to be enforced in the Federal courts. . . . I read one further decision on this subject—that case of the *Lessee of Livingstone vs. Moore.* . . .[56]

Fairman answered: "Those cases never intimated that the various requirements of the first eight Amendments really extended to the states. . . ." [Bingham] hailed *Barron v. Baltimore* as though it were a vindication of his position, and plunged on to worse confusion."[57] Fairman asserted that when Bingham invoked the Bill of Rights, Bingham was not referring to the first eight amendments. Fairman characterized Bingham as "befuddled"[58] and "confused."[59] The "obviousness" of his confusion makes sense only if certain conditions of interpretation are imposed, namely, that *Barron* was the only authoritative source on the question of incorporation. This condition, of course, is not necessary.

An alternative explanation for Fairman's view is that he simply failed to read Bingham's words carefully and that he was too hasty in his judgment. The question is, How does one establish causal factors with confidence? How can we be confident that Fairman's view of *Barron* as the only authoritative interpretation of the original Constitution shaped his interpretation of the *Congressional Globe*? First, there is structure to Bingham's history. If his assertions were simply the product of less-than-careful work, this structure would not exist; a more haphazard quality to his statements regarding Bingham, article 4, section 2, the Joint Committee on Reconstruction, jury trials, etc., would be observable. His statements on all of the subjects that he considers are linked by a set of core assumptions. (The rest of this chapter provides evidence on this point.)

The second reason that I can identify Fairman's view of *Barron* as a causal factor (and reject the "hasty work" hypothesis) has to do with peer approval. Peer approval was tremendous, and it is possible to document similar assumptions in the work of Frankfurter and the younger Justice John Marshall Harlan. (Chapter 6 considers Harlan's arguments in the 1960s.) The histories of Fairman, Frankfurter, and Harlan align. If Fairman was hasty and less-than-careful, Frankfurter and Harlan were hasty, too, in exactly the same way. This failing is highly unlikely. The patterns of their histories are much more apt to be the product of shared assumptions. The internal structure of Fairman's various works on the Fourteenth Amendment plus the structural similarities among Fairman's, Frankfurter's, and Harlan's histories are the basis for my claims about the existence of these interpretive frames.

Fairman was writing in the post-New Deal period when there was disagreement about what changed after the passage of the Fourteenth Amendment. But on the question of incorporation, consensus had been reached about the status of antebellum constitutional law. That is, the antebellum Constitution did not bind the states to the Bill of Rights. The accepted view in the 1940s was that *Barron* expressed the "right," or "true," view of the antebellum Constitution. Fairman projected contemporary orthodoxy backward. In other words, he universalized his present—the time when he was writing—and he dehistoricized then-current orthodoxy, treating it as a "natural" object.

Fairman's catholic, Court-centered understanding of the applicability of the Bill of Rights to the states during the antebellum period led him to miss (or pass over) historical materials that were arguably vital to the issue at hand. Speeches during the 39th Reconstruction Congress (1866) suggested that Republicans were highly critical of the antebellum notion of states' rights. Republicans consistently referred to antebellum political history and the Civil War. Fairman himself cited passages that contained such references. For example, during the discussion of section 1 of the Fourteenth Amendment, Bingham stated:

> The necessity for the first section of this amendment to the Constitution, Mr. Speaker, is one of the lessons that have [sic] been taught to your committee and taught to all the people of this country by the history of the past four years of terrific conflict—that history in which God is, and in which He teaches the profoundest lessons to men and nations. There was a want hitherto, and there remains a want now, in the Constitution of our country, which the proposed amendment will supply. What is that? It is the power in the people, the whole people of the United States, by express authority of the

Constitution to do that by congressional enactment which hitherto they have not had the power to do, and have never even attempted to do; that is, to protect by national law the privileges and immunities of all the citizens of the Republic and the inborn rights of every person within its jurisdiction whenever the same shall be abridged or denied by the unconstitutional acts of any State. . . .

Allow me, Mr. Speaker, in passing, to say that this amendment takes from no State any right that ever pertained to it. No State ever had the right, under the forms of law or otherwise, to deny to any freeman the equal protection of the laws or to abridge the privileges or immunities of any citizen of the Republic, although many of them have assumed and exercised that power, and that without remedy. . . . [M]any instances of State injustice and oppression have already occurred in the State legislation of this Union, of flagrant violations of the guarantied privileges of citizens of the United States, for which the national Government furnished and could furnish by law no remedy whatever. Contrary to the express letter of your Constitution, "cruel and unusual punishments" have been inflicted under State laws within this Union upon citizens, not only for crimes committed, but for sacred duty done.[60]

Fairman responded in this way:

The necessity for the first Section, Bingham tells us, is a lesson taught by the past four years of conflict. Surely this is an inapt way to express the idea that the provisions of Amendments I to VIII should be made applicable to the states! What is the great want this Section will fill? Once more we are told, the absence of power in Congress to protect the privileges and immunities of citizens of the Republic and the inborn rights of man. . . . "Contrary to the express letter" of the Constitution, states have inflicted "cruel and unusual punishments." Admit, very frankly, that this necessarily implies that the first eight Amendments were already limitations—though not enforceable by congressional action—upon the states. [Chief Justice John] Marshall's Court [in *Barron v. Baltimore*] had said they were not limitations on the states, Bingham somehow believes that they are.[61]

Now, if *Barron* is assumed to be correct, then the accompanying understanding of states' rights is that states had the legitimate right to violate the Bill of Rights. Applying the Bill of Rights to the states would constitute a "taking" from state power. This is the mind-set in which Fairman reads Bingham's statements. Bingham, remember, stated that the Fourteenth Amendment "takes from no State any right that ever pertained to it." Because Fairman assumes that states *had* the right to abridge Bill of Rights guarantees, and because Fairman *projects this view onto Bingham* (i.e., because Fairman universalizes his own assumptions about *Barron*), Fairman interprets Bingham's statement as evidence that incorporation obviously was not intended. Given Fairman's assumptions, it makes sense that he would label Bingham's statements "confused discourse"[62] and a "jumbled exposition."

But, if the assumptions are changed, Bingham's statement about the Fourteenth Amendment "tak[ing] from no State any right that ever pertained to it" will be interpreted differently. If *Barron* is challenged under the theory that the original Constitution applied the Bill of Rights to the states, but that this application was subverted and went unenforced (for any number of possible reasons), the accompanying understanding of states' rights is that states *never had* the legitimate right (though they had illegitimate power) to violate the Bill of Rights. And so explicitly applying the Bill of Rights to the states would not constitute a "taking." It would constitute merely a "return" to the preslavery-corrupted Constitution. Repudiation of *Barron* was an affirmation of "original" principles.

Republican-Northern Democratic disputes over what it meant to destroy slavery and resolve the war's issues slip right through Fairman's net. In chapters 2 and 3, I discussed Republican and Northern Democratic views of the problem with slavery and their different versions of the slavery experience. Their dispute over the criteria that marked the "end" of the slavery experience remained unacknowledged in Fairman's account. Indeed, he presented the Northern Democratic perspective as the objective view. "The Thirteenth Amendment had now put an end to slavery," he stated.[63]

Significantly, Fairman asserted that Bingham's reference to the "lesson" taught by the Civil War was "an inapt way" to express the objective of incorporating the Bill of Rights. One might think that references to slavery and the war would be relevant to an investigation of original understanding. Given that a very bloody and expensive war had just ended and that congressmen were faced with the work of reconfiguring the Union, making sense of the war was high on the political agenda. I argued earlier that Republicans and Northern Democrats waged political war by asserting different versions of the slavery experience and the war's objectives. That is why understanding the structure of Republican and Northern Democratic references to slavery and the war is vital to the question of incorporation. If Republicans saw Southern censorship as part of the problem with slavery, and if this was widely known, then their references to the Civil War and the war's "lessons" could easily be understood as an identification of a problem that the amendment would fix.

Fairman seemed largely unaware of many dimensions of slavery politics. At the time, Dunning School histories of Reconstruction, which portrayed Republicans negatively, were institutionally legitimated and accessible. W. E. B. DuBois's account of Reconstruction was published in 1935, but it received no institutional endorsement. Richard Aynes notes that Fairman and Frankfurter were both educated while the Dunning School histories were predominant. (Even in 1971, after Dunning School histories were delegitimated, Fairman used the biographical portraits that they produced. He referred to the "vindictive Radicals" and to Thaddeus Stevens as a "manipulator of men." He called the Joint Committee of Fifteen a "conspiracy."[64] In 1949, he had cited with approval a negative description of the committee by the *New York Herald*.) Aynes states that "one might expect highly educated people like Fairman and Frankfurter to be acquainted" with the works of John R. Lynch and DuBois.[65] But I doubt that Fairman was expected to mine these sources, given the white-dominated educational culture in which he was trained. It would be useful to confirm, however, if course syllabi or reading lists at the time contained DuBois's work and if professors actually expected students to read it.

Fairman did have available to him the work of Judge Timothy Farrar, Judge George Paschal, and Dean John N. Pomeroy, all three of whom published constitutional law treatises from 1866 through 1868 in which they commented on the impact of the proposed Fourteenth Amendment.[66] All three stated that the Fourteenth Amendment would apply the Bill of Rights to the states. Fairman acknowledged Pomeroy's prominence, but he made no mention of his views on the amendment. (Pomeroy's views are cited by scholars today who support the incorporation thesis.)[67]

In the 1950s, Howard Graham and Jacobus ten Broek[68] explored the antislavery background of the Fourteenth Amendment. In 1977, William Wiecek wrote that antislavery constitutionalism "developed from nontechnical popular origins that lay outside courts and legislatures. Constitutional development was (and is) not a monopoly of a hierarchic caste of judges and lawyers. It has its beginnings in the American people and

its first expressions are to be found in documents less formal than decisions and statutes."[69] In the 1990s, Michael Kent Curtis has published a
series of articles on slavery controversies involving free speech and free
press. In 1992, Akhil Reed Amar discussed the "declaratory theory" of
rights. This theory was part of the effort to gain institutional recognition
for an expanded conception of liberty, namely, the liberty of individuals against popular majorities. As discussed in chapter 2, this expanded
conception of liberty was embodied in the Republicans' political critique
of slavery, but in 1866 it was met with little institutional support.

The delegitimation of Dunning School views in the 1960s was an important development regarding legal debates over Fourteenth Amendment history. Constitutional scholars have used the 1960s histories and
resuscitated DuBois in pursuing research on slavery politics. Unlike
Curtis, Robert Kaczorowski, Amar, Aynes, and Lea VanderVelde, Crosskey did not have the work of academic historians to stand on. This made
the rejection of his history that much easier.

Fairman's prior acceptance of Dunning School history helped channel
his perception away from materials that suggested antebellum constitutional disputes existed not only over the fugitive slave clause and the
legal states of slavery in the territories, but over state denials of whites'
civil liberties as well. The existence of this last dispute and the attempt
to settle it are evident in the patterned references to the Civil War, and
the resolution of the slavery issue generally, that mark Republican and
Northern Democratic speeches on the Fourteenth Amendment.

Fairman's "understanding" of Bingham's references to *Barron* (that he
was "confused") and of his reference to the Civil War (that it was an
"inapt" way to express incorporation) were the product of several symbolic elements and interpretive conventions working together. These included the use of (not yet delegitimated) Dunning School history, the
imposition of conditions of interpretation, and the universalization of
1940s orthodoxy on *Barron* (that it was the "true" reading of the antebellum Constitution).

In sum, Fairman's frame produced a particular conception of what
evidence of incorporation would look like and what it would *not* look
like. Actually, a handful of instances could be found where Republicans
specifically referred to the first eight amendments and stated the aim
of making these amendments applicable to the states.[70] But against the
certainties produced by Fairman's frame, these references appeared as
anomalies, and Fairman discounted them.

Crosskey's Perspective on Barron

Crosskey rejected a Court-centered approach to the original understanding of the Fourteenth Amendment. As mentioned, his prior commitment to a nationalist, Congress-centered interpretation of the original Constitution played a role in shaping his perception of the *Congressional Globe* speeches in general and Republican references to *Barron* in particular.

In his 1953 book, Crosskey argued that the original Constitution placed restrictions on state authority, but the Supreme Court had destroyed them. The later section of his book discussed the Supreme Court's "destruction of the constitutional limitations on state authority," and the last several chapters made reference to the standing "constitutional law."[71] The term, constitutional law, appeared in quotations. Although Crosskey's book acknowledged the nonincorporation thesis in *Barron,* he declared that the case was "incorrectly decided."[72] The "true" view of the original Constitution was that states were bound to the Bill of Rights. Few have agreed with Crosskey on this matter, but his views on the original Constitution are relevant to the incorporation debate.

The main concern of his 1953 book was congressional rights,[73] not the treatment of disenfranchised groups or the abuses that black Americans had experienced under state governments (though "expanded congressional power" is not completely distinct from concern for blacks, since many of the most important civil rights questions concern congressional authority to legislate under section 5 of the Fourteenth Amendment). His argument in favor of incorporation supported his complaint that the Supreme Court had favored states' rights over congressional rights, and his incorporation thesis emerged in the context of (and was used to support) a claim for expanded congressional power.

This argument is significant for several reasons, not the least of which is the broad condemnation of Crosskey's Congress-centered view of the original Constitution. Even if his critics were granted their arguments about the implausibility of *all* his claims (something that not all of them were prepared to do),[74] it would be ironic that his beliefs about the original Constitution seem to have enabled him to construct a plausible account of the Fourteenth Amendment. It should be noted, however, that one need not hold a Congress-centered view of the original Constitution to believe that the incorporation thesis is plausible. One's perceptive capacities might be opened to this possibility in a variety of ways.[75]

For Crosskey, a distinction between standing law and "true" law was part of his conceptual repertoire for organizing the world. In his narrative, Bingham and the Republicans appear as reformers who wished to make the standing law "right." According to Crosskey, Bingham argued that the Fourteenth Amendment was necessary to reverse the decision in *Barron*. Crosskey's own belief that the decision was wrongly decided made it easier for him to imagine that others might reject the *Barron* decision as well. Crosskey's belief however, also made it difficult for him to imagine that the Republicans' reasons for rejecting *Barron* might be different from his own.

Fairman did not draw a distinction between standing law and "true" law. He was conceptually ill-equipped to even imagine that Bingham and the Republicans could hold such a distinction, much less act on it. Crosskey argued that there was a "law" that the courts denied, which set him apart from both Fairman (who believed the standing law was the "true" law) and someone like Holmes, who acknowledged that others drew distinctions between standing and "true" law, although such distinctions had little to do with his own legal thinking. (Holmes's famous remark that "[t]he prophesies of what the courts will do in fact, and nothing more pretentious," is what he means by "law.") [76]

Crosskey's history emphasized the relevance of Republican political thought. His reading of the *Congressional Globe* was informed by an expectation that Republican congressmen would act with a view toward antislavery/free labor goals (though Crosskey himself did not preserve the ambiguity in these terms). In other words, Crosskey held a predetermined idea of what Republican concerns could possibly be. This leaning influenced where he looked for evidence of original incorporation and what he imagined such evidence would look like. Because he associated Republican congressmen with the antislavery movement, it made sense to him to begin his story at an earlier point in time (i.e., to construct a narrative with boundaries wider than Fairman's).

For Crosskey, the not-yet-overruled decision in *Dred Scott v. Sandford* (1857) offered a critical clue in assessing Republican objectives. This decision was "undeniably relevant" to an investigation of the legislative history of the Fourteenth Amendment.

> The first feature of the prior law that is relevant to this inquiry is one of the holdings of the Supreme Court in the *Dred Scott* case: that, under the Constitution of the United States, no person of African descent, whether a slave or not, was or could be a citizen of the United States. This holding was still unoverruled when the Four-

teenth Amendment was drawn. A second relevant circumstance is that there were, at that time, in the local laws provisions denying local state citizenship to persons of African descent. . . . It was another of the doctrines of the *Dred Scott* case that all the various privileges and immunities recognized in the Constitution and its various amendments were privileges and immunities of citizens of the United States only; The foregoing doctrine, unoverruled in 1866–68 seems undeniably relevant in considering what was the meaning of the command, in the amendment then adopted.[77]

Fairman understood the overruling of *Dred Scott* narrowly, as conferring national citizenship on the former slaves. The question, of course, is what the "privileges and immunities" of national citizenship were. Fairman endorsed Miller's definition in the *Slaughter-House Cases.* Crosskey pointed to Justice Taney's own listing of "privileges and immunities" of national citizenship, which included Bill of Rights guarantees. The amendment worked off of Taney's own identification of citizenship's benefits.[78] Thus, Crosskey understood the Fourteenth Amendment in light of the Republican Party's criticisms of slave state practices,[79] Republican criticism of *Barron,* and selected aspects of *Dred Scott.* His "understanding" that congressional Republicans wanted to overrule the Court's decision in *Barron v. Baltimore* and apply the Bill of Rights to the states depended on a context that he supplied, which included both a commitment to a Congress-centered interpretation of the original Constitution and an association of congressional Republicans with antislavery thought.

This presupplied context, however, also led Crosskey away from a deeper examination of the *variety* of perspectives exhibited by Republicans on the original Constitution and *Barron.* Some Republicans appeared unaware that the Supreme Court had denied the applicability of the Bill of Rights to the states. William Kelley, for one, asserted confidently that the Fourteenth Amendment would give effect to portions of the original Constitution that had "lain dormant." Others, like William Higby (whom Crosskey quotes), said the amendment would give life to portions of the Constitution that "*probably* were intended from the beginning" to have life (my italics). Still others, like Thaddeus Stevens, harshly condemned the Founders and argued that their concessions to slavery had produced the Civil War.[80] Stevens's statements suggest that he believed the original Constitution did not apply the Bill of Rights to the states. Finally, even if most Republicans believed that applying the

Bill of Rights to the states was a practical thing to do in light of Southern intransigence, this does not necessarily lead to the conclusion that Republicans believed the Supreme Court in *Barron* destroyed provisions in the original Constitution. Crosskey's own belief in this thesis led to a simplistic representation of Republican perspectives on this matter.

In a move designed to delegitimate Fairman's reading of the *Congressional Globe,* Crosskey himself situated Fairman's reading. He asked his audience (which included Fairman) to imagine a particular set of circumstances in which *Globe* statements would be differently, but equally, clear (different, that is, from Fairman's reading). Crosskey identified Fairman's use of orthodox constitutional law in the 1940s as an interpretive baseline against which he (Fairman) read Republican statements. Crosskey explained how one could be "confused" by the historical record if one read Republican statements against the "unquestioningly accepted" views of constitutional law in the 1940s. This reading would result, he explained, in a failure to recognize the "peculiar"[81] nature of Radical thought. Fairman's failure to appreciate the nature of old Republican thought was a critical mistake that led to his "mishandling" of the evidence. Crosskey repeated the point: "It is clear that minds unaware of old Republican theories might very easily take Bingham's remarks as confused, incoherent and incompetent. And it was thus that Mr. Fairman presented them."[82]

> [I] is quite impossible to understand aright the debates over the Fourteenth Amendment . . . unless [old Republican constitutional views] are known and understood and kept constantly in mind. . . . Mr. Fairman's method was to let drop, here and there, throughout his discussion, derogatory hints and comments which gave the impression that the framers of the amendment, and Bingham in particular, were not very bright; that they held the strangest ideas about the Constitution; knew little about it, or about the decisions of the Supreme Court under it; that they were poor draftsmen; in that it was not to be expected that anything intelligible could come from their hands.[83]
>
> Read in the light of the Supreme Court's then past constitutional decisions and various other ideas of constitutional law which have since come to be unquestioningly accepted . . . statements by John Bingham undoubtedly seem a confused mass of untruths and impossibilities. But if we bear in mind the various constitutional theo-

ries set forth. . . . if we remember that these were the common faith of the Republican Party at the time; and if we remember that Bingham himself had given the plainest proof that he entertained these theories in his speech of 1859, then there is, assuredly, not much difficulty in understanding what he had to say.[84]

An understanding of old Republican thought, Crosskey argued, raised doubts about the "settled" status that Fairman attributed to certain questions, including the question of incorporation under the original Constitution. Crosskey called attention to the fact that in the 1860s the meanings of article 4, section 2,[85] and the Fifth Amendment[86] were "not actually settled."[87]

Crosskey could imagine that Republicans might assert federal oversight of certain practices that had been under (illegitimate) state control before the war. He appealed to many Republican statements to support this picture. For example, he quoted Congressman William Higby expressing his support of the Fourteenth Amendment. In Higby's view, that amendment would "only have the effect to give vitality and life to portions of the Constitution that probably were intended from the beginning to have life and vitality, but which have received such a construction that they have been entirely ignored and have become as dead matter in that instrument."[88] Crosskey interpreted this statement as evidence of Higby's support of the view that *Barron v. Baltimore* was incorrectly decided. Crosskey then quoted the Republican congressman who spoke after Higby, William D. Kelley from Pennsylvania: "Mr. Speaker, I repeat that I hold that all the power this amendment will give is already in the Constitution. I admit it has lain dormant. I admit that there has been raised over it a superincumbent mass of State and political usage and judicial decisions that . . . is mountain high."[89]

On the specific subject of section 1 of the Fourteenth Amendment, Crosskey quoted Sen. Luke Poland of Vermont:

The clause . . . secures nothing beyond what was intended by the original provision in the Constitution, that "the citizens of each State shall be entitled to all privileges and immunities of Citizens in the several States." But the radical difference in the social systems of the several States, and the great extent to which the doctrine of State rights or State sovereignty was carried, induced mainly, as I believe, by and for the protection of the peculiar system of the South, led to a practical repudiation of the existing provision [i.e., art. 4, sec. 2] on

this subject, and it was disregarded in many of the States. State legislation was allowed to override it, and as no express power was by
the Constitution granted to Congress to enforce it, it became a dead
letter. The great social and political change in the southern States
wrought by the amendment of the Constitution abolishing slavery
and by the overthrow of the late rebellion render it eminently proper
and necessary that Congress should be invested with the power to
enforce this provision throughout the country and compel its obser-
vance. . . . It certainly seems desirable that no doubt should be left
existing as to the power of Congress to enforce principles lying at
the very foundation of all republican government if they be denied
or violated by the States.[90]

Crosskey presents this statement as an expression of the Republicans'
nonenforcement doctrine, the view that the privileges and immunities
clause of article 4, section 2, applied the Bill of Rights to the states,
but with no federal enforcement or federal remedial power. The Fourteenth Amendment supplied this power by securing the Bill of Rights
against state infringement. Both national judicial authority and congressional authority were increased. Crosskey acknowledged that this view
went against the orthodox view of the privileges and immunities clause
of article 4, section 2. Fairman assumed that the orthodox view of this
article and section was the only legitimate one.[91]

    Crosskey attempted to establish that Republican references to "the
natural and personal rights of citizens" and "principles lying at the foundation of all republican government" were references to the Bill of Rights.
He paid attention to Republican language. For him, broad Republican
references to "rights that attach to citizenship in all free governments,"
found in conjunction with references to antebellum law and the decision
in *Barron,* were significant. In contrast, Fairman judged this broad language as either irrelevant to his investigation because of its imprecision
or as confirming the view that full incorporation had not been accomplished.

    Crosskey's strategy lay in showing that these broad references were
more specific and relevant than Fairman realized. He cited a sequence
of statements made by Sen. Jacob Howard and Sen. John Henderson of
Missouri. Sen. Howard, who was the first presenter of the Fourteenth
Amendment to the Senate, stated clearly (even according to Fairman)
that section 1 would make the first eight amendments applicable to the

states. Following just after Howard, Sen. Henderson stated, "I propose to discuss the first section only so far as citizenship is involved in it. I desire to show that this section will leave citizenship where it now is. It makes plain only what has been rendered doubtful by the past action of the Government. If I be right in that, it will be a loss of time to discuss the remaining provisions of the section, for they merely secure the rights that attach to citizenship in all free governments." Crosskey quoted Fairman's response to Henderson's statement: "Unless the first eight Amendments enumerate 'rights that attach to citizenship in all free governments,' Henderson's understanding is to be counted as opposed to that of Howard."[92]

As Crosskey tells it, Fairman quoted the Henderson remark in an attempt to show that there was no consensus concerning Howard's statements. "Mr. Fairman apparently thinks that such a view of the rights under the first eight amendments would be absurd, and it was his hope that his readers would think the same. But the real question is what the men in the Senate thought in 1866."[93] For Crosskey, the Henderson remark confirms Republican support for incorporation. Howard, Crosskey pointed out, had already described the first eight amendments as "fundamental rights lying at the basis of society and without which a people cannot exist except as slaves, subject to a despotism."[94]

Crosskey, then, paid close attention to the vocabularies in use at the time and the structure of Republican references to antebellum decisions. Republican references to the "fundamental rights of citizenship" that had been denied in antebellum constructions of the Constitution, and Bingham's explicit references to *Barron v. Baltimore,* led Crosskey to conclude that the Republicans aimed to reverse *Barron.* In his eyes, references to *Barron* were indeed "apt" expressions of this objective.

It is important to note that Crosskey's net led him to "lose" pieces of evidence that left holes in his analysis. These gaps in his narrative made it easier to reject his version of events. Crosskey, for example, failed to situate Bingham's references to *Barron* within a compelling explanation of when and how Republicans came to draw a distinction between "true" law and standing law. That explanation involves things like the Crittenden Resolution. As chapter 2 discussed, Northern Democrats appealed to that resolution to construct a delegitimating contradiction between postwar Republican programs and prewar Republican statements. In response, Republicans constructed this distinction and appealed to their political critique of slavery (that slavery destroyed civil liberties). They argued that the "Slave Power" (a dominant trope in antebellum rhetoric) had perverted the notion of states' rights. While Republicans acknowledged that Southern states had exercised power in suppressing personal rights in the antebellum years, they insisted that this power was illegitimate. The exercise of (illegitimate) power did not *establish* a (legitimate) state right. Republicans used the distinction between standing law and "true" law to condemn *Barron* and impose limits on state authority over rights (limits, they argued, that should have been there from the beginning). Had Crosskey offered this argument, it is uncertain what difference it would have made. But without any explanation of how the Republican distinction between "true" law and standing law developed in the context of slavery politics, Crosskey's history was that much easier to dismiss.

On Institutional Action and Political Tradition

Fairman's Perspective
Fairman brought with him a model of institutional action that understood causation (i.e., the causes of institutional action) in narrow terms. This model led him to read institutional behavior in particular ways. He presumed (reasonably) that Supreme Court justices in 1873 had "fresh knowledge" of legislative objectives. The war and war amendments were within memory (it was not "history" yet). What was more open to dispute was his assumption that possession of such fresh knowledge regarding legislative objectives would lead *only* to decisions that recognized these objectives. This view lent validity to the justices' nonincorporation thesis of the Fourteenth Amendment.[95] It was possible, however, that the justices could be aware of certain objectives, yet refuse to recognize them.

Of course, the fact that courts are supposed to follow legislative objectives provides some basis for Fairman's assumption that they will do so. But "institutional duty" is a far more complex notion than he acknowledged. Given his own attachment to state control of individual rights, it would seem that he would understand why Court justices might think it "proper" (i.e., their institutional duty) to resist a program for restructuring the state/federal relation. For the Court justices of the 1870s and 1880s, adhering to a socially and historically specific ethic of institutional duty and bowing to fresh knowledge of legislative objectives are not necessarily consistent.

Fairman also assumed that if state legislators and congressmen had

been aware of the incorporation of the Bill of Rights they would have be-
haved *only* in certain ways. State legislators would have refused to pass a
constitutional amendment that was said to annul their states' laws, and
congressmen would have refused readmittance to states that abridged
Bill of Rights guarantees. Since Southern states passed the Fourteenth
Amendment and continued practices that violated provisions in the Bill
of Rights, and since these states were readmitted to the Union, Fairman
concluded that incorporation could not have occurred.

> If it was understood in the legislatures that considered the proposed
> Amendments, that its adoption would impose upon the state gov-
> ernments the provisions of the federal Bill of Rights, then almost cer-
> tainly each legislature would take note of what the effect would be
> upon the constitutional law and practice of its own state. . . . [O]ne
> would expect to find a marked reaction. Measures would have to be
> taken to conform to the new order. Conversely if we found disparity
> [between the federal Bill of Rights and state practice] coupled with
> complete inaction, it would be very hard to believe the Fourteenth
> Amendment was understood to have that effect.[96]

For Fairman, then, conflict between state laws and the Bill of Rights
after the passage of the Fourteenth Amendment indicated that the
amendment did not apply the Bill of Rights to the states.[97] He assumed
state legislators would have either (1) refused to ratify the Fourteenth
Amendment if they understood it to conflict with their own state laws,
or (2) changed their state laws to conform to the Bill of Rights, especially its jury trial provisions. Either way, Fairman expected to see a
"marked" response to legislation that incorporated the Bill of Rights. He
did not consider that passage of the Fourteenth Amendment was politically necessary for the states of the former Confederacy, and that it was
a low-cost, formal price to pay for readmittance. As Southern Democrats knew, it was not the formal law that mattered, but Northern resolve
to suppress resistance and enforce the law by physical means. Fairman,
however, assumed that formal law mattered most to those in control in
the South. Further, Northerners attempting to assert economic control
in the South may not have had the priorities that he assumed.

If institutional action is conceived as "structured improvisation,"[98]
then one might anticipate that any number of actions might follow from
the possession of information that the Fourteenth Amendment incorporated the Bill of Rights. Institutional actors always have ranges of choices,

even if those choices are limited. Their choice of action depends on experience, training, situation, constraints, the availability of interpretive tools, etc. Supreme Court justices, state legislators, and congressmen of the Reconstruction era were all institutional actors who acted with reference to institutionally defined interests and institutionally shaped ways of thinking. (Chapter 4 offered a preliminary assessment of the institutional commitment, identities, political positions, and values of Court justices in the 1870s.)

In short, Fairman cast institutional actors as nonstrategic. He did not regard institutional action in the 1870s as "a problem" that needed explanation. In his view, institutional actors had taken the right track in asserting almost exclusive state control over citizenship. Therefore, he saw no need to dig into factors that shaped Court interpretations of the Fourteenth Amendment.

Fairman's faith in local democracy on matters of citizenship rights led him in this direction. Such faith was central to his belief system. Even if he was a nationalist when it came to federal regulation of business and labor, he remained state-centered in citizenship/electoral matters. For example, in his view, practices that lasted throughout the antebellum era signaled a "rational" distribution of state/federal power. "The freedom that the states traditionally have exercised to develop their own systems for administering justice repels any thought that the federal provisions on grand jury, criminal jury and civil jury were fastened upon them in 1868. Congress would not have attempted such a thing, the country would not have stood for it, the legislatures would not have ratified." [99]

Felix Frankfurter, concurring in *Adamson v. California,* also rejected the idea of full incorporation. He expressed his disbelief in the prospect that the Fourteenth Amendment could have imposed "the rigorous requirements of the Fifth Amendment for instituting criminal proceedings through a grand jury." This approach would have "uprooted [the states'] established methods for prosecuting crime and fastened upon them a new prosecutorial system." [100]

Fairman's faith in local democracy led him to dismiss the possibility that juries might have been seen as fundamental in the mid-nineteenth century.[101] Indeed, Republican distrust of state prosecutorial systems is widely evident in debates over the Civil Rights Act of 1866.[102] (Fairman did not begin his investigation of original understanding with those debates; rather, he focused narrowly on debates over section 1.)

For Fairman and Frankfurter, state control of jury practices had stood the test of time. But, of course, the test of time can be extended. There are no objective determinations of the end point of this test. Further, the durability of a practice also can be evidence of entrenched domination. For both Fairman and Frankfurter, the durability of the nonincorporation thesis in the postbellum period signaled its accuracy. In a companion piece to Fairman's article, Stanley Morrison attempted to look into legislative objectives by referring to Supreme Court opinions from 1873 until 1883. Morrison viewed the durability of the nonincorporation story as evidence of its accuracy. He commented sarcastically, "if it was one of the chief objectives of the Fourteenth Amendment to incorporate the Bill of Rights, it is certainly surprising that it should have taken so long to find this out." Had incorporation been intended, this information surely would have been known long before 1950.[103] Morrison apparently could not imagine an alternative explanation of how the nonincorporation story could have been initially produced by a Court with an honestly held conception of "institutional duty." He could not conceive that popular acceptance of Court decisions in the 1870s could have insulated the nonincorporation story from criticism; neither could he imagine a line of precedent accumulated so that justices could "simply" follow stare decisis. He could not understand how Dunning School history could have reinforced this line of precedent and how, finally, conditions might have been unfavorable until the 1940s for scrutinizing this account of the Fourteenth Amendment.

Crosskey's Perspective

Crosskey was more disposed to regard institutional action in the 1870s as a problem that needed explaining. This predisposition was based on his sense that such action was wrong. For him, as well, the durability of antebellum arrangements was not automatic evidence of a "rational" distribution of state/national power.

Crosskey gave some consideration (though it was limited) to the contexts in which institutional action occurred. For example, while Fairman interpreted the absence of heated debate on section 1 as evidence supporting the nonincorporation thesis, Crosskey had an opposite interpretation. According to him, this silence resulted from the noncontroversial nature of incorporation. Later sections of the Fourteenth Amendment captured more congressional attention, he explained, since these were the devices that Republicans hoped to use to push the old Southern elite out of government. "As to why the debate should have had this [relatively silent] character, there are several obvious reasons. In the first place, section 1 was not really new to the House. The other sections of the amendment were, on the other hand, entirely novel. In addition to this, they were political: they constituted the means by which the Republicans hoped to hold onto control of the national government."[104]

Crosskey explained how Fairman could interpret congressional silence as evidence of nonincorporation. "To apply the Bill of Rights to the states seems so outrageous to Mr. Fairman that he thinks a public outcry would surely have occurred in 1866–68 had it then been understood that a proposal to apply the Bill of Rights was being made. It was this state of mind that led him to count all his null results as evidence supporting the negative side of the question."[105] In Crosskey's view, Fairman's expectation of a "marked" response explains his misinterpretation of the silence. Fairman's inability to bracket (or historicize) the orthodoxy of his own era produced his "mishandling" of the historical evidence.

Crosskey emphasized the point that Republican thought contained dual impulses toward federalism, one state-centered, and one nation-centered.[106] He acknowledged the Republicans' state-centered thinking when he discussed Northern Democratic charges that the Fourteenth Amendment would destroy states. These charges struck him as absurd, and he interpreted them as a strategy to delegitimate Republican reform. Democrats frequently seized on the broad language of the Fourteenth Amendment and claimed that the amendment could be interpreted to give black citizens the vote, prohibit segregated education, and prohibit antimiscegenation laws. Crosskey pointed to Republican responses that the amendment would do none of these things. He cited Republican denials that the Fourteenth Amendment gave federal jurisdiction over voting, prohibited segregated education, or forbade antimiscegenation laws. (Of course, the Fourteenth Amendment today is seen as accomplishing all of these things.)

Crosskey emphasized that Republicans shared Northern Democratic fears of a too-powerful federal government. In his narrative, Republicans perceived federal jurisdiction over Bill of Rights guarantees as a *narrow* and limited grant of power.

Crosskey sought to make the incorporation thesis palatable to his audience in the 1950s. In defending the thesis and, significantly, its viability for twentieth-century courts, he reined in a strand of Republican nationalism. He represented this nationalism more expansively than Fairman but more narrowly than some evidence suggested (evidence such as Jacob Howard's speech introducing the Fourteenth Amendment to the Senate in which he indicated that the rights in the Bill of Rights were only *some* of those included in national citizenship). Crosskey also emphasized the Republican understanding of incorporation (that it was a narrow and limited grant of federal power). This emphasis, perhaps, was a strategy to assuage those individuals in the 1940s who worried that incorporation of the Bill of Rights would mean a huge expansion in national power. But it also was possible that Crosskey himself believed that incorporation was a narrow and limited granting of power. His thinking seemed to be that if *Republicans* thought incorporation was such a restricted ceding of federal power, then it was so. Of course, the Republicans and Crosskey could be wrong on this point.

Crosskey did not acknowledge that applying this Republican view of granting power involved uncertainty. An emphasis on the Republican understanding of incorporation did not close the case on worries over local democracy. Instead, Republican intent to prescribe a narrow role for the federal government could be interpreted in the twentieth century as legitimization for broad federal oversight of state treatment of citizens. One might acknowledge the Republican perception that elimination of the racial caste system was a narrow federal role or duty in 1866 and *still* be able to coherently defend the view that original understanding legitimated broad federal power over citizenship. In 1866 it was still possible to equate a narrow federal role with the elimination of racial caste. Experiences ranging from the Black Codes, to voting disenfranchisement, to Jim Crow, to the failure to prosecute Klan violence, etc., had not yet piled up to suggest otherwise. Crosskey failed to consider that in legitimating broad national power over citizenship, the accumulation of state-imposed and state-sanctioned practices that subordinated black Americans could enable twentieth-century interpreters of original understanding to draw on Republican desires to include black Americans in the polity.

Crosskey, as mentioned, also ignored certain aspects of the speeches that he himself cited. Republican speeches referred to the Bill of Rights as *only some* of the rights that were included among the privileges and immunities of U.S. citizens. Republican intent with regard to the privileges and immunities clause was uncertain and potentially far-reaching, and Republican speeches in support of the Ku Klux Klan Act of 1871, which Crosskey cited, speak in favor of broad federal jurisdiction. Crosskey did not explain how this stance entailed narrow and limited power. "Narrow and limited" can be subject to dispute, even when narrow means "limited to awful misuses of power." What counts as "awful" can be interpreted in many ways.

My point, I should emphasize, concerns the inherent uncertainty involved in assessing the scope of federal power as the Republicans envisioned that scope. Crosskey attempted to make the incorporation thesis manageable by ignoring some Republican statements and by suppressing the tensions that existed between apparently substantive goals and the commitment of Republicans to limited national power.

Another gap in Crosskey's analysis was his failure to explain the durability of the nonincorporation thesis. He might have used the contingency of Waite Court decisions in the 1870s and 1880s as a reason to justify departures from these decisions. Such a stance, at least, would have provided him with a response to Fairman's dogged use of durable state tradition as an *automatic* indication of a "rational" distribution of state and federal power.

*   *   *

It has been observed many times that writing history involves the imposition of the present on the past. It should be remembered, however, that present-day frames used in writing history are social and historical products. By examining the competing ways in which links were forged between documentary evidence and original meaning, this chapter has tried to illuminate one sense in which the present was imposed on the past in the incorporation debate.

Fairman's interpretive strategies were not uniquely his. His history, enabled and constrained by a set of contestable interpretive assumptions, resonated with an institutional audience that shared these assumptions. His baseline assumptions identified him as a member of a broad-based "interpretive community."[107] The success of his history was a product of contestable but widely shared interpretive assumptions.

Both the production and persuasiveness of Fairman's history must be understood in institutional terms. Situated institutional players who made up the audience for the Fairman/Crosskey dispute brought a range of pressures to bear. The term "situated" conveys location and positionality. Institutional players hold institutional values, commitments, and expectations that result from training programs, among other sources. They bring institutional ways of thinking to bear on the myriad of problems and questions that they encounter. They also have varying degrees of access to institutional resources such as law review pages and the prestige of their positions.

6

Recipes for "Acceptable" History

Fairman's and Crosskey's dueling histories met and interacted in a setting in which various institutional pressures influenced the reception of their competing accounts of the Fourteenth Amendment. As chapter 5 sought to illuminate how interpretive frames generate nets for catching phenomena, this chapter examines how the situatedness of institutional audiences shaped the acceptability of these representations.

For Fairman, Crosskey's conclusions were unbelievable. In Fairman's view, there was simply no logic or reason behind Crosskey's conclusions. Crosskey, in contrast, offered an analysis of the "believability" of the nonincorporation thesis. He explained how one's logic would lead one astray if one held particular assumptions, and he argued why evidence of intent to incorporate would take a different form than Fairman assumed.

Fairman's view of the unbelievability of Crosskey's history is clear from his response to it. He mocked Crosskey to make his point:

> Mr. Crosskey says that [John] Bingham drafted on the theory that his own very special ideas and not the Supreme Court's decision, were the standing law. I would think it plain that anyone who acted on such a view was a purblind and bull-headed draftsman. . . . So in Mr. Crosskey's theory the Fourteenth Amendment—by far the most important amendment to the Constitution—was framed and discussed under very special conditions. The movers acted on the assumption that their own peculiar ideas, and not the decisions of the Supreme Court, were the law. Time passed, and this special vocabulary was forgotten—and then Professor Crosskey discovered the Rosetta Stone and deciphered the ancient records.[1]

Fairman's sarcasm ("Either the Justices from 1873 on down—the whole lot of them, except Harlan, J.,—or else Mr. Crosskey, will be found to have fallen into error")[2] makes sense, given the network of meaning-producing associations set up by Fairman's assumptions, especially his total acceptance of *Barron v. Baltimore* as the only source of law on the antebellum incorporation question. Crosskey, and Justice Hugo Black before him, had suggested an alternative network of associations regarding Republican constitutional theory and Republican references to *Barron* that crossed Fairman's path[3] (or passed through his net) as well as the paths of many others. Black and Crosskey were literally outside the network of meaning-producing associations set up by Fairman. The Black-Crosskey incorporation thesis was not inherently unbelievable or irrational. But it was a breach that made visible some of the conventional ordering commitments of Fairman's interpretive community. When we explore the angle, movement, and scale of the Black-Crosskey breach, it becomes clearer how Fairman and those in his interpretive community were able to reassert these ordering commitments.

In explaining the success of Fairman's history, my basic argument is that Fairman constructed a history that resonated institutionally. After Fairman's article was published, his nonincorporation thesis was quickly accepted. The Fairman/Crosskey debate marked the emergence of a classic, or orthodox, legal view of the Fourteenth Amendment and of Reconstruction generally.

For those who followed, Fairman's article became a source of authority on the amendment. One of these was legal scholar Alexander Bickel, who was Felix Frankfurter's clerk and protégé. (Justice Frankfurter wrote a concurring opinion in *Adamson* that condemned Justice Black's incorporation thesis.) In a well-known article, Bickel offered a version of the legislative history of the Fourteenth Amendment as it pertained to school segregation. In a footnote, Bickel addressed the issue of incorporation and mentioned *Maxwell v. Dow* (1900). In *Maxwell,* counsel had presented Jacob Howard's speech upon introducing the Fourteenth Amendment to the Senate. Howard clearly stated that the amendment would make the Bill of Rights applicable to the states. The Court's opinion in *Maxwell* acknowledged that counsel had "cited from the speech of one of the Senators" but downgraded its significance by isolating it: "What individual Senators or Republicans may have urged in debate, in regard to the meaning to be given to a proposed constitutional amendment, does not furnish a firm ground for its proper construction, nor is it important as explanatory of the grounds upon which the members voted in adopting it."[4] Bickel reprinted excerpts from Howard's speech and then quickly resolved the issue against the incorporation thesis. For authority, Bickel cited Fairman's article.[5] Crosskey's history had appeared a year earlier, but, for Bickel, a simple citation to Fairman was sufficient. For Bickel, the matter was closed.

What lawyers and judges received in Fairman's account that they did not find in Crosskey's was, in general terms, an affirmation of state control over citizenship rights and a stabilization of the doctrine of stare decisis regarding Fourteenth Amendment history. The recipe for producing acceptable legal readings for lawyers and judges who approved of Fairman's history included (1) expressing faith in the political process and (2) weighing distrust of federal control over personal citizenship rights as heavier than distrust of state control over those rights.

The New Deal Court of the 1930s and 1940s was famous for overturning precedent,[6] which in this case concerned matters of business and labor regulation as well as personal rights. Fairman's nationalism on matters of business and economic regulation was close to Frankfurter's. He supported national control on matters concerning the regulation of business and labor.[7] On matters of individual rights, the New Deal Court used the due process clause and *Palko*'s doctrine of "ordered liberty" to accomplish its selective incorporation. The Court left the institutional version of Reconstruction/Fourteenth Amendment history untouched. Indeed, at the end of Fairman's article on Fourteenth Amendment history, he commented that Justice Benjamin Cardozo's doctrine of ordered liberty was as close as anyone could come to deciphering the objectives of the privileges or immunities clause. Thus, it is the situational state-centeredness of Fairman and Frankfurter, and their insistence that matters of individual rights be left to the political process and to local democracy, that appears to set incorporation apart from other issues dealt with by the New Deal Court.

Fairman's persuasiveness, his ability to "act at a distance,"[8] was linked to his ability to mobilize symbols that had been deeply institutionalized. He emphasized the tradition of local democracy, which appeared as a cherished achievement won against the kings of England and *the* reason for American success (no mention was made of any American failures). Fairman's story of the American Republic echoed the one told by the Northern Democrats in the 39th Congress.

Fairman, like the Northern Democrats, rooted a collective national identity in the tradition of decentralized politics. He appealed to the Revolutionary experience, which had seen local colonies fighting a central monarchy in the name of freedom. As a result of this experience, during the Founding period a strong central government was associated with tyranny and oppression. State resistance to the federal Sedition Act strengthened this association.

Not included in Fairman's version of political history were many dimensions of slavery politics. In the decades after the Revolution the invention of the cotton gin made slavery highly profitable, and a slave system became entrenched. The libertarian track record of states became tarnished. Slavery was a creation of local law; freedom was "national"[9] (though federal support for slavery existed with the fugitive slave laws and a postal system that assisted in blocking abolitionist mailings from distribution in the South). Northern experience with slave state repression produced growing support for James Madison's argument[10] that states could repress individual liberty no less than the federal government. The Revolutionary era conception of "liberty" was being reformulated, albeit outside institutional arenas.

The success of Fairman's history meant that "credible" Reconstruction history required no further examination of slavery politics beyond his own. Of course, a group of scholars took up this issue, anyway. But for the Court, institutional canons of Fourteenth Amendment construction required no additional historical testing.

Fairman's account, it should be remembered, was continuous with selected elements of the old Republican tradition. While nationalist in certain respects, Republicans shared with Fairman a suspicion of sweeping nationalizing proposals. As mentioned, Republicans were not hearty enthusiasts of broad and expansive federal power. Even if they incorporated the Bill of Rights they saw this as a conservative act. This position goes back to the difficulties of simultaneously applying the multiple dimensions of Republican intent. If Republicans understood incorporation as a conservative act (as maintaining a limited and narrow view of national power), then both incorporation and conservatism are expressions of Republican legislative objectives. In the 1950s it was clear that both these objectives could not be applied simultaneously. While the Republicans could imagine the substantive protections of rights as narrow in 1866, such protections, given the decades of experience with practices of black subordination, could not be seen in the same way in the 1940s.

Understandings of Republican conservatism might draw on the Republicans' view of a narrow role for the federal government, but these understandings do not lead inevitably to the conclusion that the Warren Court decisions were illegitimate. The Republican view of a narrow federal role was tied to the elimination of racial political violence and to the federal prosecution of racially motivated offenses against rights, generally. The removal of formal barriers to black inclusion in the polity did not exhaust Republican concerns.

The Institutional Setting

Institutional pressures played important roles in producing the "truth" status of Fairman's history. Reputation was and is one kind of institutional resource, and Crosskey's reputation had been badly damaged the year before he presented his account of the Fourteenth Amendment. His lengthy *Politics and the Constitution* earned him broad condemnation from the legal community.[11] Given the recency of that critical damage, audiences might be skeptical of his competence (or even presumed incompetence), and it is highly likely that they negatively assessed his Fourteenth Amendment history.

The damage to Crosskey's reputation, however, should not overshadow the institutional strength of Fairman's assumptions as a central reason explaining his interpretive victory. Even if Crosskey's history had appeared under someone else's name, it likely would have been rejected. Justice Black, whose reputation had not been similarly damaged, was condemned for his incorporation thesis no less severely than Crosskey (though Black was more protected from damage to his reputation because he had published other materials from which one could assess his work). Even without a damaged reputation, however, Crosskey would have faced substantial hurdles of credibility because of the broad-based nature of Fairman's interpretive assumptions and because he was a member of an expansive and powerful interpretive community linked to Harvard.[12]

There also are important connections between Fairman's and Crosskey's histories and post–New Deal shifts in political alignments. After the famous 1937 "switch in time," where the Supreme Court suddenly reversed itself and upheld President Franklin Roosevelt's federal economic programs, government was less in the hands of states. Post-New Deal debates about the "proper" judicial role revolved around recent gains in national strength and the Court's role in augmenting that strength. Fairman and Crosskey constructed their histories in the midst of this redistribution of state and national power.

Fairman's nonincorporation thesis was a defense of state autonomy on matters of individual rights, although he favored national regulation of business and labor. Crosskey's incorporation thesis worked to legitimate federal power in an area that Fairman thought should be left to the states. With one glance to recent gains in national power and the other to the past, Fairman and Crosskey built their Fourteenth Amendment histories in politically charged ways. Crosskey's book on the original Constitution was politically volatile for the same reason, a fact not lost on critics of *Politics and the Constitution*. Crosskey's version of the original Constitution, said Irving Brant, "has the flavor of congressional supremacy as we know it today. . . ."[13] One point on which Fairman and Crosskey agreed was their support for contemporary congressional control over business and labor. Crosskey's views of the original Constitution and, of course, his incorporation thesis set the two men apart.

The Mutual Construction of Past and Present

Fairman's and Crosskey's configurations of the events of Reconstruction reflected their views of the "proper" judicial role in the 1940s. In other words, historical actors of the 1860s were configured (by Fairman) and reconfigured (by Crosskey) alongside the configuration and reconfiguration of the "legitimate" judicial role in post–New Deal political arrangements. Their arguments about the past were simultaneously arguments about the present. Fairman, for example, opened his law review article by criticizing the Supreme Court's rulings of the 1940s, which were the first to apply the First Amendment and parts of the Sixth Amendment to the states.

Past and present were constructed together in a dual motion. That is, at the same time that Fairman's framework structured how he examined the past, this framework structured his judgments of "legitimate" Court action in the 1940s. His judgments in 1949 about which matters fell to the Supreme Court (to "law") and which matters fell to the states (to "political wisdom") were determined by the organizing elements that also structured his meanings drawn from the *Congressional Globe*.

This explanation pertains to the situational character of Fairman's catholic approach to constitutional meaning. While he could not imagine that the Court's decision in *Barron* might be legitimately criticized, and while he could not believe that its nonincorporation thesis in the *Slaughter-House Cases* was wrong, he *could* imagine that the Court was wrong when it began to apply portions of the Bill of Rights to the states. He was a catholic when he considered the incorporation question, but he was more protestant when he considered 1940s Court decisions that chipped away at state control over citizenship. He reserved ground on which to criticize these decisions. His nationalism was situational, and his framing assumptions determined the extent of his Court-centeredness and nation-centeredness on particular questions. Fairman's framing assumptions also are at the root of this "dual construction" dynamic.

Parameters of the Fairman/Crosskey Debate

While Fairman and Crosskey engaged in sometimes nasty exchanges over the interpretation of statements in the *Congressional Globe* of the 39th Congress, their histories—the conceptual framings (nets) implicit in their political and legal histories—converged on certain points.

The two legal scholars debated "original understanding" within parameters that both of them took as natural or self-evident. The arbitrariness of these parameters of debate was "misrecognized." Fairman and Crosskey admitted, without any questioning, a particular conception of their role as readers of the historical record (the text of the *Congressional Globe*). Neither questioned his part in locating "original understanding." In addition, both assumed the legitimacy of an originalist jurisprudence.

Fairman and Crosskey both assumed that an objectively discernible referent event (congressional debate over the Fourteenth Amendment) existed that could supply objective grounds for legitimating Court action. Referent events, in their view, supplied an independent measure of whether the "right" description of original understanding had been given. Their notion of truth was positivist not Kuhnian. The historical evidence provided the possibility of determining the absolute "true" description if one only looked at things in the right way and in the right places. Neither man considered that recovering legislative intent was contingent in any way on his own set of discursive and rhetorical practices. Neither was aware that a question of legitimacy attached to their mutual view that as readers of historical texts they played no role in constituting the meaning of the *Congressional Globe*. This convention was silent about itself as a convention.

The stance on their part does not mean that we cannot say anything meaningful about the objectives or "understandings" of actors. Proceeding as if one can talk meaningfully about somebody's aims or what somebody meant is an enabling condition of interpretation. While legal actors can plausibly believe that "original meaning," or "author's meaning," is an important concept and is provisionally recoverable, Fairman and Crosskey both believed that they could interpret or recover an absolute original meaning. They both needed enabling conditions for interpretation, as do the rest of us. But in assuming an absolute standard of truth and a conception of themselves as uninvolved interpreters, they did much more than presume that they could speak meaningfully about original understanding.

Both of them assumed that original understanding had an absolute basis of recognition, which is to say that they shared the belief that referent events provided an independent standard against which absolutely true representations could be measured. Other perspectives or approaches are possible. One perspective is that Republican objectives have *some* true basis of recognition, with "true" understood in a Kuhnian sense, and that original meaning is a moving target continually refashioned over time as legislative, popular, and court decisions are made. This view that the meaning of federal control over individual rights emerges in time is different from the notion that intentions or understandings have an absolute basis of recognition in the pages of the *Congressional Globe*.

The view that original understanding stands still—that it has an absolute basis of recognition—maintains the submergence of historiographical and hermeneutic puzzles. Contingencies and uncertainties are inherent in any recovery of the past. The sociological challenge for us is understanding how Fairman and Crosskey alternately managed these contingencies and uncertainties. Judgments about Republican objectives (or original understanding) flow from the local contexts of interpreters, and all interpreters suppress arguments about original meaning that their local contexts prevent them from imagining. The sociological task is to map the *various ways that links are forged* between the documentary evidence in the *Congressional Globe* (what was said) and its meaning or intention. Which sorts of linkages get institutionalized? How do these institutionalized linkages enable and block access to the events of the 1860s as sources of law? And what impact do these connections have on various political distributions?

Fairman's "Victory" and the Interpretive Politics of Race

My analysis of the Fairman/Crosskey dispute bears on an understanding of the way in which race hierarchy is institutionalized and reproduced in constitutional law. The tacit racial dimensions of the Fairman/Crosskey dispute are important, especially because they are difficult to see. As the modern terms of debate over original understanding were established in the post–New Deal period, a conceptual apparatus was put into place that abstracted from the particular power relations of Reconstruction. This apparatus did not prevent the emergence of the Warren Court majority, but it did link the production of credible Fourteenth Amendment history and thus a Newtonian legal standard of coherence to political distributions that harmed black citizens. Understanding how this happened means going back to the dominant conceptions of race during the Civil War period, which were discussed in chapters 2 and 3. A culturally dominant theory of race in which blacks were regarded as less deserving of membership in the people (i.e., the national collective) became implicitly institutionalized in the *Slaughter-House* cases and remained latent in Court decisions of the late nineteenth century.

Northern Democratic slavery criticism, as I discussed, was dependent on a set of racial beliefs. The elements of this slavery criticism that were adopted by the Supreme Court included a definition of slavery's destruction (formal emancipation) and a representation of slavery politics (limited to dispute over Southern demands for federal enforcement of slave law in the territories and the claimed secession right). Northern Democrats did not count ex-Confederate takeovers of political institutions in 1866 and racially motivated political violence as among the continuing problems of slavery.

Fairman's justification of the Court's nonincorporation story reinforced the Court's Northern Democratic slavery criticism and the latent theory of race on which this criticism rested. Fairman's history also reinforced the view that the Reconstruction amendments originally had little to do with the rights of whites. His Court-centered catholicism on the question of incorporation and his conception of durability maintained Justice Miller's suppression of most dimensions of slavery politics. This made it difficult for this latent theory of race to rise to the surface, much less be regarded as legally relevant.

With Fairman's interpretive victory, a conceptual apparatus for debating the Fourteenth Amendment was established. This apparatus comprised a web of methods, meaning-producing associations, and categories of thought. The theory of race on which Northern Democratic slavery criticism was contingent, and on which the Supreme Court's Civil War history depended, became conceptually inaccessible, if not buried. Said differently, the institutionalized methods and markers for identifying original meaning were not tooled to uncover the power relations of Reconstruction. Power imbalances and a view of black incapability inhered in the Court's Northern Democratic political history, but these imbalances became both difficult to perceive and redress in institutionally "strong" Newtonian ways.

It should also be remembered that the Northern Democrats thought the Black Codes, with their racial classifications, were among the choices available to local white majorities, that is, clearly constitutional. The Supreme Court eventually considered racial classifications in *Strauder v. West Virginia* (1880) and declared, against the Northern Democratic view, that local majorities could not enact racial classifications. While the formal equality model the Court endorsed might have been less than Republicans intended, this model was certainly more than Northern Democrats wanted. The Court, of course, went on to grant local majorities the choice of passing Jim Crow legislation. The *Brown* decision and the end of Jim Crow, however, did not fully expunge Northern Democratic racial beliefs from constitutional doctrine. These beliefs had been latent in other areas of law, not just in "separate but equal" doctrine. Even with the repudiation of separate but equal, the Court's Civil War and Reconstruction history was still in place.

The Persistence of Fairman's History

If Fairman's history was not self-evidently "correct," the self-propelling quality that attaches to his delegitimation of the incorporation thesis requires sociological explanation. Commitments to particular terms of debate, notions of objectivity, definitions of prestige, training programs, and assorted legal habits account for this quality. All of these things require work out of lawyers and judges. In other words, the self-propelling quality of Fairman's history from one generation to the next is a product of strategies of symbolic construction, conventions for investigation, and textual approaches—all of which involve work, all of which exist in mutually sustaining relationships with material structures, and all of which have been learned institutionally, for example, in law school and on the bench.

An investigation of the persistence of Fairman's perspective on the history of the Fourteenth Amendment is aided by research that explores the formation, nature, and dynamics of scientific theories. Echoing Simone de Beauvoir's famous remark that women are made and not born, Susan Leigh Star explains that the same is true of scientific theories.[14]

Star takes on the challenge of understanding how scientific theories are formed in a specific context (namely, nineteenth-century neurophysiology).[15] In particular, she looks at the subject of anomalies, exploring the Kuhnian idea that anomalies act as catalysts of change. (Absorption of anomalies defines a Kuhnian paradigm. When critical mass is achieved, paradigms are overturned.) Star describes theories as "stratified";[16] indeed, theories may be "obdurate."[17] She notes that while many scholars have pointed out the persistence of established perspectives and the degree to which anomalous information may be ignored if it disconfirms basic assumptions, the persistence of perspectives and the obduracy of theories have rarely been analyzed operationally—at least outside statistics.[18]

Raising the obduracy of perspectives and theories as a subject for empirical analysis, Star notes that the intensity and durability of scientific debates form a unique situation. Battle lines are drawn, and the topics of debate provide a wellspring of problems for research and publication. Star refers to Simmel's observation that conflict socializes its participants. Participation in conflict reflects and develops commitments to certain paths of action and thought.[19]

Star and others regard both internalist explanations of theories (which point to the "natural" unfolding of ideas) and externalist explanations (which point to social and political factors) as insufficient. She refutes the internal/external distinction. The success or natural quality of a theory, Star emphasizes, are only partially dependent on the logical tenets of the theory itself. "The situations that create theories are not single experiments, or moments in individual biographies. . . . Theories are the end result of many kinds of action, all involving work: approaches, strategies, technologies and conventions for investigation. The component parts of a theory become increasingly inseparable as it develops. They become thicker, or 'clotted.'"[20]

The component parts of Fairman's history became clotted in the 1950s. Even before Fairman published his history, Justice Samuel Miller's minimalist resolution of citizenship dilemmas in *Slaughter-House* had combined traditional antebellum strategies for resolving citizenship dilemmas with a mostly Northern Democratic slavery criticism, which was itself contingent on a set of racial beliefs. These elements were mutually established in that they stabilized and legitimated each other.

Crosskey challenged the narrow view of Reconstruction history *without* recognizing that his project (challenging the nonincorporation thesis) necessitated additional work: first, the work of separating the elements that the Reconstruction era Court majority had combined; second, the work of accounting for the durability of the Court's definition of abolition and its minimalist resolution strategy. Crosskey needed to struggle through the problem of balancing national citizenship with state integrity. (His answer to this problem was too pat and did not assuage those with genuine worries about central power. His confidence in his Congress-centered view of the Constitution did not lead him to worry much about this problem, at least not in his text.)

The positive reception of Fairman's history worked as a clotting agent which strengthened the perception that state control over citizenship was necessary and the *only available "coherent" strategy* for resolving citizenship dilemmas. I have been concerned throughout with definitions of legal coherence and the role that the Northern Democratic version of slavery and Civil War history played in maintaining and reproducing a definition of the term. With Fairman's victory over Crosskey, the perceptions of those in Fairman's interpretive community became even more limited regarding potential alternatives to state-centered approaches to citizenship disputes and potential sources of law for egalitarian interpretations of the Fourteenth Amendment.

The project of unclotting the component parts of Fairman's history is aided by work in cultural theory. Michael Schudson[21] offers several dimensions on which to assess the strength of cultural symbols: retrievability, rhetorical force, resonance, and institutional retention. As Schudson explains it, the retrievability of a particular cultural object is a measure of its availability or reach. Some elements of experience and culture are more readily drawn on than others. For example, individuals might be more aware of recent events, or of more dramatic or more controversial happenings. In addition to varying availability, cultural objects differ in rhetorical force. This force is achieved by the degree to which objects are powerful or memorable. The status of a speaker, for example, might supply rhetoric with greater persuasive force. Cultural objects are resonant to the degree that they connect with an underlying tradition, while resonance is a public and cultural relation among cultural object, tradition, and audience. "A rhetorically effective object must be relevant and resonant with the life of the audience."[22]

Institutional retention is Schudson's fourth measure. Many cultural objects, he observes, may be widely available, rhetorically effective, and culturally resonant, but they may fail at institutionalization. The higher the degree of institutionalization (e.g., in the educational system, in family life, in work practices, in politics), the more opportunity there is for the cultural object to exercise influence. And the more thoroughly a cultural object is institutionalized, the greater the penalty for disregard.

While Schudson does not have legal symbols in mind, his work is useful in explaining the persistence of Fairman's perspective on the Fourteenth Amendment's history. Fairman was more successful than Crosskey at mobilizing institutional symbols. What emerged powerfully in his history was a vision of collective identity rooted in the tradition of local democratic control in establishing and maintaining citizenship. The strength of the symbols that he relied on in constructing this vision can be assessed by using Schudson's dimensions.

The symbolic meaning of *Lochner v. New York* is important here and is tied to the success of Fairman's history.[23] This 1905 case involved a New York worker protection maximum hour law. The Supreme Court struck down the regulation under the Fourteenth Amendment's due process clause, saying that the regulation violated the right to contract. Today this case is widely regarded as a bad decision (although different reasons for its "badness" have been given). It is prominently displayed in law school textbooks. The extent to which *Lochner* is cited or alluded to suggests it is a memorable case; i.e., it has a high degree of retrievability.

For justices, the case has come to symbolize the wisdom of judicial deference to state legislatures and the idea that the Constitution embodies no particular political theory, whether Social Darwinian or egalitarian. "Lochnerizing" expresses the activism charge, namely, that judges are reading their own personal views into the Constitution and intervening in matters that belong to the legislatures. Fairman put this "lesson" of *Lochner* to work, appealing to the tradition of local democracy in ways that were neither personal nor idiosyncratic.

Criticism of "judicial activism" resonates deeply in American political culture. Indeed, there are good reasons to defer to legislatures. Rule by popular elected majority grew as a response to monarchy and dictatorship and is tied to Jeffersonian and Jacksonian traditions. The tradition of local democracy views state legislatures as the best arbiters over the democratization process. It is not the judge's place to intervene in this process.

Local democracy can be (and has been) put to use by those with a wide range of worldviews and political interests. Antebellum petit bourgeois democracy produced nearly universal white male suffrage in many states, which was a good thing for unpropertied white men. And in the antebellum years, many Northern states granted a handful of citizenship rights to free blacks. After an initial lack of movement in federal courts, the first victories for white women's citizenship, especially women's right to own and manage property, were won at the state level.

States' rights has justified white majorities' exclusion of blacks, but states' rights can also legitimate progressive state policies in the face of federal conservatism. Before the Civil War, radical abolitionists used the concept of states' rights to resist the nationalization of slave law. (Federal jurisdiction over the rendition of fugitive slaves meant, in practical terms, great latitude for slave catchers to use force, violence, and kidnapping.) After the war, Southern Democrats put their stamp on the concept, using it to defend home rule and condemn federal intervention on behalf of black and white Republicans. Southern exclusion of black citizens from the political process (as well as Southern landowners' control over a dependent black labor force) was legitimated through the use of the states' rights concept. Southern states' use of the concept compelled Republicans to critique the doctrine. As we have seen, Republicans argued both that concessions to slavery perverted the notion of states' rights, and the Fourteenth Amendment put checks on states that should have been there from the beginning. The Bradley/Swayne dissenting opinions in *Slaughter-House* picked up on strands of this Republican view.

The point for sociologists is to investigate how these notions of local democracy (and critiques of the notion of local democracy) have been mobilized to legitimate particular political distributions at particular historical junctures. Fairman mobilized *Lochner*'s symbolism in ways that favored white electoral majorities that desired black subordination though Fairman certainly did not argue in favor of black subordination. Nevertheless, the institutionalization of his history worked to hamper the federal judiciary's ability to intervene legitimately in state politics to stop black subordination.

Lochner is a cultural object that might be used by individuals and groups with different worldviews. Liberals supporting the substance of the prohibited legislation—that is, the regulation of corporations in the interest of worker protection—could draw on its symbolism. Conservatives condemning liberal activism could also draw on its symbolism. Because this decision has multiple meanings, sociological interest lies in examining the distribution of chances to use the case as a resource in argumentation. The strength of this object (i.e., its ability to provide authority or justification for an argument) in any particular context might be assessed using Schudson's dimensions of retrievability, rhetorical force, resonance, and institutional retention.

The traditional activism of *Lochner* is not the only way that the lessons of this case might be conceived. Cass Sunstein[24] has disputed this version of *Lochner*'s lesson. He has argued that the Court's mistake was not so much its judicial intervention into the legislative arena, but in its viewing of status quo economic distributions as natural. Sunstein explains that the Court took common law distributions as natural and used these to form a baseline for assessing state interference. New York maximum hour law was seen as "unnatural" by the Court only because it perceived status quo arrangements as natural. Had the Court regarded status quo distributions as a product of state choice, the conceptual distinction between natural economic distributions and state choice would have broken down.[25]

If the lesson of *Lochner* were conceived in the way that Sunstein suggests (i.e., viewing status quo distributions as natural is mistaken), *Lochner*'s symbolism would have been less useful to Fairman. If the Court's mistake was conceived as suggested by Sunstein, then status quo legislative policies regarding individual rights might have been scrutinized more searchingly. Such policies would not be automatically regarded as the "best" practice simply because they were longstanding; the possibility that such durability was the product of racial politics could be investigated. But Sunstein's version of *Lochner*'s lesson has not been institutionalized. So far, the traditional lesson of "activism"—the lesson that Fairman mobilized—has been institutionally retained to a higher degree.

Fairman's appeals to "tradition" (in criticizing the Court's application of the First Amendment to the states in the 1940s) worked to privilege definitions of liberty owing more to the Revolutionary period (suspicion of central, federal power) than to the slavery/Civil War period when suspicion of state power was added to the mix. In Northern Democratic history, in Supreme Court decisions during Reconstruction, and in Fairman's history of the Fourteenth Amendment, tradition appears as a singular and unified source of authority, when in fact it is neither singular nor unified. Just as the Northern Democrats and the Supreme Court privileged the Revolutionary tradition, so too did Fairman. Crosskey's history was an attempt to bring to light Republican constitutional theory, but he failed in that attempt. In other words, Fairman succeeded in deleting definitional struggles and privileging the local democracy/ Revolutionary era plot in the story of the American Republic.

Given Fairman's success at mobilizing *Lochner's* symbolism, his history should not be conceived at the level of the individual (as the labels of "arbitrary history" or "bad history" would have it). An accounting of the positive reception of his history by courts and scholars lies neither in the internal contents of his law review article or in external institutional political interests. More complex models of explanation must center on the *relation* between Fairman's interpretive framework, institutional tradition (decentralized control of citizenship), and a situated institutional audience.

The durability of state control over individual rights was important for Fairman. He cited traditional antebellum state control over juries as clear evidence of the nonincorporation thesis. This antebellum control signaled the practice's rationality, and he assumed that states would not give up this control. However, his interpretation was not the only one available. The durability of state control over juries, and over individual rights in general during the antebellum period, might be evidence of continued unfairness in the exercise of discretion. Republicans in the 39th Congress argued along these lines in attempting to draw a distinction between legitimate right and state powers illegitimately obtained. For Republicans, the antebellum durability of state control over Bill of Rights guarantees did not establish this control as legitimate.

Also, long into the twentieth century the South remained under the control of a reactionary ruling elite. The reinstated planter class enjoyed varying degrees of local dominance, and only isolated industrialization developed. In some border states, mountain Republicans held a degree of local power, and New Orleans always seemed to be a Southern exception. By the early twentieth century, racism was more deeply embedded in the nation's culture than at the beginning of the antislavery crusade. Racism became a legitimate position in pluralistic politics, dominant in the South and erratically manifested (but always latent) in the North and West.

This unexamined and untested view of durable practice as an indicator of rational distributions is troubling. Justices are not prepared (neither trained nor predisposed) to entertain the possibility that entrenched practices of subordination can explain the durability of particular practices or precedents. Stability is an institutional value. So far, justices have not found a way to reconcile this value for stability with a willingness to inquire into the possible reasons for durable practices.

In sum, sociohistorical approaches are required to explain the persistence of Fairman's perspective on the Fourteenth Amendment and the perception that state-centered strategies for resolving rights disputes are "best." This book has only begun to investigate the social production of standards of legal coherence and legal knowledge. Sketching the variety of sociological problems at hand is hard enough; producing answers is harder.

The Roots of a Subordinate History: Conditions in the 1930s and 1940s

If understanding the persistence of Fairman's history is one side of the coin, understanding the roots and maintenance of subordinated or heterodox histories is the other. In general terms, the late 1930s and 1940s witnessed changes and innovations in judicial approaches to citizenship dilemmas. During these years, fissures opened between camps of justices. (These fissures widened during the Warren Court era.) A new language appeared in Court cases, one that described racial discrimination as being "at war with our basic concepts of democratic society and representative government."[26] During the 1940s the Court handed down a series of decisions which held that black exclusion from juries was a violation of Fourteenth Amendment equal protection rights. The Court began to talk about equality in new ways. While constitutional thought had been fragmented from the beginning—multiple though differently powerful interpretive frames had always been available for use— the balance of strength among interpretive legal frames was clearly in flux during the late 1930s.[27] The larger sociological question before us is understanding how Courts use histories in different ways at different historical junctures.

Legal scholar Robert M. Cover[28] attributed changes in judicial attitudes in the 1940s to an array of causes. He suggested that the rise of fascism and Nazism sensitized the Court to the dangers that racism posed to democratic institutions. The American legal system, he stated, was a window through which the world and especially the Soviets could judge the United States. The Soviets could turn back U.S. denunciations of Stalin with the charge that the United States was hypocritical. With the beginning of the cold war, the United States needed to clean its own house.

President Roosevelt's appointments to the Court were another likely cause for the shift in its attitudes, although Cover does not discuss these. Roosevelt's appointees held a particular view of government's role. Since many of them had served in the New Deal administration, these justices not surprisingly held activist views of government, especially when it came to regulating business and labor. They did not share the nineteenth-century confidence that private gain led to public good, a position that had fueled capital growth (what Willard Hurst famously called the "release of energy").

The expansion of federal regulation of business and labor under FDR was not feared by these appointees. Indeed, an activist federal government in the service of economic welfare set a precedent of sorts for a new view of the Court. Federal activism in building a welfare state could potentially go hand-in-hand with federal activism in ensuring the health of citizenship rights and political institutions, though Fairman's nationalism did not extend this far. FDR's appointments looked backward to the opinions of Justices Holmes and Brandeis, who had written about the central role played by First Amendment freedoms in maintaining the political system's health. While shifts during the New Deal suggested that national courts might gain control over individual rights, and while Fairman condemned this development, others welcomed increased national judicial control over rights. It is important again to maintain a distinction between the New Deal's economic nationalism, which Fairman and Frankfurter supported, and the strands of political nationalism that accompanied it. While some New Dealers opposed expanded national judicial authority over individual rights, others supported it.

In 1938, Justice Harlan Stone wrote an opinion that became famous for its fourth footnote, which generated an enormous literature.[29] Support came from Justices Black, William Douglas, Frank Murphy, Wiley Rutledge, and, for a time, Felix Frankfurter[30] and Robert Jackson. Condemnation came from others. Paragraph 2, which encapsulated the Court's justification for protecting political processes, alluded to the work of Justices Holmes and Brandeis who had viewed freedom of speech and press as central values in the system. Paragraph 3 was the root of the "new" equal protection doctrine, which established "tiers," or standards, of scrutiny. State economic regulations were to be presumed rational, said Stone (thus according economic legislation the lowest level of scrutiny). Legislation that concerned the political process, especially those parts of the process that could not be relied on to include "discrete and insular minorities," was to be given a higher level of scrutiny. This sort of legislation was not presumed to be rational, meaning that states had to submit to greater federal oversight.

In chapter 2, I discussed the Republicans' concern for the political process. This concern was not institutionally preserved. Had it been, Stone might have been able to use a version of Reconstruction history to authorize in stronger institutional fashion this (re)emergent concern for political processes; perhaps he also would have had the confidence to express it in the text of an opinion rather than in a footnote.

The late 1930s marked the beginning of federal court interventions in state politics on behalf of citizens' rights. Since past interventions had been on behalf of businesses, it is clear that Court justices in the post-New Deal period were seeing social, political, and economic distributions differently than they had decades earlier.

We also can speculate that the Great Depression played a role in shifting the justices' perspectives on inequality. In the late nineteenth and early twentieth centuries, dominant explanations for poverty associated with industrialization and urbanization blamed immigrants and focused on individual depravity. Before the Depression, "protective legislation" was permitted for women but not for men because women were thought to need protection. Notions of citizenship remained linked to manhood, industry, and independence.[31] In the 1930s it became easier to imagine that bad conditions for individuals might not be the result of their failures. These new awarenesses certainly did not guarantee legal victories, especially victories for those suffering from economic dislocations. But what changed with the Depression and European fascism was that legal actors could consider as plausible resource-based and power-based explanations for social arrangements. It became easier for courts to conceive that jury exclusions, segregation, and poor facilities might not be the deserved outcome for "failing" behavior, and it became easier to persuade courts that social conditions were imposed on black men and women and hence were open to legal alteration. In short, the "naturalness" of conditions under which black Americans lived came to be more widely questioned.

The NAACP's Legal Defense and Education Fund contributed to eroding this perception of naturalness. In 1938 and 1939 the NAACP made its first major gains.[32] Richard Kluger and Mark Tushnet[33] have told the story of the NAACP's fight against legal segregation. NAACP lawyers knew at that point in time that they could not get legal segregation declared unconstitutional. Instead, their strategy was to force states to live up to the "separate but equal" requirement. In other words, the plan was to use separate-but-equal doctrine to force states to put financial resources into black schools, which, by any measure, were not equal to white schools. The NAACP documented the unequal expenditures that counties and school boards budgeted. This strategy, the lawyers believed, would force integration since the cost of building separate schools would be prohibitive. At the time, for example, Howard University Law School was the only accredited black law school. Building more black law schools to maintain the "separate but equal" standard would have been extremely expensive.

Such NAACP lawyers as Charles Houston and Thurgood Marshall, who had long lives in public service, developed a broadened conception of equality. While the cases that they litigated up to the Supreme Court affected only a few individuals, the symbolic effects of these cases undoubtedly were more substantial. The NAACP lawyers, a black male elite, exposed judges to the realities faced by Lloyd Gaines as he tried to register at the University of Missouri Law School. By many accounts, these NAACP lawyers made a favorable or strong impression on the judges who heard their cases.

The NAACP's use of separate-but-equal doctrine was an example of William Sewell's[34] axiom about the unpredictability of accumulating resources and transposing mental schemas. In applying separate-but-equal doctrine in a new context, NAACP lawyers exposed the Roosevelt Court to the living, working, and educational conditions faced by black men and women. New symbolic resources, among them a conception of "equal citizenship," created greater opportunities for the Warren Court majority to craft contradictions between constitutional guarantees and contemporary social and political arrangements.

These societal developments in the third and fourth decades of the twentieth century created possibilities for transformation in constitutional law, although they did not determine specific outcomes. Justices' perception patterns shifted, and their institutional imaginations opened to new explanations for existing social and political conditions. Not only were justices able to authorize their new protections of political processes, but Justice Black was able to persuade three of his colleagues that the first eight amendments in the Bill of Rights were protected against state infringement. Incorporation now appeared not only "doable" but also necessary.

Legal conservatives, however, could resist legal transformation, and they appealed persuasively to older sources of law and a Newtonian model that had been institutionalized for generations. Institutional standards of "coherency" that grew from a Newtonian model naturalized durable practices and precedents. Deeply integrated into the vocabularies, commitments, and conventions of the Court were symbolic meanings that made it easier to defend state-centered approaches on citizenship and Charles Fairman's perspective on the incorporation question.

Checking History

The 1960s witnessed the delegitimation by professional historians of Dunning School Reconstruction history. Dunning School histories had portrayed Republicans in unflattering terms. Southern "Redeemers" were the heroes of the period. Progressive histories of Reconstruction, in which Republicans were cast as self-interested economic actors, were also delegitimated in the 1960s. Republicans emerged in these new histories as genuinely concerned for black rights (and suspicious of monopolies and big business). Eric Foner, author of what is now regarded as the standard account of Reconstruction, acknowledged his great debt to W. E. B. DuBois, whose *Black Reconstruction in America* was published in 1935. The availability of these more recent works has played an important role in keeping Crosskey's Fourteenth Amendment history circulating today.

In discussing the checks that operate on historians, a leading intellectual historian, Martin Jay, suggests that two kinds of checks "militate against the unfettered freedom of historians to narrativize arbitrarily."[35] First, statements and texts bear on the plausibility of historians' reconstructions. These sources—the stuff of historians' narratives—are not raw, prelinguistic material, says Jay. Rather, they are already inflected with meaning for those who initiate or suffer them in their own lives. Jay calls these statements "first-order narratives," and he views them (not unlike social scientists view data) as a check on the freedom of historians.

Second, other historians read and judge historians' work. This community of scholarship, however imperfect, also operates as a check. History, as Jay observes, "is not a single historian's emploting of the past, but rather the institution of historians . . . trying to convince each other about the plausibility of their reconstructions. It is not so much the subjective imposition of meaning but rather the intersubjective judgment of meanings that matters."[36]

Jay bows in Habermas's direction, relying on a discursive community that shares standards and procedures of communicative rationality which are more inclusive than the communities from which their members derive. Historians win assent for their narrative reconstructions "by redeeming validity claims through procedures that satisfy conditions of rationality."

Communities of judges and law professors, however, are different from communities of historians. Diversity in the community of practitioners (greater in universities and colleges than on courts and in law schools) and institutional formulations of legitimacy and credibility play crucial roles in the process of checking legal history. In a sense, my entire project translates Jay's description of the checks that operate on historians into an empirical question about the checks that operate on justices and law professors. I have been investigating how checks on histories work in constitutional law, where communities of historians read and evaluate histories under one set of institutional constraints, while communities of justices and law professors assess and employ histories using different conceptual practices under different sets of institutional constraints.

It is necessary, then, to be sensitive to the range of institutional knowledges, even on the same subject, and the range of institutional practices for accrediting knowledge across society. The full scope of knowledge about Reconstruction, thankfully, is not limited to what courts have taken to be knowledge about Reconstruction.

* * *

Fairman's study refurbished the Court's history of the Fourteenth Amendment. Hugo Black was able to challenge the authorized account of the amendment to such a degree that Fairman felt it necessary to respond, but Fairman was successful at reasserting the ordering commitments of his interpretive community.

Part of an assessment of the Fairman/Crosskey dispute depends on how one views what happened in the post-*Adamson* cases. Most of the rights protected by the Bill of Rights were made applicable to the states, but a notion of "ordered liberty" and the due process clause were the vehicles for this selective incorporation. Black and Crosskey won in the sense that most of the Bill of Rights was incorporated. But Frankfurter and Fairman won in the sense that they supplied an institutional version of Republican intent on the Fourteenth Amendment and on Reconstruction history, generally.

7

History as an Institutional Resource:

Warren Court Debates over Legislative

Apportionment

In the 1960s the Warren Court majority's interpretation of the Fourteenth Amendment and their expansions of rights carried the day. On historical grounds, however, the majority's decisions were perceived as weak. My purpose in this chapter is to investigate the nature of this weakness and to argue that a century's worth of debate over Reconstruction history helped produce it. This perceived weakness has provided grounds for intellectual reaction against Warren Court expansions of rights.

My argument is that the institutional account of Reconstruction undermined the Warren majority's ability to ground its decisions in certain traditional sources of law (e.g., legislative history, precedent) even while the majority had access to other legal sources. This institutional account rendered their decisions vulnerable. Mark DeWolfe Howe once said that the Supreme Court can bind us with its rulings, but it cannot bind us with its history. In one sense, this is certainly true. Historians such as Leonard Levy have shown that the Court has gotten its history wrong, and academic historians have been there to provide alternate histories. But if a taken-for-granted history of the Civil War and Reconstruction put in place by the Supreme Court in the 1870s worked to deny the Warren majority the use of traditional sources of law and if this deficiency rendered those decisions vulnerable to criticism and rollback, then the Court's history can shape its rulings. In this way, the Court's history can bind (if temporarily) and affect various political distributions.

The Apportionment Cases

Warren Court decisions, in general, were high-profile conflicts between justices with consistently different answers to the question, "Which battles should the Supreme Court resolve, and how?" Were such matters as access to contraception, procedural protections for criminal defendants, or legislative apportionments for state legislatures, to be overseen solely by state courts? Or were these matters within the reach of federal courts? Was unfairness in the basis of representation a "proper" issue for the Court to resolve? Approximately equal votes might be a good thing, but could that ideal be coherently defended according to accepted legal standards?

No better example of the Warren majority's "disregard for the Constitution" existed, according to Robert Bork, "than the legislative apportionment cases, which created the principle of one person-one vote."[1] Bork reserves some of his harshest criticism for *Reynolds v. Sims* (1964), which imposed population-based apportionment on the states. For this reason, I consider the apportionment cases here.

The Warren majority had trouble persuading its critics that state apportionments were matters for federal courts and that equal protection required the one-person, one-vote standard. Indeed, one searches with little success for positive reviews of the majority's reasoning in the legislative apportionment cases, even among those who supported the outcomes. The Warren dissenters argued against the one-person, one-vote standard as a constitutional principle. That is, they argued that the standard was acceptable if a state wanted it, but that it should not be imposed on other states. The Warren dissenters asserted that the Fourteenth Amendment did not require population-based representation, although it permitted states this choice. The dissenters relied heavily on historical argument in asserting that an equally weighted vote was not a federal right (i.e., was not constitutionally required).

Fairman's history helped block the Warren majority from using 1860s history and the language of section 2 of the Fourteenth Amendment as sources of law. The political events of the 1860s could have been used (i.e., interpreted, mobilized) to support both sides in the Warren Court disputes. But over time, Justice Miller's version of what the Civil War was about had become accepted, and the Northern Democrats' local democracy doctrine had become deeply embedded within legal vocabularies and practices. The Warren dissenters' argument that the equal protection clause did not require the one-person, one-vote standard (and the dissenters' state-centered federalism, generally) relied on supporting practices and warrants already in place.[2]

Fairman's history had participated in establishing and reinforcing these supporting practices (legal conventions) and warrants, which included (1) the view that state control over citizenship rights had proven "best"; (2) a version of the slavery and Civil War experience; (3) the view that the Fourteenth Amendment did not invigorate national citizenship; (4) the convention of viewing durable Court precedent as an indicator of its "correctness"; and (5) the convention of viewing long-standing legislative choices as an indicator that they are "best."

These conventions and beliefs together defined what I am calling institutional standards and definitions of coherency. The Warren dissenters' argument that the Fourteenth Amendment left most aspects of citizenship in the hands of the states drew institutional strength from these already-in-place practices and beliefs. While it was easy for the Warren dissenters to call on traditional sources of legitimacy (constitutional language, history, precedent), it was hard for the majority to appeal persuasively to these sources. Complex social processes had produced for the Warren majority and the dissenters unequal access to the history of the 1860s, including the history of the Fourteenth Amendment as a source of legitimacy.

The approval of Fairman's history was an endorsement for Justice Felix Frankfurter, who had criticized Justice Hugo Black's incorporation thesis in *Adamson* (1947). Frankfurter and Fairman had provided the "right" view of Fourteenth Amendment history, and the alignment of Fairman's and Frankfurter's arguments is noteworthy because Frankfurter supplied some of the key historical arguments for the Warren dissenters in the apportionment cases.[3] Using the same historical approach that produced his defense of the nonincorporation thesis in *Adamson*,[4] Frankfurter argued (in dissent) in *Baker v. Carr* (1962) that the Fourteenth Amendment left apportionment in the hands of the state legislatures.

History: On the Side of the Dissenters?

Several questions confronted the Warren Court justices in the apportionment cases. (1) What should be done about the deliberate failure of states to institute state constitutional requirements to reapportion?[5] (2) Did population growth and shifts in population concentration[6] constitute an emergent set of facts that required the Court to frame new principles to protect recognized constitutional rights? (3) How was the Republican articulation of a principle of equal representation to be assessed? (4) How were Republican critiques of unfairness in the practice of voting to be assessed? and (5) What was the meaning of the Republicans' choice in 1866 to refrain from intervening in state regulation of voting and then their later decision to pass the 1870 and 1871 Enforcement Acts, as well as their later passage of the Fifteenth Amendment, which barred race as a basis for exclusion from suffrage? The meaning of the choice not to intervene in state regulation of voting in 1866 was not obvious, especially in light of the fact that only a few years later Republicans did intervene. My critique of the cases striking down the Enforcement Acts remains relevant here.

There was also the matter of judicial concern with the use of apportionment as a device to dilute black votes. It is difficult to get a good measure of such concern. High-profile congressional hearings on the Dirksen amendment to the Constitution came after the *Reynolds* decision. Sen. Everett Dirksen introduced this popular sovereignty amendment in 1964, which declared that "the right and power to determine the composition of the legislature of a State and the apportionment of the membership thereof shall remain in the people of that State." The amendment stated that "[n]othing in this Constitution shall prohibit" a state from using "factors other than population" in apportioning one house of a bicameral legislature. The hearings on the Dirksen amendment brought out arguments about the implications of nonpopulation-based apportionment for black voting rights. The National Committee for Fair Representation pressed a black rights argument, stressing that the amendment could make possible severe dilutions of newly won black voting strength. Witnesses for the committee also argued that the language in *Reynolds* left latitude for such dilutions as well. The amendment failed 57 to 39, lacking the necessary two-thirds majority.[7] While these hearings made clear the racial dimensions of the apportionment cases, it would be helpful to know if such arguments were brought to the justices' attention or if justices discussed such arguments among themselves before *Baker* or *Reynolds*.

The racial dimensions of the apportionment cases exist in the shadows. In offering a historical defense of the apportionment cases, I consider these dimensions. The contentious issue of racial gerrymandering is often triggered in discussions of apportionment. However, my historical defense of the one-person, one-vote standard should not be construed as a defense of the practice of creating majority-minority voting districts. This practice can be both defended and criticized on principled grounds. Rather, my purpose is to show how the playing field of historical argumentation has come to be uneven and what the impact of this has been on a group of cases where historical arguments play a significant role. In fact, Republican versions of Reconstruction do not lead inevitably to one side or the other on the subject of minority-majority districting. By rebutting the view that the apportionment cases are objectively weak historically, my eye is actually set on affirmative action case law, not majority-minority districting. I touch on these cases in the conclusion.

First, a brief summary of the justices' arguments in the apportionment cases is in order. In an early apportionment case, Justice Frankfurter argued that apportionments were a "political thicket."[8] He also argued that Congress had exclusive remedial authority over state districting. Justice Harlan agreed in *Wesberry v. Sanders* (1963).[9] In 1962, Frankfurter argued in his *Baker* dissent that longstanding usage of non-population based apportionments was enough to make the Court uphold the scheme. Frankfurter had articulated this argument in response to the Warren majority's assertion that "the fundamental principle of representative government in this country is one of equal representation for equal numbers of people." This was the majority's rationale for imposing population-based apportionment on the states. Frankfurter argued that state apportionments were not matters for federal courts. Gerrymandering that favored rural counties over urban counties did not present a matter of federal law (did not involve rights under the federal Constitution).

In *Reynolds v. Sims* (1964), Justice John M. Harlan (also in dissent) extended Frankfurter's historical arguments and added his own on legislative history. The legislative debates over section 2 of the Fourteenth Amendment,[10] asserted Harlan, provided "conclusive evidence" that the Framers had knowingly acquiesced in state control over voting. Harlan argued that the Framers did not view the equal protection clause of the Fourteenth Amendment as requiring the one person, one vote standard.

Harlan offered detailed historical arguments in *Wesberry v. Sanders* and *Reynolds v. Sims* to support the argument that the equal protection clause did not require the one-person, one-vote principle. He argued that the history of article 1, section 2 of the original Constitution and the language and history of the Fourteenth Amendment both showed that states retained full control over apportionments.

In *Wesberry,* the Court majority relied on article 1, section 2 as the source of law justifying the ruling that imposed population-based apportionment on state congressional districts. The majority argued that the phrase "by the People" in article 1, section 2 meant that the Framers favored a principle of equal representation in federal elections. Harlan argued that "by the People" did not mean what the Court majority said it meant. As evidence, he cited the three-fifths clause, the exclusion of women from the vote, and the scant sympathy for popular democracy on the part of many Framers. These exceptions were evidence that the original Constitution did not contain the principle of equal representation. Harlan asserted, "The Constitutional right which the Court creates is manufactured out of whole cloth." For Harlan, *Wesberry* was not "a case in which an emergent set of facts required the Court to frame new principles to protect recognized constitutional rights." [11]

In *Reynolds,* Harlan cited the language of section 2 of the Fourteenth Amendment and debates over the postwar basis of representation to support this conclusion.[12] He was harshly critical of the Warren majority's "failure" to consider these factors.

> The Court's constitutional discussion [in *Reynolds*] . . . is remarkable for its failure to address itself at all to the Fourteenth Amendment as a whole or to the legislative history of the Amendment pertinent to the matter at hand. . . . The failure of the Court to consider . . . the understanding of those who proposed and ratified [the Amendment], . . . the political practices of the States at the time the Amendment was adopted . . . [and] numerous state and congressional actions since the adoption of the Fourteenth Amendment . . . cannot be excused or explained by any concept of "developing" constitutionalism. It is meaningless to speak of constitutional "development" when both the language and history of the controlling provisions of the Constitution are wholly ignored. Since it can, I think, be shown beyond doubt that State apportionments, as such, are wholly free of constitutional limitation . . . the Court's action now bringing them within the purview of the Fourteenth Amendment amounts to nothing less than an exercise of the amending power of the Court.[13]

Harlan cited and discussed a number of statements made by Thaddeus Stevens, who had introduced the Fourteenth Amendment to the House of Representatives, John Bingham, and Jacob Howard. Stevens had said, "I believe it is all that can be obtained in the present state of public opinion. Not only Congress but also the several States are to be consulted. Upon a careful survey of the whole ground, we did not believe that nineteen of the loyal States could be induced to ratify any proposition more stringent than this."[14]

The next statement that Harlan cited was also from Stevens. "If any State shall exclude any of her adult male citizens from the elective franchise, or abridge that right, she shall forfeit her right to representation in the same proportion. The effect of this provision will be either to compel the States to grant universal suffrage or so to shear them of their power as to keep them forever in a hopeless minority in the national Government, both legislative and executive."

Harlan included statements by Bingham, among which he italicized this entire portion of a Bingham speech: "The amendment does not give, as the second section shows, the power to Congress of regulating suffrage in the several states. . . . The second section excludes the conclusion that by the first section suffrage is subjected to congressional law. . . . The exercise of the elective franchise, though it be one of the privileges of a citizen of the Republic, is exclusively under the control of the States."[15] The last speech Harlan quoted was made by Howard when he introduced the Fourteenth Amendment to the Senate:

> The committee was of opinion that the States are not yet prepared to sanction so fundamental a change as would be the concession of the right of suffrage to the colored race. We may as well state it plainly and fairly, so that there shall be no misunderstanding on the subject. It was our opinion that three fourths of the States of this Union could not be induced to vote to grant the right of suffrage, even in any degree or under any restriction, to the colored race. . . . The second section leave the right to regulate the elective franchise still with the States, and does not meddle with that right.[16]

To provide additional support for his historical readings, Harlan attached an appendix containing twenty statements made during congressional debate on section 2. About them, he said, "the speakers stated repeatedly, in express terms or by unmistakable implication, that the

States retained the power to regulate suffrage within their borders."[17] Listed below are the first ten statements that he reproduced:[18]

> As the nearest approach to justice which we are likely to be able to make, I approve of the second section that bases representation upon voters. (Garfield [R])

> Would it not be a most unprecedented thing that when this [former slave] population are not permitted where they reside to enter into the basis of representation in their own State, we should receive it as an element of representation here; that when they will not count them in apportioning their own legislative districts, we are to count them as five fifths (no longer as three fifths, for that is out of the question) as soon as you make a new apportionment? (Thayer [R])

> The second section of the amendment is ostensibly to remedy a supposed inequality in the basis of representation. The real object is to reduce the number of southern representatives in Congress and in the Electoral College; and also to operate as a standing inducement to negro suffrage. (Boyer [D])

> Shall the pardoned rebels of the South include in the basis of representation four million people to whom they deny political rights, and to no one of whom is allowed a vote in the selection of a Representative. (Kelley [R])

> I shall, Mr. Speaker, vote for this amendment; not because I approve it. Could I have controlled the report of the committee of fifteen, it would have proposed to give the right of suffrage to every loyal man in the country. (Kelley [R])

> But I will ask, why should not the representation of the States be limited as the States themselves limit suffrage. . . . If the negroes of the South are not to be counted as a political element in the government of the South in the States, why should they be counted as a political element in the government of the country of the Union? (Broomall [R])

> It is now proposed to base representation upon suffrage, upon the number of voters, instead of upon the aggregate population in every State of the Union. (Raymond [D])

We admit equality of representation based upon the exercise of the elective franchise by the people. The proposition in the matter of suffrage falls short of what I desire, but so far as it goes it tends to the equalization of the inequality at present existing; and while I demand and shall continue to demand the franchise for all loyal male citizens of this country, and I cannot but admit the possibility that ultimately those eleven States may be restored to representative power without the right of franchise being conferred upon the colored people, I should feel myself doubly humiliated and disgraced, and criminal even, if I hesitated to do what I can for a proposition which equalizes representation. (Boutwell [R])

Now, conceding to each State the right to regulate the right of suffrage, they ought not to have a representation for male citizens not less than twenty-one years of age, whether white or black, who are deprived of the exercise of suffrage. This amendment will settle the complication in regard to suffrage and representation, leaving each State to regulate that for itself, so that it will be for it to decide whether or not it shall have a representation for all its male citizens not less than twenty-one years of age. (Miller [R])

Manifestly, no State should have its basis of national representation enlarged by reason of a portion of citizens within its borders to which the elective franchise is denied. If political power shall be lost because of such a denial, not imposed because of participation in rebellion or other crime, it is to be hoped that political interests may work in the line of justice, and that the end will be the impartial enfranchisement of all citizens not disqualified by crime. Whether that end shall be attained or not, this will be secured: that the measure of political power of any State shall be determined by that portion of its citizens which can speak and act at the polls, and shall not be enlarged because of the residence within the State of portions of its citizens denied the right of franchise. So much for the second section of the amendment. It is not all that I wish and would demand; but odious inequalities are removed by it and representation will be equalized, and the political rights of all citizens will under its operation be, as we believe, ultimately recognized and admitted. (Eliot [R])

In Harlan's estimation, all these statements, plus the speeches by Stevens, Bingham, and Howard, showed "beyond any possible doubt" that the Fourteenth Amendment did not reach state apportionments (that the equal protection clause did not require population-based apportionment). Harlan summarized the situation this way:

> (1) Congress, with full awareness of and attention to the possibility that the States would not afford full equality in voting rights to all their citizens, nevertheless deliberately chose not to interfere with the States' plenary power in this regard when it proposed the Fourteenth Amendment; (2) Congress did not include in the Fourteenth Amendment restrictions of the States' power to control voting rights because it believed that if such restrictions were included the Amendment would not be adopted. . . . There is here none of the difficulty which may attend the application of basic principles to situations not contemplated or understood when the principles were framed. The problems which concern the Court now were problems when the Amendment was adopted. By the deliberate choice of those responsible for the Amendment, it left those problems untouched.[19]

The Warren majority offered no counterinterpretation of these statements. They said only that "considerations of history alone do not justify deviations from the equal-population principle."[20] The dissenters interpreted the majority's lack of response as evidence that the majority's outcome was based on political preferences, not the Constitution. The majority did attempt to use history in a generalized way, arguing that "history has seen a continuing expansion of the scope of the right of suffrage in this country,"[21] and extracting a principle of equal citizenship from a number of historical documents. "The conception of political equality from the Declaration of Independence to Lincoln's Gettysburg Address to the Fifteenth, Seventeenth and Nineteenth Amendments can only mean one thing: one person, one vote. . . . The concept 'we the people' under the Constitution visualizes no preferred class of voters but equality among those who meet basic qualifications."[22]

I will return to the majority's arguments. First, though, I will consider the factors that shaped Justice Harlan's conclusions and the strategic moves he accomplished. I will then consider competing, plausible interpretations of legislative history and Fourteenth Amendment language.

Harlan's view that apportionment was a matter of politics, to be left with the states, was shaped by a number of legal conventions and taken-for-granted assumptions. These conventions and assumptions enabled Harlan to bind, or limit, the meaning of national citizenship and so resolve the dilemma about whether the basis of representation was a question of federal law or of state politics. The interpretive work accomplished by him included (1) decontextualizing the Republicans' "deliberate choice" to leave matters of voting to the states; (2) decontextualizing state legislative choices in favor of nonpopulation-based apportionment; and (3) deleting references to the Republican principle of equal representation and Republican discussion about the relationship between citizenship and political inclusion. Harlan took for granted two especially important things: the institutional version of what the Civil War was about and a faith in the political process. These beliefs both played vital roles in structuring the meaning that he extracted from the legislative debates and helped produce the decontextualization patterns in the dissenters' opinions. (The Warren majority's opinion contained different decontextualization patterns, which will be examined later.)

The Dissenters' Decontextualizations
Harlan emphasized repeatedly that the Republicans made a deliberate choice to leave state regulation of voting unaffected. In 1945, Justice Frankfurter stated that apportionments were natural and eternal "political thickets,"[23] adding that "[t]he one stark fact that emerges from a study of Congressional apportionment is its embroilment in politics, in the sense of party contests and in party interests."[24] Apportionments therefore were not appropriate for judicial determination. Battles over apportionment were best carried out in the legislatures through state politics.

The Warren majority might have framed the Republicans' "deliberate choice" as a concession to dominant racial ideologies, which were a nonpermanent dimension of apportionment fights.[25] The majority might have argued that the Republicans' "deliberate choice" to leave state regulation of voting unimpeded in 1866 was no longer controlling as a result of the growing public rejection of the nineteenth-century racial doctrines that necessitated that choice. Pragmatic concessions to white supremacist doctrines should not establish the legitimacy of state control over voting in the 1960s, especially when the public acceptability of those doctrines had shifted and when major precedent (Brown) disavowed those doctrines. The strength of white supremacist doctrines lessened in the 1960s (which is not to say that racial egalitarian sentiment flowered), and white supremacist doctrines should not be permitted to acquire legal legitimacy because they have been strong and entrenched in the past.

It also could have been argued (though, again, the majority did not argue it) that Court precedent from the 1940s which upheld state jurisdiction over apportionment was not controlling in the 1960s. The reason, again, was the growing public rejection of the racial doctrines that helped produce malapportionment in the 1940s (though race was not the explicit issue in the apportionment cases since the plaintiffs were white suburbanites). Court precedent from the 1940s that upheld state jurisdiction over apportionments could have been distinguished. The facts of those cases could have been restated to emphasize the continued public legitimacy of the view that black citizens did not belong in state legislatures. It also could have been argued that by the 1960s the lessons of racism taught by Nazi Germany had come to be more widely appreciated.[26] Thus, these examples would justify the departure from Court precedent.

This argument, it should be noted, rests on a methodology of constitutional interpretation that many people do not accept, namely, that later events shape the meaning of operative language in constitutional clauses. My point is not that this argument would have persuaded everyone. Rather, I am suggesting that this argument was available, that it could rest on history, and that it was coherent. Had the majority chosen to use this sort of argument, criticism would exist, certainly, but this criticism would revolve *not* around its avoidance of history, but instead would center on its choice to regard later events (the erosion of white supremacist doctrine) as a relevant factor shaping the meaning of the equal protection clause. This choice at least can be coherently defended, while the majority's avoidance of history and its claims that precedent was left intact cannot.

Harlan, significantly, did not discuss Republican concerns with the political process (e.g., illegitimate political power held by ex-Confederates, political violence directed against white and black Republicans). The Warren majority might have identified these concerns which were tied to the Republicans' political critique of the planter elite and used them to defend a principle of "equal representation." The majority's discussion of citizenship in *Reynolds* actually evoked the Republican concern for "equal representation," but the justices made no explicit appeal to the history of the Civil War or legislative history.

Chapter 2 presented Republican arguments about slavery's corruption of the political process and the need for a change in the basis of representation. Republicans, in fact, argued against population-based apportionment because this would produce unequal results. In 1866 Republicans knew that Southern states would exclude black men from voting, although a black individual would now count as a "whole" person, not three-fifths of a person, for purposes of apportionment. The states of the former Confederacy would thus increase their strength in the national Congress while denying political participation to blacks. (Little support existed at that time for federally imposed black manhood suffrage.) Republicans attempted to avert this outcome with section 2. It was a notion of fairness in representation that mattered most.

Republican support for nonpopulation-based apportionment could be presented as evidence that the Warren majority's imposition of population-based apportionment went squarely against Republican objectives. But this Republican preference also could be contextualized in a way that would provide support for the "equal representation" principle and federally imposed population-based apportionment. Such a contextualization would turn legislative history and the language of section 2 into resources for the majority.

Republicans argued against population-based apportionment in a context where they did not have the political strength to curb Southern exclusions of blacks from the political process. If apportionment was population-based (which meant counting blacks for the purposes of determining the number of congressmen assigned to Southern states), those states would increase their national political strength. If blacks participated freely in voting, then some of this increased Southern political strength would be in their hands. But if ex-Confederates could exclude blacks from voting, they would reap the benefit of the increased number of blacks, though they excluded blacks from the political process. Section 2 was originally understood as an attempt to avert this. Republicans, arguably, were concerned with fairness in representation. Their rejection of population-based apportionment and the language of section 2 could be put forth under a principle of equal representation. (Northern Democrats favored population-based apportionment; they called it the most democratic method of apportionment.)

In 1866 it was clear that most Republicans did not support suffrage for black men even though they did not want Southern states to gain congressional seats in the manner described above. (Black women, of course, did not get the vote until white women did in 1920.) Most Republicans felt that voting rights were not fundamental to citizenship, although Radical Republicans opposed that position. Moderate Republicans, however, supported voting rights in 1870 as experiences with Southern resistance to their reforms piled up. They were no longer willing to concede state authority over voting rights. This concession in 1866 had produced their back door method (section 2) for maintaining fair representation. The Fifteenth Amendment can be seen as the Moderate Republicans' revision of their 1866 presumption that the vote was not necessary. This revision can be made relevant in rendering the "original understanding" of section 2. Of course, the Fifteenth Amendment was passed for a variety of reasons. Some Republicans, for instance, had come to believe that voting rights were indeed necessary while others saw the granting of suffrage as a way to rid Congress of responsibility for the safety and inclusion of blacks.

Republican concerns about ex-Confederate takeovers of state legislatures can also be made relevant. The Reconstruction Act of 1867 imposed military rule on the South and set up the Reconstruction governments. This obviated, for a time, some Republican concerns about the former elite returning to power. Republican slavery criticism had targeted the planter aristocratic elite. This group had gained political power illegitimately in the antebellum period, according to Republicans. Numerous comments in 1866 suggest that Republicans were alarmed by their return to power after the war and sought political checks on this group. The Hayes-Tilden Compromise of 1877 removed military rule, thus reintroducing problems in the political process Republicans had tried to address. Republicans, of course, had lost political strength by this time. Whig Republicans and business concerns had taken hold.

My point is that congressional debates over reforming the basis of representation do not *naturally* support the view that federally ordered population-based apportionments are illegitimate. History and language are open to multiple readings. For Harlan, only one reading was possible: his own.

Justice Frankfurter used a decontextualizing strategy in his dissenting opinion to *Baker v. Carr* (1962). One question that the Warren Court justices encountered in the apportionment cases was whether a state's refusal to apportion every ten years as required by its state constitution had a federal remedy. Frankfurter argued that no federal remedy existed. He showed little concern for the Tennessee legislature's refusal to reapportion. Instead, he characterized the state constitution as "dead words of written text" and called the refusal of the legislature to reapportion "truer law."[27]

Frankfurter, here, endowed malapportionment practices with value because the practices were explicitly chosen and durable. State refusal to reapportion was therefore, in a sense, more "authentic," more worthy of judicial deference, than the state constitutional requirement that had been rejected. Frankfurter emphasized that equal representation for equal numbers of people had never been the dominant choice of state legislatures. Population-based apportionment was not the colonial system, was not the system predominantly practiced at the time of the Fourteenth Amendment's adoption, and was not predominantly practiced in the 1960s. The widespread choice of nonpopulation-based apportionments was evidence that it was the "best" scheme.

If the work of judging is to proceed, judges must make a general practice of according deference to state choices that have proven durable. But if chosen practices automatically accrue "trueness" over time, a byproduct is that chosen abuses (exclusions driven by white supremacist doctrines) can also accumulate "legitimacy." Dissenting opinions in Warren Court cases were generally characterized by historical narratives of progressive emergence in which the durability of the state legislative practice was taken as evidence of a law's natural fitness. The danger associated with historical narratives of progressive emergence is that an ethical system may be smuggled in so that the law becomes legitimate, if not necessarily right. Legal history becomes a history of the victors. Certainly, it makes sense to value durable traditions of local government. But difficulties arise when traditional deference to state choice threatens to tie the hands of federal courts when historic abuse of state discretion has occurred.

The problem, then, is balancing the value of local government with the value in remedying patterns of local abuse. Justice Frankfurter's solution to this balancing dilemma was to rely on the political process to correct local abuses. He imagined that in the long run, elected elites would be more responsive than judges. In his dissenting opinion in *Baker v. Carr,* he consistently chose to rely on "the people" to correct political injustice. Frankfurter had argued in *Baker* that even if apportionment was being used as an exclusionary device, and "if Congress failed in exercising its powers whereby standards of fairness are offended, the remedy ultimately lies with the people."

Where historic demonstrations of unfairness have occurred in the exercise of state discretion, faith in the political process might be called into question. How long is the Court supposed to wait for the political process to correct the injustice? There is no clear or obvious answer. What if little flexibility is evident elsewhere in the political structure? How is flexibility to be assessed? The Warren majority might have raised these questions, but they did not. The Warren dissenters assumed that flexibility existed, that the years between 1900 and 1962 were sufficiently long to establish the "rationality" of the state choice even though these were the years of Jim Crow and encompassed the Great Migration of blacks from the South to the North and from rural to urban areas generally. State legislative refusal to reapportion according to state constitutional requirements during these years was *not* viewed by the dissenters as having any relation to these shifting arrangements. State refusal was "truer" law than state constitutional requirements.

The Dissenters' Assumptions

The legal conventions and symbolic elements that the Warren dissenters used to bind the meaning of citizenship circumscribed national power, generally, and the federal courts, specifically. Among these conventions was the institutional version of Civil War and Reconstruction history, which included (1) nonrecognition of disputes over the definition of "established" states' rights, (2) a Northern Democratic/Whig definition of slavery's destruction, and (3) a denial that the Fourteenth Amendment invigorated national citizenship.

Institutional images of the Civil War and Reconstruction helped the dissenters to strike their particular balance between the value of local government and the need to remedy local abuses. In other words, these historical images worked to bind the dissenters' meaning of citizenship. The dissenters could decide that representation was a matter of politics because they felt assured that the political process would provide an eventual remedy and that other parts of the governmental structure were sufficiently flexible. Institutional images of what the war "was about" helped provide this assurance.

Institutional history of the war also influenced the dissenters' use of precedent. The Warren dissenters treated antebellum precedent as obviously relevant. They did not defend it as relevant. Had Republican versions of the problems with slavery been institutionalized, the relevance of this antebellum precedent could not have been treated that way and its relevance would have had to be defended. (This precedent was not obviously irrelevant either. My point is that a real argument would have been required to support its relevance. The dissenters presented no such argument; it was simply assumed to be relevant.)

For example, as part of the claim that nonpopulation-based apportionment denied them "equal suffrage," the voters in the underrepresented urban counties argued that self-interest in retaining their seats motivated the legislators' refusal to reapportion. Relying on doctrine beginning with *Fletcher v. Peck* (1810) (a case on contracts), the dissenters argued that "unworthy or improper motives" were irrelevant if it appeared that the nonpopulation-based apportionment was a rational policy. Since the weighting of the rural vote was a rational policy to protect "agricultural interests," Justice Harlan concluded that legislators' motives were irrelevant.

In relying on antebellum doctrine concerning the legal relevance of legislative motives, the dissenters froze the meaning of *Fletcher*. A by-product was the removal from relevance of the motives of ex-Confederate legislators who returned to power in 1866 and then again after the fall of the Reconstruction governments. Such motives concerned Republicans in 1866 (they were one reason for passage of the Reconstruction Act of 1867, which set up Northern military rule in the South). Republicans identified deep-seated "prejudice"—against white Republicans as well as against blacks—as among the continued threats of slavery. These prejudices motivated what Republicans saw as defects in the political process.

Ex-Confederates had the motive and the ability to disenfranchise their opponents in 1866 as well as when they returned to power in 1877. (The Reconstruction Act of 1867 only temporarily helped secure safeguards to the political process. Process defects were a central concern for Republicans.) But the appeal to *Fletcher* excluded motives, including racial motives, from legal relevance. Institutional Civil War history, which suppressed recognition of a range of Republican concerns, facilitated this exclusion. The Warren majority might have argued that Frankfurter's solution (handing the issue of apportionment off to the "vigilance of the people") was a denial of federal responsibility because it denied federal jurisdiction in the face of known and long-standing general abuses of power and the specific use of white supremacist doctrines. Gradual public rejection of white supremacist doctrines could provide the legitimacy for distinguishing *Fletcher*. But without an alternative version of Civil War history to stand on, this argument would be weak.

In his famous *Plessy v. Ferguson* dissent, the elder Justice John M. Harlan argued that antebellum precedent should be seen as inapplicable in certain respects because the cases were rendered prior to adoption of the Reconstruction Amendments. He stated, "those decisions cannot be guides in the era introduced by the recent amendments of the supreme law, which established universal freedom. . . . [S]ome were made at a time when public opinion, in many localities, was dominated by the institution of slavery." While certain elements of Harlan's *Plessy* opinion had been resuscitated by the *Brown* Court, other elements had not, among them his analysis of antebellum precedent.

The Warren dissenters' arguments revolved around the idea of "activism," namely, that the Constitution reserves to democratically elected bodies the determination of "political wisdom" and that the federal courts should deal only with "law." But if the Warren dissenters' determination of the "proper" boundary between state and federal authority (i.e., between matters "properly" left to democratically elected bodies and matters for the federal courts) depended on an interpretive framework that shaped perceptions of "naturalness," and if an institutional account of the Civil War and Reconstruction was one element in that interpretive framework, then the traditional notion of "activism" is misconceived.

The Warren Majority's Argument for One Person, One Vote

The most salient aspect of the majority opinion in *Reynolds v. Sims* was its emphasis on citizenship. The opinion echoed the words of Republicans in the 39th Reconstruction Congress, even though the majority made no mention of them. The majority's concern for the political process also was reminiscent of the concerns expressed by Republicans. It is uncertain if the majority was aware of this or not.

Chief Justice Earl Warren wrote the majority opinion in *Reynolds*. He stated, "each and every citizen has an inalienable right to full and effective participation in the political processes of his State's legislative bodies. . . . To the extent that a citizen's right to vote is debased, he is that much less a citizen."[28] Inhering in citizenship, stated the justices, is the opportunity for "equal participation" and "equal access" to the electoral process.

> The right to vote freely for the candidate of one's choice is of the
> essence of a democratic society, and any restrictions on that right

strike at the heart of representative government. . . . As long as ours is a representative government, and our legislatures are those instruments of government elected directly by and directly representative of the people, the right to elect legislators in a free and unimpaired fashion is a bedrock of our political system. . . . Full and effective participation by all citizens requires that each citizen have an equally effective voice.[29]

The majority justified its interpretation of the equal protection clause in this way:

Logically, in a society ostensibly grounded on representative government, it would seem reasonable that a majority of the people of a State could elect a majority of that State's legislators. To conclude differently, and to sanction minority control of state legislative bodies, would appear to deny majority rights in a way that far surpasses any minority rights that might otherwise be thought to result. Since legislatures are responsible for enacting laws by which all citizens are to be governed, they should be bodies that are collectively responsible to the popular will. And the concept of equal protection has been traditionally viewed as requiring the uniform treatment of persons standing in the same relation to the governmental action questioned or challenged. With respect to the allocation of legislative representation, all voters, as citizens of a State, stand in the same relation regardless of where they live. Any suggested criteria for the differentiation of citizens are insufficient to justify any discrimination, as to the weight of their votes, unless relevant to the permissible purposes of legislative apportionment. . . . We are cautioned about the dangers of entering into political thickets and mathematical quagmires. Our answer is this: a denial of constitutionally protected rights demands judicial protection; our oath and our office require no less of us.[30]

In chapter 4, I used Duncan Kennedy's concepts of "freedom and constraint" to elucidate certain dimensions of the conditions under which Court justices worked in the 1870s. Kennedy's work is helpful here as well.

Let us begin by assuming that the Warren majority wanted to impose population-based apportionment. What was the situation in which the justices worked? They must have encountered immediate resistance: a large "perceived obviousness gap"[31] between federal imposition of population-based apportionment (their answer to the citizenship problem) and a long line of precedent (refusing federal intervention in apportionment). As Kennedy explains: "The skill of legal argument is to close a big obviousness gap with minimal disturbance of the elements of the field. It is the skill of combining the different moves—restating facts and holdings and rules and policies and stereotypes—in such a way as to achieve multiple goals at minimal costs. . . . How much you can change the field through argument is a property of yours, that is, it is determined by your skill as well as the property of the field."[32]

Both "liberal" and "conservative" judges can encounter such obviousness gaps. In the Warren cases, the liberal justices confronted this gap. Given the criticism of the majority's opinion, it seems reasonable to conclude that the Warren dissenters were not persuaded by the majority's attempt to close this gap. Again, Kennedy: "The probability that a judge will move the law so as to achieve any given result is smaller in proportion as the work and the credibility risk involved are greater, and that the total quantity and quality of work available from the judicial labor force limit the total amount of legal movement we can expect in any one direction."[33]

The difficulty for the Warren majority, as we know, was not an inability to impose federal remedies. They were able to institute a series of federal protections of citizenship rights—ranging from access to contraceptives, to procedural guarantees, to an equally weighted vote. Their difficulties, instead, had to do with meeting certain institutionally accepted standards. They had trouble mobilizing authorities (e.g., constitutional language, legislative history and precedent) for their federal interventions.

The Warren majority needed to argue for exceptions to the presumption that the durability of nonpopulation-based apportionment justified the legal meaning that this practice was "rational" and "legitimate." To the extent that they succeeded in arguing this position, the majority's departures from past practice would have appeared less arbitrary and antidemocratic. The majority justices needed to challenge the dissenters' faith that the political process would correct injustices, and they needed to carve out an exception to the a priori view that long-standing state choices in matters of apportionment were rational. In addition, the majority needed to restate earlier rulings (by distinguishing their fact situations) that denied federal jurisdiction over apportionment rather than simply declare (as they did) that those holdings were consistent with the rulings in *Baker* and *Reynolds*. Their simple claim of consistency strained believability, even for those friendly to the outcome. The majority argued that they were not overturning precedent, even though it was clear by any account except their own that overturning precedent was precisely what they were doing. The majority also asserted that population-based apportionments were traditionally favored, even though it was easy to point to widespread use of nonpopulation-based apportionment.[34]

In Kennedy's terms, the majority, then, had trouble "moving the law." Did their failure result from a lack of skill? Was it a product of the properties of the field in which they worked? Imagining himself a judge in order to explain the work of judging, Kennedy states:

> If I fail to develop a plausible legal argument . . . I won't know whether the reason was that I lacked skill in manipulating the field or that the "inherent properties of the field" were such that there was nothing I could have done. Did I screw up, or was I doomed from the start? . . . When someone else does what I couldn't do[,] I learn that my failure was a failure of skill; and there is suggestive evidence in the failure of others that my failure was a consequence of the properties of the field. But it isn't possible to prove convincingly that there was just no way to make it fly. You can't prove it can't be done.[35]

Kennedy poses the question, what determines the outcome of the interaction between the field and How-[the Justices]-Want-To-Come-Out?: "From inside the practice of legal argument, the only possible answer to this question is that I determine the outcome. As I work to manipulate the law field in the direction of How-I-Want-to-Come-Out, I have a strong feeling that I am acting in the world, remaking it to fit my intentions. If I manage to restate the law so that it plausibly requires my preferred outcome, I will see this as my accomplishment."[36]

Kennedy's answer is based more in an existentialist phenomenology than on a discursive structuralism. "The messages that constitute the field are on one level just a set of verbal formulae. On another, they are speech I imaginatively impute to the 'ancients.' On a third level, the resistance of the field is another name for my ambivalence about whether or not I should do X. To the question, 'who is the field,' the answer has ultimately to be that the field is me, resisting myself."[37]

If, as I am suggesting, the institutional history of the Civil War and Reconstruction, explicitly justified by Fairman, undercut the Warren majority's ability to develop alternative resolutions to the problem of citizenship that met certain traditional institutional standards, then Kennedy's conclusion that "the field is me" does not strike the right balance between agency and structure. The authorized account of Reconstruction has an objective existence in addition to living in the heads of justices. If we are to accept Kennedy's conclusion that "the field is [the judge] resisting [himself/herself]," then Kennedy needs at minimum a theory of how socially constructed conceptual mechanisms get into judges' heads.

By the 1960s the Court's reconstituted accounts of the Civil War and Reconstruction had been accepted for generations. They had survived the initial dissenting opinions in the *Slaughter-House Cases*, the dissenting opinions of the elder Justice Harlan in the late nineteenth century, and the Black-Crosskey incorporation thesis.

This historical image, without doubt, got into the heads of the majority as well as the heads of the dissenters. But the difficulties faced by the majority in manipulating the legal field, which included various legal materials such as holdings, fact cases, policies, and historical images, was a product of the *relation* between objective institutional mechanisms and taken-for-granted symbols. As new cohorts of judges learn in law school that systems of meaning are socially constructed, as new critical techniques become available, as the flow of cases changes, and as the culture of judges (for now, mainly organized around objectivist notions of realism) shifts, this relation will change.

It is difficult to know for sure whether the justices in the Warren majority accepted (believed in) the authorized account of Reconstruction. It is difficult to know whether they had doubts about that story but were unwilling to overtly challenge it. Had they put forward a challenge, it would have been clear that Newtonian assumptions of constitutional law were not holding up. It also would have been clear that the Court had been wrong about its history for ninety years, and Court legitimacy would have been damaged. Perhaps the justices in the Warren majority believed the authorized story but found constitutional authority for principles of egalitarianism elsewhere. This view is plausible, though it does not cancel the point about the damage to constitutional assumptions and the doctrine of stare decisis that would accompany challenges to the authorized account of Reconstruction.

The Decontextualization and Contextualization of the Majority

The majority's strategy for defending its view that the basis of representation was a matter of federal law was to pitch its discussion of representative government at an abstract level. Fairness in voting was presented as a general need. The majority offered *no* discussion about exclusionary motives or historical abuses in the use of apportionments, although this approach was possible. In Alabama (the state involved in the *Reynolds* case), as in other states with high percentages of black voters, the targets of disfranchisement campaigns during Reconstruction and the 1890s were black men and women. Literacy tests, poll taxes, and apportionments were used by many Southern states to keep blacks from the polls.

But the reasons for malapportionment in 1960 were complex, involving population growth, shifts in the concentration of population, and race hierarchy. Class hierarchy was a reason for historical malapportionment. Before exclusionary motives were aimed at black citizens, they were aimed at poor whites. In the 1960s, rural-urban splits among whites were developing, and the apportionment cases involved them.

A brief look at the disfranchisement campaigns launched by Democrats in the late 1880s and the reasons behind the first Jim Crow laws passed during that period convey the complex dynamics behind some schemes of malapportionment. A handful of white populists attempted to mold biracial political alliances with black farmers and tenants, but most white farmers with small holdings refused such alliances. In rural areas where populism was strong, legislators from those counties sought to protect white, agrarian interests. These interests were sometimes aligned with elite white interests, but often they were not. C. Vann Woodward suggests that many populists used blacks as a convenient scapegoat for their political frustrations.[38]

Charles Lofgren in his well-known study of *Plessy v. Ferguson* (1896) argues that agrarian support for Jim Crow legislation enacted between 1887 and 1892[39] antedated the point when real frustration set in for the agrarians. Anti-black feeling among populists, then, could not be fully explained by political frustration. Lofgren argues that white agrarians desired segregated railway cars, for this would permit them to avoid contact with black men and women. (Wealthy whites already could afford first-class, largely segregated cars.) Jim Crow legislation permitted poor whites to exploit their race privilege, gaining status from their white skin despite their class (which had previously consigned them to the second-class cars that railways often left unsegregated). Populists also favored corporate regulation and viewed Jim Crow restrictions as a form of regulation. A class-based protest, then, also helps to explain populist support for separate railway cars.

The passage of Jim Crow laws during the same period when Democrats began in earnest to exclude blacks from the political process is also significant. (In the late 1880s, with the exception of Kentucky, states that passed separate car laws also initiated campaigns of black disfranchisement.) The growing threat of populism led the dominant Democrats to push franchise restriction, with black voters the target, but not always the only victims. Thus, a complex intersection developed between Democratic campaigns of black disfranchisement, which included the use of apportionment schemes, and agrarian support for Jim Crow and black disfranchisement. Because there were multiple groups of "victims" and multiple "victimizers," with white populists in both groups, sorting out a judicial response would be difficult.

The Warren majority could have provided a context like this one to establish that malapportionment involved a pattern of abuses. But to provide such evidence would have opened a can of worms. Different kinds of abuses appear in the situation described above. And apportionment was only one of many devices of exclusion. How was the Court to handle this complex of sentiments and abuses? How was it to set criteria for deciding which states were "guilty"? Furthermore, population growth and shifts in population concentration are not the product of political exclusion, though such shifts provide a motive for state legislators to refuse to reapportion every ten years as their state constitutions require (their self-interest lies in retaining their seats).

To contextualize apportionment practices in this way would have brought the majority face to face with complicated dynamics of race, class, urban-rural politics, and city-suburb politics. Redressing the exclusion of blacks would have been hard enough (see *Wright v. Rockefeller* for the degree of difficulty in establishing a racial motive in districting). Redressing the exclusion of poor whites would have been especially difficult because they never have been a recognized class for legal protection under the Fourteenth Amendment.

Thus, decontextualization was as essential for the majority as it was for the dissenters. Distinctions had to be flattened between the different reasons for exclusion in voting and the different target groups in apportionment practices. Only by erasing these differences could the majority avoid the problems of drawing lines that accompany contextualization. Decontextualization was necessary, then, to reduce the unwieldy nature of historical accountings of malapportionment. Generalized rhetoric on citizenship was a way out of this problem.

The majority in *Reynolds* did use a strategy of contextualization to reject the "federal analogy." (Alabama argued that its bicameral legislature, with only one house apportioned by population, was analogous to the federal Congress and was thus constitutional.) Chief Justice Warren found the federal analogy inapposite and irrelevant to state legislative districting schemes. "The system of representation in the Federal Congress arose from unique historical circumstances. . . . [It was] conceived out of compromise and concession indispensable to the establishment of our federal republic. . . . At the time of the inception of the system of representation in the Federal Congress, a compromise between the larger and smaller States on this matter averted a deadlock in the Constitutional Convention which had threatened to abort the birth of our Nation."[40]

The justices contextualized the "specific historical concerns" that produced the Great Compromise in order to distinguish between the structure of state governments and that of the federal Congress. "State legislatures are historically the fountainhead of representative government in this country," Warren argued. "Full and effective participation by all citizens in state government requires that each citizen have an equally effective voice in the election of members of his state legislature. Modern and viable state government needs . . . no less."[41]

The majority rejected the view that apportioning only one of the two houses of a state legislature according to population sufficiently ensured the right to "equal representation." "The right of a citizen to equal representation and to have his vote weighted equally with those of all other citizens in the election of members of one house of a bicameral legislature would amount to little if States could effectively submerge the equal-population principle in the apportionment of seats in the other house. . . . [The] probable result would be frustration of the majority will through minority veto in the house not apportioned on a population basis."[42]

The problem, then, was a "minority stranglehold"[43] on the state legislature that could not be broken by political processes. Those processes could not be relied on since the legislators (the only ones who could decide to reapportion) and the people who elected them had an interest in rejecting reapportionment. The majority could reject the "federal analogy" argument by contextualizing only because the contextualization could be controlled. The contextualization of apportionment-as-an-exclusionary-device was difficult to control or limit.

Both the majority and dissenting justices in *Reynolds v. Sims* used de-contextualizing methods, which are a byproduct of the use of taken-for-granted interpretive elements. Thus, *all* strategies for deciding whether questions of citizenship are questions of "law" or of "politics" involve decontextualization. But decontextualization occurred in different ways and to varying degrees in both majority and dissenting opinions.

By definition, law might be strategic decontextualization. But some strategic decontextualizations might become more powerful than others. The dissenters' decontextual interpretation of the Republicans' deliberate choice to refrain in 1866 from intervening in state regulation of voting was powerful because it was reinforced by legislative history, precedent, and original meaning. The dissenters' decontextual meaning of state choices to use nonpopulation-based apportionment (even though some of those choices were aimed at abusing discretion) was reinforced by the legal convention of viewing long-standing state choices as automatic indicators of "true law."

In contrast, the majority's decontextualization was less powerful, mainly because it stood alone. The use of this decontextualizing strategy (i.e., the choice to pitch the argument for the one-person, one-vote standard at a high level of abstraction, relying on principles of representative government) required that the majority argue for *exceptions* to many legal conventions. It also required that the majority challenge the versions of political history provided by the Court in the 1870s. The majority did neither of these things; indeed, it tried to argue that federally ordered population-based apportionment was a product of legal conventions and historical authorities. These moves rendered their opinions vulnerable.

Certain arguments did gain legitimacy for the apportionment decisions. While the majority chose to avoid certain contexts, they emphasized others. The majority held a version of history as progress. The franchise had regularly expanded, and *Reynolds* was simply the most recent development. The majority also alluded to the social and political context created by Jim Crow laws: unpunished violence against blacks, differential sentencing, all-white juries, etc. Black citizenship, the majority argued, was threatened if black men and women could not protect themselves by voting. These arguments have been found persuasive by many, in spite of the logical and historical weaknesses of the opinions themselves. This persuasiveness accounts for the legitimacy of the Warren decisions. My point is not that this legitimacy is undeserved. My aim has been to identify the social and historical production of institutional historical "standards" that weakened the majority's opinions.

To build a fully coherent and historically grounded argument which considered the passage of the Fourteenth Amendment, the majority had to challenge the authorized version of Civil War and Reconstruction history. Had they been preserved, Republican versions of slavery and Reconstruction history—which cautioned against leaving power in the hands of those who had misused it, which identified abuses against whites' rights as well as blacks' rights, which challenged the definition of "established" states' rights, and which condemned abuses of the political process—might have supplied symbolic resources for the Warren majority. To be sure, uncertainty derived from Republican versions of history. The scope of federal power remained in question. Republican history did not command the Warren majority's outcome, but it permitted it. Interpretive work would have been necessary to mobilize this history, but at least it would have been accessible. Instead, the majority was confronted with an authorized version of Reconstruction that looked to support the dissenters' judgments. Again, my point concerns the structured access to history as a source of authority: Who has access? For whom is access blocked? How did this happen? What are the effects?

Interpretive Frames and the Resolution of Citizenship Dilemmas in the 1960s

As previous chapters have shown, the ways in which judges resolve citizenship dilemmas and sort through history is historically and socially shaped. The presumption that politically passed legislation is legitimate (this presumption itself is a historical product) has usually been a starting point for judges in resolving citizenship dilemmas. But of course uncertainties arise about how one then proceeds. Since ambiguities inhere in the distinction between "political questions," which are not appropriate for judicial consideration, and matters of "law," which are, we can investigate the mechanisms that shape this sorting process. As Justice William Brennan has stated, "Unlike literary critics, judges cannot merely savor tensions or revel in ambiguities. . . . [J]udges must resolve them."[44]

Dilemmas about whether questions of citizenship are questions of law or of politics have been resolved partly through the articulation of bases for choosing essential principles of citizenship. Judges have limited themselves to a few central principles of citizenship (and chosen basic "units of citizenship," for example, individuals, not family heads or races) that become subject to court enforcement.

Judges might choose principles of citizenship according to widespread legitimacy so that even those disadvantaged and/or those with the power to generate disorder and violence give some support. This is a pragmatic consideration, for there are practical difficulties in enforcing "just" laws on unwilling majorities.[45] It makes sense, then, to allow delays but not indefinite ones for political institutions to work out ways of achieving norms of citizenship. Judges should rely on a difficult, though not impossible, amendment procedure for those basic rights, a procedure which ensures that basic changes occur through democratic processes.

But these bases for choosing a few principles of citizenship are indeterminate. Allowing lengthy but not indefinite delays does not answer the question, How long? When do "very long" delays shade into "indefinite" ones? How much opposition, and by whom, is enough to veto a judgment of widespread legitimacy? How much unrest can be or should be risked for a "just" decision? How can enough flexibility be ensured in aspects of the governmental structure other than the enforcement of rights? What is a sufficient basis for assuming that this flexibility exists?

Warren Court justices in the apportionment cases faced these uncertainties, and the justices needed ways of managing them. This task was accomplished by invoking taken-for-granted cognitive sets, or interpretive frameworks, which moved the judges from general bases for choosing principles of basic citizenship to actual judgments in the legislative apportionment cases. These cognitive sets did critical work in shaping the justices' determinations of the "proper" boundary between federal and state jurisdiction. In other words, these sets managed the indeterminacies inherent in legal conventions for resolving citizenship dilemmas.

All strategies (or "recipes") for resolving citizenship dilemmas involve taken-for-granted—hence, undefended—elements. The elements in Justice Harlan's and Justice Frankfurter's recipe included an assumed faith in the political process and an assumed flexibility in other parts of the governmental structure. Also included were historical images of the Civil War and Reconstruction. All of these elements made up the justices'

interpretive frameworks. Absent in their frameworks was any knowledge that Republicans and Northern Democrats disputed the definition
of "established" states' rights and the definition of slavery's destruction.
Also absent was a view of Reconstruction in which the problems of
democracy were reconceptualized. Had such knowledge been institutionalized, confidence could not so easily be derived from the belief that
the basis of representation was so "obviously" a matter for the states.

To say that the legal category of "jurisdiction" is socially constructed
means that the line between matters of "law" and matters of "political
wisdom" is set by the operations of socially and historically produced
cognitive sets. These sets include versions of history, categories of race,
gender, property, contract, conceptions of religious morality, etc.

The roots of both the majority and dissenting opinions in *Reynolds* extend deeply into the political history of the United States, reaching back
to early debates about federalism and slavery. Disputes about the distribution of state and federal power began with the Federalists and Antifederalists in the 1780s and continued throughout the antebellum period
among the Free-Soilers, (later the Republicans), the Stephen Douglas
Democrats, and the slaveowners. These debates did not end with the
Civil War but carried over into the Reconstruction congresses. Republicans and Northern Democrats were the new protagonists in 1866 in this
ongoing debate about the distribution of authority over citizenship. The
Supreme Court supplied a resolution in the 1870s that quieted debate
until the 1930s.

When the debate was reopened in the 1930s and 1940s, the arguments
were shaped in a legal field packed with various political traditions, compromises with slavery, and a civil war. By the time that Warren Court
justices debated questions of citizenship in the 1960s, disputes over the
distribution of power between the states and the federal government had
become laden with accumulated layers of argumentation and resolutions.

One device that the Supreme Court had used in the 1870s to provide
its minimalist resolution of citizenship dilemmas—Northern Democratic
versions of the slavery experience and Northern Democratic definitions
of slavery's destruction—became layered over with the sediment of Court
precedent endorsing this strategy. As a result, the field within which Warren Court justices worked contained closed accounts of slavery and Reconstruction history. These accounts were mutually entrenched, or co-
produced,[46] with Justice Samuel Miller's state-based minimalist strategy
for resolving postwar citizenship dilemmas. The closed nature of these

accounts, as we have seen, enabled Warren dissenters, but not the Warren majority, to use the history of the 1860s as an institutional resource.

*   *   *

In the 1960s a narrow definition of slavery's destruction along with a version of the war's issues worked to the rhetorical advantage of Southerners who sought black political exclusion and subordination. Even those who did not seek black political exclusion could believe that the Warren Court's imposition of population-based apportionment was the product of politics not law.

In arguing for federal jurisdiction over apportionments, the Warren majority had resources available to it that previous judges favoring nationalist solutions to questions of citizenship lacked (e.g., a notion of equal citizenship developed by the NAACP in the 1930s, an expanding awareness of racism and totalitarianism brought about by World War II). But in arguing that apportionments were matters of "politics," unfit for judicial appraisal, Warren dissenters could call forth a story about Reconstruction and the Civil War that had been reaffirmed in Court precedent since 1873. Fairman's "victory" over Crosskey, along with widespread condemnation of the nationalist "substantive due process" line of cases culminating with *Lochner,* strengthened the state-centered account of the Fourteenth Amendment.

As the majority opinion in *Reynolds* shows, those justices attempted to develop nationalist solutions to citizenship dilemmas without challenging the institutional account of Reconstruction. This attempt was bound to be unpersuasive to a segment of the legal community, given that the authorized history of Reconstruction had become entrenched with legal conventions for binding the meaning of citizenship. The majority needed to take on all of it—authorized history and conventions together—in order to build a fully coherent and historically grounded (from 1866–1960) opinion. The majority's refusal, or inability, to confront this issue was a virtual guarantee of incoherence and historical vulnerability. If we are to understand the roots of intellectual reaction against the Warren Court, we need to understand how the legal project of developing antisubordination solutions to citizenship dilemmas is indissolubly linked with the legal project of challenging the institutional account of the Civil War and Reconstruction.

8

Constitutional Law as a "Culture
of Argument": Toward a Sociology
of Constitutional Law

In 1990 J. B. White conceptualized law as a "culture of argument," as a
set of ways of making sense of things. This concept, which I reformulate
to some extent, is probably the best one available for capturing the dynamics at work in the previous chapters. I turn at this point to develop a
sociology of constitutional law, gathering and melding concepts, sometimes critiquing them, from scholars who have had other things in mind
than constitutional law. I build a linguistic turn into a theory of social
structure and discuss how Fourteenth Amendment doctrine may be seen
as an institutional mode of social reproduction and social change. I offer
some high-order generalizations about how an institutional history of
Reconstruction was built, established, used, and challenged, though I do
not offer new constitutional theory in the traditional sense.

Ships in Bottles

When Supreme Court justices look at the social world, their perceptions and pieces of knowledge are like ships in bottles.[1] The ships—their
bits of knowledge about social arrangements and events—are so firmly
lodged inside the bottles of validity that it looks as if they always must
have been there. And ships in bottles look as though they could never
get out. Judges, as much as other cultural actors, lack a sense of accomplishment as they sort through events for purposes of adjudication,
even while they do feel that they have accomplished something as they
rearrange precedent and restate rulings. Like other cultural activities,
judges' orderly ways of seeing the world are built upon what phenome-
nologists call a taken-for-granted reality. "Those trained in the law learn

to see the world in particular ways, and the particular ways come to be seen unproblematically as the only truth there is. There seems to be no question or choice about it. It just is."[2] Far from pulling free of taken-for-granted ways of seeing, justices adjudicate in a legal arena full of ships already within their bottles. Theorizing institutional practices of work and legitimation requires attention to these captive vessels.

Legal knowledge of Reconstruction is like our ship. This book has been about the production and impact of "credible" Reconstruction history. A mostly Northern Democratic version of Civil War/Reconstruction history got institutionalized, and this "knowledge" had an impact on judicial approaches to civil rights disputes in the twentieth century. Many groups of social actors, acting within specific social relations and across many generations, produced the "truth" value that has attached to this account of Reconstruction. Neither a materialism nor an idealism is exclusively adequate for conceptualizing this production process.

This study of the production and impact of credible Reconstruction history suggests that the theoretical link between constitutional inter-pretation, social structure, and production of knowledge must be tightly drawn. By giving prominence to a series of questions about how institu-tional legitimacy is achieved and sustained, won and lost, I make a case for the central relevance of the sociology of knowledge (the production and mobilization of various knowledge claims) in the theorization of social structure and institutional Court legitimation.

On Dependent and Independent Variables

At times, in examining the process by which a mostly Northern Demo-cratic slavery criticism gained "truth" value, I have used the language of dependent and independent variables. However, inherent difficulties with these designations arise in conceptualizing the act of judging as a social practice.

The judgment of the Warren dissenters in *Reynolds v. Sims* that the one-person, one-vote ruling was illegitimate resembles a traditionally defined dependent variable. I have explained the dissenters' judgment of illegitimacy by pointing to factors (institutional symbolic structures) that also are found in the texts. Thus, I did not explain the dissenters' textual judgments with traditionally recognized sociological variables outside the texts. Rather, I treated a set of institutional mechanisms, stabilized against each other, as independent variables. These variables produced the dissenters' judgment about the illegitimacy of federally ordered population-based apportionment and through textual analysis these mechanisms were identified. The way that these mechanisms *arrived in the text* was investigated by moving outside the text.

In examining the historical process by which one of these mechanisms — the account of the Civil War and Reconstruction reconstituted in the Supreme Court's opinions from 1873 until 1883 — gained value as "truth," I did not treat the reconstituted historical account as a dependent variable except for identification purposes, as when I called it the Northern Democratic account to place it in the context of post–Civil War political discourse and political arrangements. I did not explain the content of the Northern Democrats' historical representations with reference to independent factors outside the texts. While I pointed to the role played by a theory of race in generating and sustaining this account, I attempted to convey a dynamic interaction between the Northern Democrats' representations of political history and social arrangements at that time.

The Supreme Court's representation of the political history of the 1860s, supplied under a distinct set of social and political arrangements during the 1870s, had a series of determinative effects on the social order — briefly, the healing of the divisions of the Civil War at the expense of federal guarantees of black citizenship. Instead of explaining the text of the reconstituted account of Reconstruction given from 1873 through 1883 with reference to the context of Reconstruction politics, I again attempted to set both against each other. Duncan Kennedy's notions of legal fields and degrees of freedom and constraint were used to model this dynamic interaction.

Pierre Bourdieu understands institutional mechanisms generally as "an objectification of accumulated social energy." History, Bourdieu suggests, is objectified in institutional structures. I have investigated the history of the institutional account of the Civil War and Reconstruction with the purpose of giving a concrete sense of what an "accumulation of social energy" looks like in the realm of constitutional decision-making.

This kind of a situation, where the authorized representation of Reconstruction is stabilized against other institutional symbolic structures (such as conceptions of durability), and where the authorized representation of Reconstruction has gained value as "truth" through a complex social-historical process, makes it difficult to model the relation between constitutional arguments and society. Thus, in the preceding chapters, I have analytically frozen the process as a series of points.

My strategy for analyzing the production and use of historical meanings has been to place constitutional history, political history, and social history in mutual relation—without (I hope) reducing it all to mush. I have avoided such traditional categories as the state and class interest. And I have not arrayed my evidence (which has ranged from political rhetoric about slavery, race, and Republic, to postbellum labor contracts, to Grant administration civil rights policy) under a single heading. I did not call my analysis "competition between modes of production," "conflict over the control of state power," or "modernization of ideals of citizenship to fit an urban economy," though the story was about all these things. The designation that I prefer is a "sociology of constitutional law."

What I have done, most generally, is place constitutional law in relation to another specific cultural practice, namely, the sociology of knowledge. One cannot read the whole (of culture) in the part (of textual representations of Reconstruction legislation). But in building a story about the multiple and divergent accounts of "the problem" with slavery and "what happened" during Reconstruction (supplied by Republicans, Northern Democrats, federal judges, Supreme Court justices, academic historians, and law school professors) and in charting the process by which a mostly Northern Democratic account of Reconstruction gained institutional value as "truth," I have tried to establish networks of cultural relations that resist totalization.

By conceiving of the constitutional field as fragmented and conflicted, but also as symbolically weighted, my historically oriented sociological criticism of legal representation resists closure on an account of Reconstruction. Closure of the official account has permitted legal conservatives to use that account as institutional authority for their judgments. That representations of Reconstruction are not closed for everyone, especially academic historians, in part has made this project possible.

Theorizing Social Structure: Taking the Linguistic Turn

Sociologists do not typically take Supreme Court opinions as data, much less use them as a basis for theorizing social structure. But the production and use of legal symbols in practices of judicial work do not fit neatly into a formulation of social structure as mutually sustaining sets of mental schemas and resources. The challenge for theories of social structure, of course, is to overcome the divide between semiotic and materialist visions of structure. William Sewell's formulation of structures as mutually sustaining sets of (virtual) mental schemas and (actual) resources offers no conceptual home for institutional symbols that exist simultaneously in both forms: as virtual elements of schemas and as actual objective resources. I have tried to show how the institutional account of Reconstruction exists in both forms at the same time.

Attention to institutional discursive structures confounds attempts to maintain a conceptual distance between mental schemas and resources. Sewell's notion of structure is not fully adequate for conceptualizing the range and complexity of signifying practices that have been examined in previous chapters, practices that took place across different social arenas and at different levels of society, from the institutional to the collective to the individual.

Whenever institutional actors (like judges) act, and whenever they build justifications for their actions, they invoke knowledge systems. The knowledges brought to bear on the myriad of problems that institutional actors encounter are institutional—particular to time and place. This chapter builds a theoretical link between social structure and the production of knowledge. I make a case for bringing sociological attention to the processes by which institutional actors come to know what they know. Under what conditions and circumstances do they come to know it? As just noted one of the most important, and most difficult, tasks of social theory is to connect discursive analyses of signifying processes with structural analyses of institutions. One aspect of this task is getting a historical grasp of the structuredness of the discursive relations and conditions into which institutional actors inevitably enter.

Sewell begins his essay on social structure by acknowledging it to be profoundly cultural in nature. Taking his cue from cultural anthropologists who have defined culture as "what people know," Sewell designates mental schemas as the virtual dimension of structures. Mental schemas (what people know) are actualized or put into practice in an undetermined range of situations. He explains that such schemas organize action and activate the exchange value of resources.

But while Sewell places great emphasis on cultural knowledge systems, he finds linguistic models of structure extremely limited. Why? According to him, the power of linguistic structures is "unusually slight.

The enactment of phonological, morphological, syntactical and seman-
tic structures in speech or writing in itself has relatively modest resource
effects."[3] In addition, "one danger that arises from accepting the linguistic model is a tendency to think of structures as composed purely
of schemas, while ignoring the resource dimension." Sewell, then, in
finding linguistic models of limited use, does not conceive of linguistic
structures as having "resource dimensions." This results from his use of
phonological, morphological, and syntactical structures of language as
the *basis* for linguistic models.

Sewell finds the linguistic analogy of limited use because he unnecessarily limits what might serve as the basis for linguistic models. What
is commonly called discourse now operates as the basis for formulating
linguistic models of structure. To take Claude Lévi-Strauss's work as representative of linguistic models, which Sewell does, misses the fact that
such models have been the subjects of intense debate. Nancy Fraser[4] describes postmodernism as springing from "the imperative of theorizing
from within the horizon of the linguistic turn," and she groups theorists
such as Foucault, Habermas, Bourdieu, and Gramsci. As she explains,
much of the debate in social theory today is over the question of how to
conceive the processes of signification.

Linguistic models no longer are far removed from dynamics of power,
domination, and social change. When discourse operates as the basis for
formulating linguistic models, state and political structures are no longer
"particularly poor candidates," as Sewell calls them, for the linguistic
analogy. Sewell actually refers to the U.S. constitutional system, calling
it an unusual political structure because it is both "immensely powerful"
and relatively deep. However, he offers no explanation for this unusual
combination. Had he used discourse (instead of phonology, morphology,
and syntax) as the basis for formulating models, an explanation might
have been closer to hand.

The depth (durability) and power of the constitutional system are in
part functions of the discursive relations into which institutional actors
inevitably enter. Unless attention is given to the structuredness of these
discursive relations, an explanation of this combination of depth and
power will remain out of reach. When a theory of structure is oriented
around a discursive problematic, then social structure is linked more
tightly to the production of knowledge. This objective is central to this
chapter, and it also is relevant to the study of institutions beyond courts.

Drawing a tight theoretical connection between social structure and knowledge production is not easy. One must approach this task while keeping in mind the actual historical diversity of meanings, knowledge systems, and subject positions.[5] A basic imperative is to preserve existing conflicts of interpretation and struggles over meaning, in this case disputes over the history of the Fourteenth Amendment and Reconstruction. An adequate framework must be sensitive to specificity and historicity (e.g., of the contest to tell authoritative Civil War history in the 39th Congress, or of the Fairman/Crosskey contest to reconstruct original understanding), yet it also must grasp the overall historical trajectory of the Northern Democratic version of Reconstruction.

The problem in cultural studies, as pointed out by Stuart Hall,[6] comes in identifying the relation between the logic of thinking and the logic of historical processes. The objective is to think of both the specificity of different practices and the forms of unity that they constitute. But if culture is fragmented and structures multiple and intersecting, we must investigate the competition between logics of thinking. What are the social and historical circumstances in which competitions to build "credible" meanings occur? On what distributions are interpretive "victories" contingent? How do early victories constrain and enable competitors in subsequent periods?

An adequate framework must be rooted in a relational and contextual way of thinking that connects various elements of the (fragmented and nonunified) social totality, ranging in levels from the structural to the institutional to the collective to the individual. The outline offered below is preliminary; it needs refinement and elaboration. An adequate framework for building a tight theoretical link between social structure and knowledge production must do the following:

1. Accomplish the (now) basic work of showing the constructed and contingent character of what passes for necessary, inevitable, natural, or unalterable. Also show how social arrangements and hierarchies inhere in the naturalization and reification of contingent meanings.

2. Demonstrate not just *that* meanings are socially constructed but map *how* this process happens. What are the historical genealogies (i.e., the careers) of institutional symbols, and what are the contemporary effects of institutional meanings? By what processes are meanings both built *and* resisted? By focusing on such processes, the meanings used in both the reproduction and erosion of domination are rendered socially

and historically specific. The delegitimation of received and taken-for-granted meanings opens space for producing altered meanings and for challenging traditional legitimization strategies while eroding hierarchy. So far the combination of material and discursive conditions under which this opening occurs is inadequately understood.

3. Attend to the relation between "subject positions" and institutional knowledge systems, and investigate how assumptions shape practices. Interpretive frameworks, or frames, are one analytic formulation of the meeting point between individual institutional actors (e.g., Court justices, or lawyers, or law professors) and societal and institutional levels of structure. It also would specify and remain sensitive to the various levels of structure: from macro societal levels, to institutional levels (within society), to collective levels (within institutions), to individual levels (within collectives inside institutions). Meanings circulate within and across each of these levels. At the institutional level are resources that include reputation, "capital" of various sorts, and accredited knowledges. Within institutions at the collective level are competing interpretive communities that use competing interpretive frames. At the individual level are the relatively isolated or unique positions and arguments carved out by institutional actors. Constitutional interpretation proceeds through the invocation of taken-for-granted interpretive frameworks, although this procedure does not mean that judges are cultural dopes. Neither does it mean that material factors play a secondary role in generating Court outcomes. Again, the challenge is to model the mutually sustaining relations between material and discursive relations. Judges, like all institutional actors, always act within socially constructed ranges of possibilities.[7] Judges might be viewed as rational actors, so long as the meaning and limits of rationality are defined within specific institutional, historical, material, and cultural contexts.

4. Attend to the interplay of constraint and maneuver (degrees of constraint and freedom for institutional actors) that is the complex result of using particular frameworks within particular fields. In law, legal fields are composed of legal materials: rules, case precedent, policies, historic images, messages from the ancients about how ethically serious people ought to proceed.

5. Attend to the competition in sense-making between judges and judicial frameworks as well as the contrasting play of meanings and resources in their different recipes for institutional action. Attention would

be paid to mapping both the divergences and overlaps between institutional interpretive frameworks. That is, understand what is disputed and what is not disputed. What implicit validity claims are never subjected to critique? What questions of legitimacy are raised?

6. Attend to the *careers* of the symbols and interpretive conventions that make up interpretive frameworks, for example, movement from a disputed to undisputed status, or vice versa, and movement from heterodoxy to orthodoxy, or vice versa. Attention also would be given to the different statuses and amounts of symbolic power that attach to legal symbols at particular times. The historical careers of legal symbols (and mental schemas, generally) are associated with the reproduction and reconstitution of social hierarchies as well as with limited adjustments in those hierarchies. One reason for questioning the careers of legal symbols is to increase our understanding of *how it happens* that citizenship guarantees are rendered vulnerable or denied in court, and, consequently, how they might be established or made more firm. The emphasis on social and historical contingency keeps us true to the Everett Hughes dictum that "it could have been otherwise."

7. Attend to the distribution of chances among institutional actors to use a document, event, person's writings, etc., as a resource or source of justification or support. This distribution could be conceived alternately as "communicative silences and imbalances" or in more power-laden terms as "access to symbolic resources." On the flip side is focusing on how legitimacy claims are debunked by bringing critical attention to the differential distribution of chances.

8. Identify various kinds or forms of discursive constraints and offer a detailing of the effects of specific communicative constraints, for example, the effects of blocked chances to use a document, event, or person's writings as a source of institutional support. How are these different kinds of constraints concretely institutionalized? What kinds of material constraints exist in mutually sustaining relationships with these discursive constraints?

9. Conceptualize the interpretive work required for institutional actors (in this case, judges) to "legitimately" avoid the problems of contingency and uncertainty inherent in their work. These problems derive, for example, from the existence of multiple perspectives on events and from the contingencies of social, political, and economic arrangements.

10. Address the persistence of certain institutional perspectives and

the stratified nature of perspectives. How do particular representations become "clotted" together or mutually entrenched? What is the relation between interpretive frameworks, institutional traditions, and the audiences that evaluate the actions of particular institutional actors? What role do institutional interpretive communities and institutional surroundings play in the accreditation of particular perspectives?

11. Conceptualize the relation between symbols as they exist in different forms. Legal symbols, as stated, exist in at least two forms: as objectified mechanisms (things), which might be mobilized and used consciously to support a particular argument; and as components in taken-for-granted interpretive frameworks. Legal symbols are used explicitly and implicitly in the course of judicial work, both with and without the conscious awareness of judges. One challenge for a discursive problematic is modeling legal symbols as they are used, simultaneously, in their different forms. Phrased more abstractly, how do the different gears turn inside the "black box"[8] of argumentation?

A key dimension of constitutional decision-making is the dialectical relation between taken-for-granted interpretive frames and objective institutional mechanisms. Identifying this dialectical relation is central to understanding the practices of judicial work and explaining the pathways of institutional action. Modeling this relation is difficult, especially as judicial practices become conventional and habitual over time, as new arrays of resources are produced, and as old categories are identified as outdated. Social relations become frozen in both objective institutional mechanisms and in taken-for-granted interpretive frameworks. Shifts in social relations, which must be explained and theorized as part of any theory of institutional legitimization, can be traced through adjustments in taken-for-granted legal symbols, shifts in established conventions, and changes in the menus of objective mechanisms (e.g., when the status of a symbol becomes closed or reopened).

Putting Structure into Motion

What does it mean to put a theory of structure into motion? Sewell's theory of structure retains Anthony Giddens's emphasis on structure as a process.[9] Discussing the notion of agency, Sewell explains that actors' ability to creatively extend and apply mental schemas (defined as "what people know") in unanticipated ways makes social change possible. Sewell's emphasis on the dynamics of constraint and maneuver puts certain elements of structure into motion.

But before social actors can apply and extend mental schemas, they first must hold them. How do social and institutional actors come to know what they know, and under what conditions do they come to know it? These questions put the concept of structure into motion in new ways. The institutionalization of certain knowledges, certain vocabularies, and certain categories of thought affects the pathways of institutional action and change. The historical careers of institutional symbols and mental schemas, generally, are associated with the reproduction and reconstitution of social hierarchies as well as with limited adjustments in those hierarchies.

When constitutional interpretation is considered, the (familiar) problem arises of modeling the patterned and structured nature of judicial thought, argumentation, and behavior without falling into a rigid determinism, thereby wiping out agency, innovation, and all possibilities for criticism, change, and transformation. An adequate discursive framework for theorizing institutional action would attend to these needs.

Constitutional Decision-Making as an Institutional Mode of Social Reproduction

The reproduction of the social order and the persistence of race, gender, and class hierarchies are central problems for sociologists. In this advanced capitalist era, sociologists investigate a wide array of institutions in search of answers about how modes of social reproduction are organized and sustained. On the opposite side, of course, are questions about how and when institutional modes of social reproduction are disorganized and rendered precarious. Research has shown that political,[10] economic,[11] cultural,[12] educational,[13] and familial[14] institutions all tend to reproduce class, race, and gender hierarchy. When these institutions are weakened, the hierarchies are rendered more vulnerable. This same research demonstrates that social arrangements are reproduced by seemingly neutral mechanisms and institutionalized structures of thought (i.e., networks of interpretive practices that systematically order and give meaning to the social world). Individual malice and intent to reproduce hierarchy are not necessary to perpetuate the system.

The question of social reproduction, however, is usually met with answers that are totalizing yet incomplete. Appeals to social structure (material or economic conditions or cultural logics) tend to wipe out agency, leaving no critical leverage for social transformation. Appeals to cultural categories of gender and race, while greatly needed, are frequently insufficient. Matters of institutional explanation are complicated enormously by the ways in which sets of institutional mechanisms, including categories of race and gender, interact to reproduce and legitimate social arrangements.[15] We also are in the early stages of understanding how delegitimation of such categories renders those arrangements (and the categories themselves) more vulnerable.

A consensus is growing that categories of thought and knowledge play critical roles in reproducing social hierarchy. Social theorists Peter Berger and Thomas Luckmann[16] observed this process more than twenty-five years ago. Today, theorists like Pierre Bourdieu make the same point: the symbolic power to impose principles by which the social world is made meaningful is a significant dimension of social power. By imposing certain principles of meaning, particular distributions and differentiations along race, gender, and class lines are legitimated. (This means, of course, that any symbolic power possessed by feminist and antiracist legal scholars has the opposite effect.) Thus, the production of authoritative knowledge is, at the same time, social and political. The investigation of institutional modes of social reproduction, then, is increasingly understood to involve exploration into the production of institutionalized knowledges.

Courts are institutions where stratified social orders are reproduced and occasionally changed in limited ways. In Court opinions, the structures of thought and signifying practices that produce, undergird, and justify Court action are especially accessible. Court opinions offer extensive records of institutional justification. Law, as Bourdieu notes, is one of those fields in which practitioners must be above suspicion. Judicial sensitivity to the slightest slur or innuendo of political decision-making makes Court opinions a site where institutional justification is given express attention. And importantly, judicial strategies for achieving and sustaining Court legitimacy are not unique to the constitutional field.

The concepts of judicial work and legal resources are important to my theorization of constitutional law (though my definition of a legal resource differs from Sewell's). Legal resources are sources of law and legitimation. And resources exist in multiple arrays. It is important to remember that legal resources do not exist objectively in the world. Rather, they *become* objective through social and historical processes.

Legal resources are rare and worthy of being sought.[17] Not every version of Civil War or Reconstruction history, for example, can be used to gain legitimacy for a Fourteenth Amendment decision. Not every memory of Jim Crow can be used to argue that race employed as a relevant factor in districting (i.e., in the creation of majority and minority districts) is unconstitutional. In constitutional law, avenues of argumentation are structured; arrays of resources are differently powerful (in the sense that they vary in their ability to provide standards of meaning and interpretation); and various theories of action are stratified. Different vocabularies are more or less embedded institutionally, requiring judges with their particular ways of thinking to invest more or less constructive work in building arguments. In this sense, different ways of thinking are more or less easily extended in law.

The field of constitutional law is relatively autonomous[18] in the sense that it is characterized by its own agents (lawyers, justices, scholars, graduate students), its own accumulation of history, its own logics of action, and its own forms of resources. Like culture generally, the constitutional field is fragmented and conflicted.[19] It is not a unified system or an integral whole but the site of a variety of contested claims. Constitutional thought, like history in general, is not characterized by a gradual unwinding of tradition. Rather, significant breaks occur "where old lines of thought are disrupted, older constellations displaced and elements, old and new, are regrouped around a different set of premises and themes."[20]

Legal texts have drawn the attention of only a handful of sociologists. This relative lack of interest stems, in part, from constitutional law being designated as the turf of political scientists. Thus, law school professors, political scientists, and legal historians rather than sociologists have noted that interpretations of the Fourteenth Amendment in twentieth-century civil rights cases (even in Warren Court decisions) have generally tended to reproduce unequal distributions of political power and social hierarchy, even taking into account Court decisions favoring black voting rights and anti-stereotyping rules.

The claim that legal knowledge systems (systems imposing certain principles of meaning) are "social" is by now old news. But the *sense* in which legal systems of knowledge are social products remains a difficult question. An answer requires that we be able to identify social and institutional forces in various periods that shape decision making without denying the individual and critical capacities of judges.

In addition to being a system of knowledge, constitutional law designates certain legal protections as *federal* guarantees. These protections usually are backed up with federal force. For a guarantee to be federal means that it has been authorized, in some sense, as "fundamental." Constitutional debate about federal guarantees focuses on what it means to be an American citizen and what it means to participate in the national collective. Because of its symbolic importance, constitutional decision-making at the very least, is an important site for sociological inquiry and theorizing.

All established orders tend to produce the naturalization and legitimation of their contingent relations and formations. It is through these processes that social arrangements are reproduced. Denaturalization, therefore, has become a standard tool of social and legal critics, showing the contingent and constructed character of what passes for natural and inevitable. What makes constitutional decision-making an *institutional* mode of social reproduction is that Supreme Court justices work in a field in which objective mechanisms—that is, symbolic structures—already have been established or authorized. Each new justice does not need to re-create these symbolic structures from scratch. Noninstitutional modes of domination must be re-created in every generation, and they have to be enforced face-to-face. Importantly, too, there must be individual intent to enforce a relation of dominance and subordination.

In contrast, institutional modes of domination do not happen face-to-face. Justices need not intend to reproduce relations of domination for these relations to be reproduced.[21] Thus, what makes constitutional decision-making an institutional mode of social reproduction is the establishment in the constitutional field of objective mechanisms with the capability of reproducing both themselves and social distributions without the conscious intention of Court justices.

The bases of all judicial ethics of conduct are misrecognitions of the contingencies that underlie social arrangements and the uncertainties that underlie legal interpretations of facts and rules. The availability of multiple meanings and multiple accounts of events, not just single meanings and single accounts, creates some of these uncertainties.

Different judicial "philosophies" are really different interpretive frameworks that structure different *sorts* and *degrees* of misrecognitions. Constitutional decision-making is always strategic (though not always conscious) decontextualization, but the dimensions of context that are submerged (rendered legally irrelevant) vary from framework to framework. What a theory of constitutional decision-making must address is how certain ways of seeing (the use of certain frames) rather than other ways have been *more or less easily* extended and made coherent in legal discourse.

In constitutional law, social arrangements that are the product of "action" and are, hence, controllable come to be conceived as part of the natural order and beyond legal remedy. Dominant sets of mechanisms often work to legitimate unequal distributions of resources (understood broadly) across race, gender, and class lines. Unequal distributions (e.g., in wealth, status, titles, access to what is defined as rare and worthy of accumulation) come to be conceived as beyond control and outside federal remedy. In this way, unequal distributions are legitimized by means of judgments of the "proper" relation between states and the federal courts, that is, through judgments of jurisdiction.

In law, the naturalization of contingent social relations is an interpretive practice that often works to delegitimate nationalist, anti-subordination strategies for resolving dilemmas concerning the definition of citizens' rights and the scope of both state and federal power over those rights. Determinations of jurisdiction, for example, are socially constructed. It is the operations of interpretive frameworks that determine judgments of the "proper" boundary between state and federal authority.

Judges' "legitimate" avoidance of dilemmas and "legitimate" use of presentational devices might be conceived in terms that Bourdieu has popularized, namely, in terms of the availability and mobilization of "symbolic capital." In the legal field, symbolic capital takes the form of both legal conventions (e.g., a view of history as progressively emergent) as well as specific symbols such as particular versions of historical events or particular categories of gender or property.

At this point, notions of legal resources and symbolic power come into play. Legal symbols vary in the degree to which they have been institutionalized or taken-for-granted. They vary in symbolic power, that is, in their ability to impose standards of meaning. Judges using different interpretive frameworks find it more or less easy to mobilize legal resources depending on a number of things: the status of historical accounts (open or closed, discredited), the availability of newly produced resources, the weight and direction of precedent, and shifts in field configurations.

Constitutional Law as a "Culture of Argument"

As earlier mentioned, James Boyd White conceived of law "as a culture—as a 'culture of argument'—or, what is much the same thing, as a language, as a set of ways of making sense of things. . . ."[22] The "culture of argument" concept, as White observes, is far more complex than theories such as "law as façade" (for ruling-class interests), or "law as rules," or "law as rules plus principles"[23] would have it.

While White introduced the phrase, he did not expand it to encompass the competition over meaning (e.g., over what determinations of jurisdiction and what uses of evidence are to count as "legitimate") that occurs among Court justices. White painted an idealistic picture of the exchange and communication potential that law carries, but his conception of law as a "culture of argument" can in fact capture quite the opposite, that is, the socializing effects of conflict where battle lines are drawn and established. Particular ways of seeing might become entrenched, and blocked avenues of argumentation might result. The "culture of argument" concept might be reformulated to capture the politics of sense-making that is at the heart of legal interpretation. White himself steered away from the political dimension of interpretation and meaning production.

The idea of frames, developed in chapter 5, is central to the notion of a culture of argument. As discussed, all human beings make use of vocabularies—clusters of terms and classification systems—in order to make sense of their experience. Kenneth Burke and, after him, Erving Goffman have demonstrated how experience is organized within frames.[24] Goffman described frames as the basic elements that organize accounts of "what is happening," or "what happened" (or put more technically, as a definition of the situation and its embedded actions, intentions, tools, and inevitabilities). The interpretive tools that make up frames are made available at the cultural level. That means, of course, that judges are constrained in terms of their access to interpretive tools. A varied though limited menu is offered to them, and items on the menu are institutionalized to different degrees.

Frameworks structure a judge's sense of limits, of what is proper institutional action. More generally, interpretive frameworks organize sets of enduring judicial dispositions or orientations to action. These symbolic structures organize definitions of "acceptable" Court behavior. To the extent that dominant symbolic structures are weakened, their ability to organize notions of acceptable or legitimate legal opinions is eroded.

The kinds of symbolic structures that make up frameworks include conceptions of race, gender, and property; a sharp distinction between "speech" and "action"; historical images of the Civil War, Reconstruction, and Jim Crow; a structuring of temporality; and notions of religious morality.

Frameworks of course both enable and constrain arguments. Judicial arguments are explanations and justifications for court decisions. Argumentation involves forwarding claims, staking out grounds, and establishing warrants.[25] It is an umbrella term because it encompasses many suboperations or subpractices. In order to make an argument, a situation must be defined, "relevances" must be established, evidence must be gathered and assessed, and "authorities" must be established. All of these operations take place with reference to preexisting frames.

Burke's interest in language led him to explore how divergent perspectives offer both opportunities and limitations in analyzing human behavior. He insisted on the need to understand meanings if we are to understand social life. Indeed, as anthropologists have shown, it is through cultural forms of thought (categories, classification systems, mental structures in general) that we give meaning to all our actions, institutional and noninstitutional alike. This interest in language puts Burke's investigations of frames closer to investigations of social structure and social hierarchy.[26] But Burke, as Joseph Gusfield[27] notes, was vague about the relation between frames and social structure.

Studies of institutions that focus on how institutional actors generate meanings and how they build arguments to legitimize their actions are central to an understanding of how social orders are reproduced and altered. Investigations into the production of meaning are key to the investigation of institutional legitimacy as well, that is, how legitimacy is disputed and negotiated. Given that frameworks enable and constrain legal meanings, the study of legal frames—how they emerge (how they are built and under what circumstances) and how they are used—offers a sociological inroad on long-standing challenges of unpacking legal interpretation.

The notion of legal argumentation as a culture of argument is the broadest conception of law yet available that makes it possible to explain how "legitimate" and "logical" outcomes are produced that favor dominant social groups and how they are found persuasive by large segments of legal communities. An important characteristic of this culture of argument is that, as a whole, it has to admit the possibility of another side winning. In other words, the culture assumes that "reasonableness" and "persuasiveness" can be attained by any judge. This assumption buries domination (e.g., blocked avenues of argumentation, differential access to legal resources, communicative silences and imbalances) in an atmosphere of fairness. The oppressed group that actually wins in limited ways occasionally validates the atmosphere.

The culture of argument idea conceives of multiple groups of social actors, acting across multiple generations, producing the value that attaches to legal resources. With this conceptualization, the sharp distinction between legal texts and social practices is rendered artificial.

The notion of a culture of argument captures the idea that argumentation, which includes the assessment of historical meaning, is not an idiosyncratic activity but is deeply patterned. Interpretive frames exhibit historical trajectories, although they tend to remain constant over temporary periods. Frames enable judges to handle a wide variety of situations, and snapshots of these frames may be taken at various times. These frames structure the improvisation of judges. Continuities in sense-making become observable because the process of making sense out of individual cases is an apparatus-driven process.

Dilemmas involving rights are resolved through the invocation of interpretive frameworks. Since the elements that make up such frameworks are institutionalized through cultural and historical processes, Bourdieu's notion of "regulated improvisation" and symbolic power offer a means of closely linking explanations of judicial decision-making with social structure and the production of knowledge systems. Bourdieu, of course, is noted for his attempts in classical social theory to transcend the opposition between objectivist and subjectivist approaches to understanding social life.[28] His notion of habitus (as a system of enduring dispositions that is simultaneously objective and subjective) attempts to transcend the opposition between structure and agency.

Bourdieu's effort to go beyond the opposition between structuralism and existentialism has parallels in recent sociolegal research that explores the ways in which legal discourse is not only socially grounded and expressive of preexisting social categories (i.e., constituted) but creative as well (i.e., constituting). Legal discourse can forge, shift, renew, and sometimes jolt social relations. A growing body of sociolegal scholarship shows law as continually determining and being determined by a historical period's ideology.

In the past two decades the crude legal realist equation of "the social" with "ruling-class interests"—an equation that maintains the materialist primacy of social class and the economic—has given way in feminist and critical race scholarship to more sensitive examinations of the points of view and angles of vision that have been built into law.[29] By showing how reality is made meaningful in law from dominant male, white, and middle-class perspectives, feminist and critical race scholars strip the universal pretensions of law as they show the formative powers of legal discourse.[30]

Bourdieu's emphasis on enduring orientations is especially useful when it comes to the analysis of constitutional decision-making. Judicial practices are objectively regular (patterned) without being the product of rules, on the one hand, or consciously rational (calculated, self-interested, or driven by policy preferences) on the other. Judicial work is best conceived, I think, as structured, or regulated, improvisation. This conceptualization is more supple and nuanced than a notion like point of view in that it encompasses the degrees of constraint and freedom which characterize judicial work. In this way, Bourdieu's widely used notion of habitus becomes useful here as well. "The habitus is the source of a series of moves which are objectively organized as strategies without being the product of a genuine strategic intention—which would presuppose at least that they are perceived as one strategy among other possible strategies."[31]

Critical to this conceptualization of judicial decision-making is a limited awareness of choices and strategies. Hence, my previous formulation that the basis of *all* ethics of judicial conduct is a misrecognition of contingency and uncertainty. Different brands of misrecognition are found in the different ethics of different camps of judges. Their interpretive frameworks decontextualize in different ways and to varying degrees. The shared practices of judges in different camps are significant in that they tacitly exclude control over certain mechanisms of social reproduction from the area of legitimate competition.

Bourdieu's notion of "interest" counters the idea that practices in non-

economic fields, such as the legal, are disinterested. His notion of interest is highly contextual. "[T]he concept of interest as I construe it has
nothing in common with the naturalistic, transhistorical, and universal
interest of utilitarian theory. . . . Far from being an anthropological invariant, interest is a historical arbitrary, a historical construction that
can be known only through historical analysis, ex post, through empirical observation, and not deduced a priori from some fictitious—and
so naively Eurocentric—conception of 'Man.'"[32] The point which Bourdieu thinks rational choice theorists do not understand is that choices
are made available and preferred within cultural systems. Agents act and
make choices within socially constructed ranges of possibilities.

*   *   *

The culture of argument in the constitutional field can be modeled by
using the social constructionist "onion model." Onion models are especially useful for conceptualizing the ongoing clashes of judicial perspectives, the careers of legal symbols, and the trajectories of specific interpretive frameworks. They also capture the idea that legal meanings are
always pealed down to empty cores, that interpretations of the Constitution always rest on other interpretations that rest on yet other interpretations. As I stated at the outset, however, this does not mean that
we cannot "know" anything.

Onion models are useful for modeling the series of contests which
constitute the histories of legal resources that dot the fields in which
judges work. Legal fields are populated by arrays of resources and legal
symbols, all of them more or less powerful. The symbolic power of the
institutional account of Reconstruction must always be assessed in concrete situations because it is in such situations that justices accomplish
judicial work. Shifting variables, such as cultural ideologies, the Court's
cast of characters, accumulating precedent, and the question at hand,
produce differently configured legal fields.[33] Field configuration, in conjunction with judicial frameworks, shape access to resources.

Of course, there has never been just a single way of reading the Constitution. This results, in part, from the fact that the U.S. constitutional
system was built on the competing principles of majority rule and minority rights. In addition, the original Constitution contained compro-

mises with slavery, which were developed by those supporting slavery into a states' rights doctrine (except on the fugitive slave question), parts of which were judged "legitimate" by the Reconstruction-era Supreme Court. Of course, the competition between state-centered and nation-centered visions of federalism continues today. The coexistence of principles of majority rule and minority rights and the coexistence of state and federal jurisdictional systems (stemming from inherent ambiguity in the term "federalism," which refers to state/federal relations) means that each half of these pairs provides a symbolic resource for citizens and justices. Citizens (their lawyers, anyway) and justices always have the argument available to them that the balance has tipped too far in one direction. But while the argument is at hand, that does not mean it will persuade a majority of Court justices.

Justices in the course of their work must manage the instabilities generated by the dual principles of majority rule and minority rights and by the dual systems of state and federal jurisdiction. Justices must create certainty, stability, and the appearance of timelessness under conditions of uncertainty, instability, and historicity. They accomplish this task by making some choices that go unnoticed (even by them) and undefended. Many choices, of course, are consciously made and defended.

The roots of every judicial framework extend back into American political history to early debates about federalism and slavery, although twentieth-century developments have significantly shaped the contours of judicial frames and the availability of legal resources. Disputes about the distribution of state and federal power were implicated in the Civil War in complex ways. These debates did not end with the Civil War but carried over into the Reconstruction congresses. In 1866, Republicans and Northern Democrats were the new protagonists in this ongoing debate about the distribution of power and the legitimacy of Court intervention in state politics. In the 1870s, the Supreme Court supplied a minimalist, state-centered strategy for resolving citizenship dilemmas, an approach that quieted this debate until the 1930s.

When the debate concerning the "legitimate" approach to citizenship dilemmas reopened in the 1930s and 1940s, the arguments were shaped in a legal field packed with various political traditions, compromises with slavery, and a civil war. By the time that Warren Court justices debated questions of citizenship in the 1960s, legal disputes over the distribution of power between the states and the federal government had become laden with the accumulated layers of previous argumentation and resolutions.

One device that the Supreme Court had used in the 1870s to provide its minimalist resolution to citizenship dilemmas—a mostly Northern Democratic version of the causes and objectives of the Civil War—accumulated "truth" status over succeeding generations. This Northern Democratic version of 1860s history was mutually entrenched, or co-produced, with Justice Samuel Miller's state-based strategy for resolving postwar citizenship dilemmas. The closed nature of this account enabled Warren dissenters to use it as a resource in argumentation; it was a component in their taken-for-granted interpretive framework—one that played a crucial role in shaping the dissenters' assessment of the "proper" boundary between state and federal jurisdiction in disputes over rights. As a result of the institutionalization of a Northern Democratic version of Civil War and Reconstruction history, that history appeared to be on the side of the Warren dissenters, who had privileged and unearned access to the "history" of the Fourteenth Amendment as a source of law and legitimation, even though nothing in the events of the 1860s determined this outcome. For each historical event or period, the sociological task is to examine whether there is uneven access to that event as an institutional resource, and how it came to be this way.

Developments in the 1930s and 1940s, owing to appointments to the bench by Franklin D. Roosevelt, produced new arrays of symbolic resources for the Court majority. Among these was a notion of "equal citizenship" developed by the NAACP as part of its strategy against legal segregation. In 1937 and 1938, the ability of justices to create certainty and the appearance of timelessness broke down. Instability and historicity became visible.[34] The possibility appeared of transformation in the constitutional field. These developments enabled Justice Hugo Black to put forward his full incorporation thesis. FDR's Court appointees mobilized new arrays of resources, the availability of which helped enable the Warren majority more than a decade later to authorize a nationalist and egalitarian view of the Fourteenth Amendment, despite the rhetorical advantages held by the dissenters.

While new conditions enabled Justice Black in 1947 to challenge the authority of the selective incorporation account of the Fourteenth Amendment's due process clause, Charles Fairman succeeded at fending off this move. Fairman's history was taken, by Justice Harlan, as proof that "historical reasons . . . are wholly lacking"[35] for the full incorporation thesis. Older lines of thought were disrupted in the late 1930s, but they did not disappear. Old interpretive practices not only remained available, but they retained symbolic power (i.e., authority). Understanding how stores of symbolic power are accumulated, maintained, and lost is one of the basic objectives of a sociology of constitutional law.

9

Conclusion

Sometimes, political figures attempt to control history by directly manipulating documentary evidence.[1] At Stalin's direction, a multitude of figures in a series of photographs were airbrushed out of existence. The altered and unaltered photos, placed in juxtaposition, provide an immediate and striking demonstration of how historical "truth" may be produced. In my examination of the production of historical truth there has been no equivalent to "vanishing commissars."

I have examined disputes over a documentary record. I have looked into three rounds of argumentation: between Northern Democrats and Republicans in the 39th Reconstruction Congress, between Charles Fairman and William Crosskey in the 1950s, and between Warren Court justices in the legislative apportionment cases. In tracking part of the history of interpretive dispute about Reconstruction, I have tried to develop a sociologically based way of investigating the construction of history and the impact of historical knowledge on institutional action. All contestants in these disputes—the builders and users of Reconstruction history—were embedded in institutionally specific relations, of which further investigation (especially of the power dimensions of these relations) is needed. While I have not fleshed out the institutional embeddedness of these history-builders and users or devoted extended attention to the experiential and material dimensions of interpretive disputes over Reconstruction history, a more fully developed history of this interpretive dispute would include such analyses.

Seeing the Past Through the Eyes of the Present?

It seems appropriate to conclude by emphasizing the complexity of the dynamics that regulate exchanges between past and present (i.e., inquiries into the past and the effects of past practices on present arrangements). Hayden White's thesis that interpretive frameworks structure the making of historical narratives focuses attention on contemporary lenses: the past seen through the eyes of the present. Walter Benjamin expresses this idea differently (and with different concerns in mind) when he refers to history as "time filled by the presence of the now. . . . Every image of the past that is not recognized by the present as one of its own concerns threatens to disappear irretrievably."[2]

Benjamin's objective is to hold in contention the ways that constructions of history are used to legitimate and preserve power. He perceives the permanent threat that "tradition" might become a tool for dominant classes. While one can hardly disagree that constructions of history are used in this way, it is important to recognize that Benjamin *starts with* dominance. In other words, a "ruling class"[3] already has been established. Hence, his undifferentiated and uncomplicated use of "now" as a concept. Because Benjamin starts with the dominance of a ruling class, he creates a false break between the "now" (where dominance is already established) and the "history" that ruling groups appropriate to legitimate their power.

The concept of "now," or the "present," is more complex than Benjamin lets on. Implicit in the idea that the past is seen through the eyes of the present is another question about how various ways of seeing, or frameworks, have been established and institutionalized. How do interpretive frameworks come to be institutionally embedded, and hence powerful, to various degrees? This question, in effect, doubles back on the understanding that the past is reconstructed through the eyes of the present. For if competing and differently powerful articulations of present concerns have been shaped by earlier practices, struggles, and subordinations, then an emphasis on the present threatens to falsely separate "now" from "then." Said differently, if the contemporary frameworks used to investigate the past are themselves products of past practices and struggles, no sharp break can occur between "now" and "then." After all, frameworks and the knowledge systems that they reference are historical products. Sociological investigations of the trajectories of various versions of history help shed light on the production and politics of historical knowledge.

Many groups of social actors, acting across many generations, produced the values that attached to the mostly Northern Democratic account of Reconstruction. In 1866, Republican and Northern Democratic congressmen gave different versions of the slavery experience in order to advance their different postwar visions, which included a vision of citizenship. Republicans portrayed the antebellum notion of states' rights as somehow dysfunctional, and they warned against leaving power in the hands of those who had misused it. Northern Democrats articulated a postwar version of the doctrine of white popular sovereignty that, while no longer permitting local elected majorities to enact slave law, permitted those majorities to hold extensive informal control over black rights.

In the 1870s the Supreme Court offered a postwar model of thinking about citizenship that satisfied Republican governments in the North and Democrats in the South. (This resolution quieted debate until the 1930s.) The Court cited the Civil War as momentous, and the Court recognized the lowest common denominator that tied Northern factions together (ending formal slave law), but the Court gave no recognition to the fundamental interpretive disputes (over the original Constitution, the war's objectives, and the definition of slavery's destruction) that configured congressional debate in 1866. In producing its own mix of Northern Democratic and Republican thinking, the Court suppressed the Moderate and Radical Republican visions of what it meant to resolve the slavery issue. As I have emphasized, Moderate and Radical Republican versions of Reconstruction are indeterminate with respect to legal outcomes. But the institutional preservation of them would have enabled the Warren Court majority to use 1860s history and constitutional language to authorize their expansions of rights in stronger institutional fashion.

When Justice Black reopened debate over the Fourteenth Amendment in the post–New Deal period, the battle to offer credible Reconstruction history took place in legal and political fields packed with various political traditions, compromises, and subordinations. Charles Fairman's history was judged more "credible" than William Crosskey's in the 1950s, but the contingencies of this judgment were drained as Fairman's account became a standard and legitimate resource/citation on Fourteenth Amendment history.

In subtle ways, the institutional account of Reconstruction supplied a rhetorical and institutional advantage to those in the legal community who viewed Warren Court expansions of rights as illegitimate. This account undercut the ability of the Warren majority to redress state practices of black political exclusion in ways that were regarded as institutionally strong. The account provided institutional footing for the politics-not-law charge. In the 1960s it looked to the Warren dissenters, legal conservatives, and even academic historians such as Charles Miller that "history" was on the side of the dissenters. It appeared as if "history" supported the view that the Fourteenth Amendment left apportionment under the control of states. But again, while this institutional history of Reconstruction gave the Warren dissenters a rhetorical advantage, mobilization of this resource did not enable the justices to win (to gain a Court majority), nor did it block the Warren majority from gaining access to certain resources. Understanding the shifting tides of resource mobilization by Court justices in different historical periods is the larger sociological project of which this study is only a part.

I have tried to show how the institutional account of Reconstruction obscured dynamics of black subordination. As a theory of race was implicitly institutionalized with the Court's version of Reconstruction, and as the power relations of Reconstruction became conceptually buried with Fairman's interpretive victory over Crosskey in the 1950s, constitutional law worked to marginalize black experience. It became increasingly difficult to identify the presence of Northern Democratic racial concepts, much less to expunge them.

A Brief Comment on the "Color-Blind" Standard

As I mentioned in the introduction, Rehnquist Court decisions lie implicitly in the background of this book. The *form* of Rehnquist Court reaction to Warren-era decisions could be taken to mean that I am making much ado about nothing, that is, that institutional history is not as significant as I make it out to be. If it were so significant, then would not the Rehnquist majority have resuscitated the historical arguments of the Warren dissenters in employing the "color-blind" standard? And cannot Rehnquist Court decisions be seen as a triumph of Republican nationalism? Are not the current inheritors of Northern Democratic doctrine states such as North Carolina, whose legislature approved the majority-minority district struck down in *Shaw v. Reno* (1993), and Texas, whose state law school in Austin approved the affirmative action program struck down in *Hopwood v. State of Texas* (1996)? Some brief comments are in order.

First, the current strength of Justice Scalia's originalism does not mean historical justifications have been banished forever from the Court. The institutional history of Reconstruction remains a latent source of authority even if originalists do not now tap it. Unless the institutional history of Reconstruction is challenged, the occasion at which it is brought back will be characterized by an imbalance not mandated by the events of the 1860s. I stated earlier that there are multiple sources of legitimation in law, the institutional history of Reconstruction among them. I also indicated that the sociological problem is explaining the mobilization of different sources of legitimation in different historical periods. To state the obvious, we are in a different period than we were in the 1960s. Originalism, with its disavowal of legislative history, has become a stronger doctrine. This requires explanation (no small feat) because the tenets of originalism are not self-evidently correct. The form of Rehnquist Court reaction to Warren-era jurisprudence does not necessarily mean that the institutional history of Reconstruction is not important, for we can easily extend into the future the time frame for assessing the significance and impact of this history. Simply because historical appeals are not explicitly made today does not mean historical appeals will not be made in the future. My bet is that this institutional history will be back.

But even if historical justification has been less favored of late, there remains an indirect relationship between the institutional account of Reconstruction and Rehnquist Court decisions. The institutional, taken-for-granted account of Civil War and Reconstruction history makes a formal equality, color-blind model seem natural and reasonable. This account of history contains the Northern Democratic definition of slavery's destruction—formal emancipation—and this definition fits the formal equality model. The institutional history of Reconstruction suppresses the Republican refusal to regard formal emancipation as the definition of slavery's destruction. Also, this history suppresses the Republican concern with private, racially motivated denials of civil/economic rights and personal rights, a concern that persisted after most states had repealed the racially specific provisions in the Black Codes. The Supreme Court, of course, endorsed the formal equality model of the Fourteenth Amendment when it articulated the state action doctrine.

More light needs to be shed on the subject of Republicans and formal equality, and the study of debates over the Enforcement Acts of 1870–

71 might provide this. But the evidence presented in chapter 3 showing Republican condemnation of political violence in 1866 suggests that Republicans regarded private, racially motivated denials of civil rights and personal rights (Bill of Rights guarantees) as violations of the Thirteenth Amendment. Further evidence, however, is needed to substantiate this conclusion. Evidence that Republicans continued to identify such actions as against the Reconstruction amendments, even after formally equal statutes replaced the Black Codes, would thus be significant.

Justice Harlan's appeal to a color-blind Constitution in his *Plessy* dissent is also relevant to the discussion on Republicans and formal equality. Harlan's appeal has been a source of authority for the Rehnquist Court's color-blind standard. When Justice Harlan articulated the general principle of color-blindness, however, only one *kind* of race consciousness was in his experience, namely, the kind of race consciousness motivated by a belief in white superiority. This kind of race consciousness supported and maintained white advantage and white dominance. When originalists seize on his principle, they cut out this contingency. Of course, we can call attention to this contingency by referring to Harlan's principle of color-blindness in conjunction with this one kind of race consciousness. We cannot know for certain that if Harlan had experienced race consciousness in the form of affirmative action, he would have distinguished it from Jim Crow. However, certainty is arguably not necessary. We do not need to be certain that Harlan would have distinguished between Jim Crow and affirmative action; we only need to be *un*certain that he would have equated them.

This uncertainty is enough because there is historical evidence that Republicans were concerned with white supremacist–motivated denials of rights, and there is contemporary evidence that white privilege continues to operate privately today to deny "free labor" opportunities to blacks.[4] Whites, for example, get unearned presumptions of competence that lead to unequal distributions of economic opportunity. Indeed, this evidence of continuing white privilege can be used to challenge the Rehnquist Court's definition of discrimination directly.

Such historical and contemporary evidence, furthermore, would mean that when states enact affirmative action and set-aside policies they lay claim to *certain* pieces of Republican thought, but not others. It needs to be remembered that Republican thought cannot be reduced to nationalism. This reduction produces the too simplistic view that states such as North Carolina and Texas are the current inheritors of the Northern Democratic position. Pieces of the Northern Democratic position rejected by the states in these instances include Northern Democratic race theory. Thus, Rehnquist Court decisions represent the triumph of only a few strands of Republican thought. In these decisions, Republican nationalism has been cut loose from the Republican "free labor" commitment to real opportunity and the Republican concern with denials of civil, personal, and later political rights motivated by white supremacist belief systems.

My hope is that this book has offered a new and useful look at the Fairman/Crosskey debate, linked the institutional history of Reconstruction to the institutional strength of the politics-not-law charge leveled at the Warren Court majority, and raised preliminary ideas about the role of this history in current controversies. Understanding how the ideas of political minorities (like the Northern Democrats and conservative Republicans immediately following the Civil War) can gain the support of Court majorities, and how the ideas of political majorities that pass legislation (like Moderate and Radical Republicans in the aftermath of presidential Reconstruction) can be restricted to a minority voice on the Court, is critical to our understanding of American political structures and the nature of the challenges that face American democracy.

Notes

1 Introduction

1 *Black Reconstruction in America, 1860–1880* (New York: Atheneum, 1985; 1935), 3.

2 In law, see, e.g., Patricia J. Williams, *The Alchemy of Race and Rights* (Cambridge, Mass.: Harvard University Press, 1991); Charles Lawrence, "If He Hollers, Let Him Go," *Words That Wound* ed. Mari Matsuda et al. (Boulder, Colo.: Westview Press, 1993). Kim Lane Scheppele gives an overview of the literature on legal storytelling, which has roots in the law-and-literature movement, in "Foreword: Telling Stories," 87 *Michigan Law Review* 8 (1989). In history, see Hayden White, *The Content of the Form: Narrative Discourse and Historical Representation* (Baltimore: Johns Hopkins University Press, 1987); Saul Friedlander, ed., *Probing the Limits of Representation* (Cambridge, Mass.: Harvard University Press, 1992). In anthropology, see Donna J. Haraway, *Simians, Cyborgs, and Women: The Reinvention of Nature* (New York: Routledge, 1989). In science studies, see H. M. Collins, *Changing Order: Replication and Induction in Scientific Practice* (London: Sage, 1985); Susan Leigh Star, *Regions of the Mind: Brain Research and the Quest for Scientific Certainty* (Stanford, Calif.: Stanford University Press, 1989).

3 Major contributors to the legal literature include Harold M. Hyman and William Wiecek, *Equal Justice Under the Law: Constitutional Development, 1835–1875* (New York: Harper and Row, 1974); Phillip Paludan, *A People's Contest: The Union and the Civil War, 1861–1865* (Lawrence: University Press of Kansas, 1988); Michael Les Benedict, *A Compromise of Principle: Congressional Republicans and Reconstruction* (New York: Norton, 1974). Harold M. Hyman provides a brief history of Reconstruction historiography, *The Radical Republicans and Reconstruction* (Indianapolis: Bobbs-Merrill, 1967), xvii–lxviii.

4 William E. Nelson, *The Fourteenth Amendment: From Political Principle to Judicial Doctrine* (Cambridge, Mass.: Harvard University Press, 1988), 11. See Nelson's overview of lawyers' and historians' debates over the objectives of the Fourteenth Amendment and the nature of Reconstruction (1–12). See also Har-

old M. Hyman, *A More Perfect Union* (Boston: Houghton Mifflin, 1975), 290; Herman Belz, "The Civil War Amendments to the Constitution," 5 *Constitutional Commentary* 115, 139–40 (1988).

5   Historians have differed in their definitions of Radicalism. See Eric Foner on the distinctions between Radical and Moderate Republicans, *Free Soil, Free Labor, Free Men: The Ideology of the Republican Party Before the Civil War* (New York: Oxford University Press, 1970), 103–48; 186–225; Foner, *Reconstruction: America's Unfinished Revolution, 1863-1877* (New York: Harper and Row, 1988), 238. The Congressional Joint Committee on Reconstruction was controlled by centrists (Benedict, *A Compromise of Principle*, 144). According to Hyman, the committee "became radical," *The Radical Republicans*, 320. Foner states that the Radicals were "vindicated by events," *Reconstruction*, 238–39. A substantial group of Republicans defies categorization, and many Republicans shifted in their views. Foner offers a number of defining characteristics of the Radicals, including a persistent refusal to compromise with the South on any question involving slavery (*Free Soil*, 104, 144); agitation against the Gag Rule (*Free Soil*, 113); defenses of black rights in courts in the 1850s (*Free Soil*, 263); initial support for Southern emancipation as a goal; development of a "comprehensive program of political agitation against slavery, one which would not breach the constitutional barrier against direct federal interference with slavery in the states" (*Free Soil*, 115–17); refusal to restore the Missouri Compromise (Moderate and Conservative Republicans agreed to restoration) (*Free Soil*, 120). No economic policy was shared among the Radicals.

    Moderates held the balance of power in the Republican Party between 1856 and 1860. They included Sen. William Pitt Fessenden (Maine), Sen. James W. Grimes (Iowa), Sen. John Sherman (Ohio), Rep. Shuyler Colfax (Indiana), Rep. Nathanial P. Banks (Massachusetts), and Sen. Timothy O. Howe (Wisconsin). Many supported Lincoln because they believed his election would preserve the Union by ending the slavery controversy (Foner, *Free Soil*, 219). Unlike the Radicals, the Moderates were willing to wait for slavery's demise. According to Foner (*Free Soil*, 209), it was "the course of events in the 1850s rather than firm ideological commitments that led Moderate Republicans to side more often with radicals than conservatives." The Kansas-Nebraska Act of 1854, the Dred Scott case of 1857, and the Lecompton Constitution (1857) convinced Moderates that the Radicals' claims regarding the Slave Power were justifiable. During the secession winter, most Moderates refused compromise. After the war, Moderates embraced civil rights for blacks (Foner, *Reconstruction*, 242–44); however, they were not enthusiastic about black manhood suffrage. The Moderates' dilemma, according to Foner, "was that most of the rights they sought to guarantee for blacks had always been state concerns. Federal action raised the specter of undue centralization of power" (*Reconstruction*, 242).

6   The main battles over Reconstruction legislation occurred along party lines, with the Moderate and Radical Republicans voting in the majority. The Fourteenth Amendment passed the House by the comfortable margin of 128 to 37. *Cong. Globe*, 39th Cong., 1st Sess., 2545 (May 10, 1866). Nineteen members of

the House did not vote. The vote in the Senate was 33–11. *Cong. Globe,* 39th Cong., 1st Sess., 3042 (June 8, 1866).

7   Their work began to address Hyman's complaint, registered in 1967, that "in almost everything written on Reconstruction since 1865, only post-Appomattox events are considered in depth" (*The Radical Republicans,* lxiv). Hyman urged that the Civil War and Reconstruction be rejoined and understood as a unit. Lea S. VanderVelde, too, connects post-Appomattox Republican congressional intent with pre-Sumter Republican belief. VanderVelde, "The Labor Vision of the Thirteenth Amendment," 138 *University of Pennsylvania Law Review* 437 (1989).

8   The emerging issue in constitutional scholarship today is whether the Reconstruction Amendments were added to the Constitution according to normal procedures, that is, according to procedures laid down in art. 5 of the Constitution. Bruce Ackerman challenges the view that the Reconstruction Amendments were normal amendments (i.e., procedurally unoriginal). He sees the need for a richer set of interpretive categories that "allow us to express the kind of constitutional transformation envisioned by the nineteenth-century Americans who supported the Reconstruction proposals." Ackerman, *We the People: Foundations* (Cambridge, Mass.: Harvard University Press, 1991), 42–46, 92. Debate over the Fourteenth Amendment as an art. 5 amendment is only now beginning, and thus it is not yet amenable to analysis along the lines mentioned here.

9   For David A. J. Richards the primary attraction of Fourteenth Amendment debate is the Republicans' revolutionary constitutionalism. He states: "Antebellum American political history set the stage for the amendments; but the dramatic focus for our purposes was the interpretive agon over the meaning of the U.S. Constitution as a central feature of that political history." *Conscience and the Constitution: History, Theory, and Law of the Reconstruction Amendments* (Princeton, N.J.: Princeton University Press, 1993), 17. While Richards takes an interpretive stance on the Constitution, he tends to be uninterpretive on the events of slavery. "The Reconstruction Amendments were as much the result of internal reflections on the revolutionary constitutionalism of 1787–88 as they were external criticisms of that constitutionalism in light of the bitter experience of its antebellum decadence" (114–15). Northern Democrats surely experienced the split of the Democratic Party and Southern secession as "bitter." The events associated with "antebellum decadence" were more narrowly defined by Northern Democrats than by Republicans.

10   Arthur Bestor, "The American Civil War as a Constitutional Crisis," 69 *American Historical Review* (1964), 327–52. This is a shortened version of a manuscript first published in 1961. Bestor argued that constitutional ambiguities in the fugitive slave clause along with ambiguities about the clause dealing with the territories led to a standstill over a single question: Who had the constitutional authority to make decisions with respect to slavery in the territories?

11   M. I. Finley notes that while slavery existed all over the world, the U.S. South was one of only five places that had not merely slavery, but a racially based

slavery society. See *Ancient Slavery and Modern Ideology* (New York: Viking Press, 1980), 9. For Americans, notes David Brion Davis, "race has always been the central reality of slavery." "Slavery and the American Mind," in *Perspectives and Irony in American Slavery,* ed. Harry P. Owens (Jackson: University Press of Mississippi, 1976), 59. See, generally, Orlando Patterson, *Slavery and Social Death: A Comparative Study* (Cambridge, Mass.: Harvard University Press, 1982), vii. For a discussion of racial views in the North, see Leon F. Litwack, *North of Slavery* (Chicago: University of Chicago Press, 1961).

12   Historians have recognized that the periodization of history—the segmenting of time into discrete periods—is a constructive act that takes place with reference to particular concerns and points of view. On the significance of period constructs in shaping scholarly research and knowledge on the American presidency, see Stephen Skorownek, *The Politics Presidents Make: Leadership from John Adams to George Bush* (Cambridge, Mass.: Belknap Press, 1993), 4–8. Period constructs, it seems, have shaped scholarly research on the Reconstruction debates as well. If one starts with the assumption that slavery ended in 1865, then much of the nature of the interpretive contest in the wake of the Thirteenth Amendment will be missed. After all, if one assumes that slavery ended in 1865, how could debate that followed be about the criteria that marked slavery's destruction? One more likely will classify post-1865 arguments as debate about the definition of freedom.

13   Hyman, *The Radical Republicans,* lxii–lxiii.

14   In *The Alchemy of Race and Rights,* Williams comments on her choice of categories, stating that she prefers "African-American" in conversational usage because it "effectively evokes the specific cultural dimensions" of her identity. In her book, she uses the term "black" most frequently in order "to accentuate the unshaded monolithism of color itself as a social force" (257). Color as a social force is at issue in the present book, so I have chosen to use the term "black."

15   Foner, *Free Soil,* 59. Foner comments (115) that Charles and Mary Beard made a mistake in taking Republican pledges of noninterference with Southern slavery as proof that slavery had little if anything to do with the coming of the war.

16   Sanford Levinson, "Slavery in the Canon of Constitutional Law," 68 *Chicago-Kent Law Review* 1087 (1993). Derrick Bell, "Learning the Three 'I's' of America's Slave Heritage," 68 *Chicago-Kent Law Review* 1037 (1993).

17   Levinson, "Slavery in the Canon of Constitutional Law," 1104.

18   Bell, "Learning the Three 'I's' of America's Slave Heritage," 1041.

19   *Slaughter-House Cases,* 83 U.S. (16 Wall.) 36, 72.

20   Even with the *Jones v. Alfred Mayer Co.* (1968) decision that resuscitated the Thirteenth Amendment, interpretation of the amendment has remained fairly narrow.

21   General accounts of Reconstruction in the tradition of the Dunning School include William Dunning, *Reconstruction, Political and Economic, 1865-1877* (New York: Harper and Row, 1907); Walter Fleming, *The Sequel of Appomattox* (New Haven, Conn.: Yale University Press, 1919); Claude Bowers, *The Tragic Era* (Cambridge, Mass.: Harvard University Press, 1929).

22 See, e.g., John Burgess, *Reconstruction and the Constitution, 1866–1876* (New York: Harper and Row, 1902), and George Milton, *The Age of Hate: Andrew Johnson and the Radicals* (New York: Coward-McCann, 1930).

23 In 1967, after a wave of Reconstruction historiography that delegitimated earlier Dunning School and Progressive histories, Hyman noted that Reconstruction historiography had its own history. Hyman (*The Radical Republicans,* xvii) quoted Fawn Brodie, who had asked in 1962, "Who won the Civil War anyway?" In surveying the literature on the war, Brodie found evidence of a Southern victory, a victory in "the war of words," as Hyman put it, that led historians in the 1960s to reassess Reconstruction and resuscitate W. E. B. DuBois's writings.

24 *United States v. Classic* 313 U.S. 299 (1942); *Screws v. United States* 325 U.S. 91 (1945).

25 In the decade before the *Adamson* decision, the Supreme Court handed down a series of decisions that required states to guarantee certain sections of the First and Sixth Amendments.

26 The analogy of ships in bottles comes from H. M. Collins, "The Seven Sexes: A Study in the Sociology of a Phenomenon, or the Replication of Experiments in Physics," *Sociology* 9:205 (1975). He expands the metaphor in *Changing Order: Replication and Induction in Scientific Practice* (London: Sage, 1985).

27 See Michael Kammen, *A Machine that Would Go of Itself: The Constitution in American Culture* (New York: Knopf, 1986). Organic, living models of law have grown in reaction to the mechanistic Newtonian model, but that model retains legitimacy. For a critique of the Newtonian model, see Morton Horwitz, "Foreword: The Constitution of Legal Change: Legal Fundamentality Without Fundamentalism," 107 *Harvard Law Review* 30 (1993).

28 See Charles A. Miller, *The Supreme Court and the Uses of History* (Chicago: University of Chicago Press, 1969), 119–48. According to Miller, the dissenters had the better historical arguments.

29 More comprehensive critiques of originalism are available elsewhere. For a recent articulation of the fallacy of textualism, i.e., that meaning does not lie independently in words themselves but in social conventions and expectations that attach to words, see Mark E. Brandon, *Free in the World: American Slavery and Constitutional Failure* (Princeton, N.J.: Princeton University Press, 1997), 15–17. Brandon notes that Antonin Scalia concedes this point but continues to defend originalism on the grounds that it is less flawed than non-originalist approaches. Brandon responds (p. 26), "it is not clear what one should make of such a defense when the fundamental reason for originalism cannot be sustained." See Scalia, "Originalism: The Lesser Evil," 57 *University of Cincinnati Law Review* 849, 862–865 (1989).

30 See, e.g., Kim Lane Scheppele, *Legal Secrets* (Chicago: University of Chicago Press, 1991); Ronen Shamir, *Managing Legal Uncertainty: Elite Lawyers in the New Deal* (Durham, N.C.: Duke University Press, 1995).

31 The term is James Boyd White's in *Justice as Translation* (Chicago: University of Chicago Press, 1990).

32 Duncan Kennedy, "Freedom and Constraint in Adjudication: A Critical Phenomenology," 36 *Journal of Legal Education* 518 (1986).

33 The idea that resources exist in "arrays" is William H. Sewell's. See "A Theory of Structure: Duality, Agency, and Transformation," *American Journal of Sociology* 98:1 (1993).

34 See Steve Woolgar, *Science: The Very Idea* (London: Tavistock, 1988), and Susan Leigh Star, "Introduction," special issue, *Social Problems* 35:3 (1988).

35 Star, "Introduction," 198.

36 By "closed," I mean taken for granted by judges as true (or fully institutionalized). This version is not "closed" for everyone.

37 See Stanley Fish, "The Young and the Restless," in *The New Historicism*, ed. Aram Vesser (New York: Routledge, 1989).

38 Fish, "The Young and the Restless," 310.

39 Foundationalist theory for that matter cannot guide or underwrite practice either. Fish explains: "A realist will know, by virtue of his theory, that there is something beyond or behind the conventions that are currently established, but that knowledge will not help him either to set those conventions aside or to determine which of them is a better approximation of what the facts 'really' (independently of convention) are. . . ," Stanley Fish, *Doing What Comes Naturally* (Durham, N.C.: Duke University Press, 1989), 382–83.

40 Fish states: "The belief that facts are constructed is a *general* one and is not held with reference to any facts in particular; particular facts are firm or in question insofar as the perspective (of some enterprise or discipline or area of inquiry) within which they emerge is firmly in place, settled; and should that perspective be dislodged (always a possibility) the result will not be an indeterminacy of fact, but a new shape of factual firmness underwritten by a newly, if temporarily settled perspective," "The Young and the Restless," 308.

41 This is paraphrased from Fish, "The Young and the Restless," 325.

2   Slavery as an Interpretive Issue: The Northern Democrats

1 See Abraham Lincoln, "Second Inaugural Address," delivered March 4, 1865, in Don Fehrenbacher, *Abraham Lincoln: A Documentary Portrait through His Speeches and Writings, 1858–1865* (Stanford: Stanford University Press, 1977), 686.

2 See Michael Kent Curtis, "The 1837 Killing of Elijah Lovejoy by an Anti-Abolition Mob: Free Speech, Mobs, Republican Government, and the Privileges of American Citizens," 44 *UCLA Law Review* 4 (1997).

3 See William W. Freehling, *The Road to Disunion: Secessionists at Bay, 1776–1854* (New York: Oxford University Press, 1990), 308–52.

4 See Michael Kent Curtis, "The 1859 Crisis over Hinton Helper's Book, *The Impending Crisis:* Free Speech, Slavery, and Some Light on the Meaning of the First Section of the Fourteenth Amendment," 68 *Chicago-Kent Law Review* 3 (1993).

5 Sen. James Henry Hammond issued the famous statement that black slaves

provided a "mudsill" on top of which a democracy of white men could be built. *Cong. Globe,* 35th Cong., 1st Sess. 961–62 (March 4, 1858).

6 Free blacks in the antebellum South were denied the right to testify against whites in court, banned from schools and certain professions, forbidden from owning firearms, and limited in their physical mobility. See, generally, Ira Berlin, *Slaves Without Masters: The Free Negro in the Antebellum South* (New York: Pantheon, 1974); John Hope Franklin, *The Free Negro in North Carolina, 1790–1860* (Chapel Hill: University of North Carolina Press, 1969).

7 U.S. Constitution, amend. 13, sec. 1. "Neither slavery nor involuntary servitude, except as a punishment for crime whereof the party shall have been duly convicted, shall exist within the United States, or any place subject to their jurisdiction."

8 Quoted in Hyman, *The Radical Republicans,* 244.

9 See, e.g., Foner, *Reconstruction,* xxvii: "Reconstruction was not merely a specific time period, but the beginning of an extended historical process: the adjustment of American society to the *end* of slavery" (emphasis added). VanderVelde, "The Labor Vision," 485: "It appears that many members of Congress envisioned, or came to envision, *slavery's repeal* as only a way station on the path to attaining the ideal of free labor in substantive terms . . ." (emphasis added). When scholars present "freedom" as a concept subject to multiple meanings but "slavery" as a period objectively marked out by formal slave law, they naturalize and depoliticize the notion of "slavery's destruction." This presentation inadvertently contributes to the symbolic strength of perspectives on the nation's slavery experience developed and used by Northern Democrats and conservative Whig Republicans during debate over the Fourteenth Amendment.

10 VanderVelde, "The Labor Vision," 495.

11 Foner, *Free Soil,* 11–72; *Politics and Ideology in the Age of the Civil War* (New York: Oxford University Press, 1980), 57–93; *Reconstruction,* 124–75.

12 Foner, *Politics and Ideology,* 23; see also *Free Soil,* 59.

13 See Foner, *Free Soil,* 304, 309. Massachusetts Conscience Whigs like Charles Sumner and Henry Wilson, who advocated equal rights for blacks, accepted nonextension as the goal of the war. Foner, *Free Soil,* 313–14.

14 Foner, *Free Soil,* 11. As Foner explains, the line between the capitalist and worker was to a large extent blurred in the antebellum Northern economy, which centered on the independent farm and small shop. Many Republicans were also "deeply suspicious of corporations and of economic concentration." *Free Soil,* 15, 22.

15 Foner, *Free Soil,* 44–47, 64.

16 Foner, *Politics and Ideology,* 73. See also Foner, *Free Soil,* 27, 55. The future shape of western society, i.e., its economic development, was of interest to all Northerners and hence could not be left to local majorities (as the popular sovereignty doctrine would have it).

17 Foner, *Politics and Ideology,* 78.

18 Quoted in Foner, *Free Soil,* 130.

19 Republicans tended to think that the Irish lacked the qualities of discipline and sobriety essential for social advancement. Foner, *Free Soil*, 33.

20 Foner, *Politics and Ideology*, 60.

21 Foner, *Politics and Ideology*, 40.

22 Foner, *Free Soil*, 306.

23 Foner, *Free Soil*, 308.

24 Hyman, *The Radical Republicans*, 40–41; Foner, *Reconstruction*, 4–5.

25 Foner, *Free Soil*, 116.

26 Hyman, *The Radical Republicans*, 85.

27 Martha Hodes, *White Women, Black Men: Illicit Sex in the Nineteenth Century* (New Haven, Conn.: Yale University Press, 1997), 9.

28 Quoted in Foner, *Free Soil*, 294. See Foner's discussion, "The Republicans and Race," *Free Soil*, 261–300.

29 *Cong. Globe*, 39th Cong., 1st Sess. 2252 (April 28, 1866).

30 An amendment to this effect passed both the House and the Senate less than a week before Lincoln's inauguration on March 4, 1861. *Cong. Globe*, 36th Cong., 2nd Sess. 1285 (March 2, 1861). Northern Democrats supported this amendment because it was consistent with their view that questions of slavery were municipal questions that fell to the territories. The rejection of this amendment by the proslavery forces, according to Arthur Bestor, is evidence of the fact that slavery was an expanding institution.

31 Grosvenor was a Yale graduate, a professional journalist, and an abolitionist when abolitionism was still unpopular. Hyman, who includes some of Grosvenor's writings in his anthology on the Radical Republicans, calls Grosvenor an "unusually competent observer" (*The Radical Republicans*, 151).

32 Quoted in Hyman, *The Radical Republicans*, 152. Republicans make strikingly similar remarks in the 39th Congress.

33 During the Lincoln-Douglas debates, Douglas stated: "I hold that under the Constitution of the United States, each state of this Union has a right to do as it pleases on the subject of slavery. In Illinois we have exercised that sovereign right by prohibiting slavery. . . . I approve of that line of policy. . . . We have gone as far as we have a right to go under the Constitution. It is none of our business whether slavery exists in Missouri. . . . Hence I do not choose to occupy the time allotted to me in discussing a question that we have no right to act upon." Speech at Quincy, Illinois. *The Collected Works of Abraham Lincoln*, vol. 3, ed. Roy P. Basler (New Brunswick, N.J.: Rutgers University Press, 1974), 266–67. In Chicago, Douglas stated: "It is neither desirable nor possible that there should be uniformity in the local institutions and domestic regulations of the different states of this Union. The framers of our government never contemplated uniformity in its internal concerns. . . . They well understood that the great varieties of soil, of production and of interests, in a republic as large as this, required different local and domestic regulations in each locality. . . . Diversity, dissimilarity, variety in all our local and domestic institutions is the great safeguard of our liberties." In *Created Equal?* ed. Paul Angle (Chicago: University of Chicago Press, 1958), 18–29.

34   Gordon S. Wood discusses the Revolutionary-era conception of liberty. *Creation of the American Republic* (Chapel Hill: University of North Carolina Press, 1969), 24–25, 60–61.

35   Akhil Reed Amar discusses the declaratory theory of rights in "The Bill of Rights and the Fourteenth Amendment," 101 *Yale Law Journal* 6 (1992), 1203–17. The declaratory theory of constitutional construction was steeped in common law methods and was used by those who viewed the Bill of Rights as applicable to the states during the antebellum period. In the fifteen years before *Barron* "a considerable number of weighty lawyers implied in passing or stated explicitly that various provisions in the Bill did limit states" (1203). In the 1840s, high-profile "*Barron* Contrarians" included New Hampshire Governor C. P. Van Ness and Chief Justice Henry Lumpkin of the Supreme Court of Georgia, a proslavery body.

36   Nelson, *The Fourteenth Amendment,* 91–109.

37   The Antifederalists were not opposed to federalism (i.e., to distributing power between the states and the national government), but they had a particular view of the best balance between state and federal power. They felt that the Constitution gave too much power to the central government. Some Antifederalists were opposed to changes in the Articles of Confederation that might limit the scope of local government. Others were certain that states were the largest political unit at which popular sovereignty and republican government could be maintained. These men wanted nothing more than a loose confederation of states. Still others thought that a confederation government might be given a greater amount of power than was coded to the states, but not so much as to threaten state sovereignty. Cecelia Kenyon, "Introduction," *The Antifederalists* (Indianapolis: Bobbs-Merrill, 1966).

38   *Cong. Globe,* 39th Cong., 1st Sess. 2097 (Smith, April 28).

39   *Cong. Globe,* 39th Cong., 1st Sess. 2080, 2082 (Nicholson, April 28).

40   *Cong. Globe,* 39th Cong., 1st Sess. 2394 (Phelps, May 4).

41   *Cong. Globe,* 39th Cong., 1st Sess. 1107 (Stewart, March 1).

42   Several times, Hyman remarks on the need felt by Northern Democrats to distance themselves from Southern Democrats, referring to the "burdens of associate guilt that secession and copperheads had fastened upon them." *The Radical Republicans,* 248, 299, 366.

43   *Cong. Globe,* 39th Cong., 1st Sess. 2254 (April 28).

44   *Cong. Globe,* 39th Cong., 1st Sess. 2501 (May 9).

45   *Cong. Globe,* 39th Cong., 1st Sess. 2394 (Phelps, May 4).

46   *Cong. Globe,* 39th Cong., 1st Sess. 2411–12 (May 5). See also 1171 (Kuykendall, March 3).

47   *Cong. Globe,* 38th Cong., 1st Sess. 712 (Cox, Feb. 17, 1864).

48   *Cong. Globe,* 38th Cong., 2nd Sess. 242 (Jan. 12, 1865).

49   *Cong. Globe,* 38th Cong., 1st Sess. 1123 (March 1).

50   *Cong. Globe,* 38th Cong., 1st Sess. 2412 (May 5).

51   *Cong. Globe,* 39th Cong., 1st Sess. 2412 (May 5).

52   *Cong. Globe,* 39th Cong., 1st Sess. 2408 (Randall, May 5).

53   *Cong. Globe,* 39th Cong., 1st Sess. 2412, 2413 (May 5).

54   *Cong. Globe,* 39th Cong., 1st Sess. 1107 (March 1); 1112 (March 1); 2096 (April 21).

55   In his annual message to Congress, Dec. 4, 1865, Johnson stated: "the evidence of sincerity in the future maintenance of the Union shall be put beyond any doubt by the ratification of the proposed amendment to the Constitution [the Thirteenth] which provides for the abolition of slavery forever within the limits of our country. The adoption of the amendment reunites us beyond all power of disruption. It heals the wound that is still imperfectly closed." Johnson's speech is quoted by Phelps, *Cong. Globe,* 39th Cong., 1st Sess. 2395 (May 5).

56   *Cong. Globe,* 39th Cong., 1st Sess. 2098 (Ritter, April 21).

57   *Cong. Globe,* 39th Cong., 1st Sess. 2394 (May 5).

58   *Cong. Globe,* 39th Cong., 1st Sess. 2460 (May 8).

59   *Cong. Globe,* 39th Cong., 1st Sess. 1134 (March 2).

60   *Cong. Globe,* 39th Cong., 1st Sess. 2397, 2398 (May 5).

61   *Cong. Globe,* 39th Cong., 1st Sess. 1286 (March 9). See also Shanklin's portrait of the South, 2510 (May 9).

62   *Cong. Globe,* 39th Cong., 1st Sess. 2408 (Randall, May 5).

63   See, e.g., *Cong. Globe,* 39th Cong., 1st Sess., 2093 (Smith, April 21); 2096, 2097 (Ross, April 21); 2253–55 (Harding, April 28); 2394, 2397 (Phelps, May 5); 2505, 2506 (Eldridge, May 9); 2465 (Boyer, May 8); 2501 (Shanklin, May 9); 2530–32 (Strouse, May 10); 2530 (Randle, May 10).

64   A. J. Rogers, for example, made multiple references to the "disunionists of either the South or the North." See, e.g., *Cong. Globe,* 39th Cong., 1st Sess. 2413 (May 5). Rogers refers to Wendell Phillips ["he had been a disunionist for thirty years"] and Horace Greeley ["he held out an invitation to the Southern people to secede"], 2411 (May 5). See also 2464 (Finck, May 8).

65   *Cong. Globe,* 39th Cong., 1st Sess. 2465 (Boyer, May 8).

66   *Cong. Globe,* 38th Cong., 1st Sess. 712 (Feb. 17, 1864).

67   *Cong. Globe,* 39th Cong., 1st Sess. 2413 (May 5).

68   *Cong. Globe,* 39th Cong., 1st Sess. 2079 (Nicholson, April 21); 2411 (Rogers, May 5). See also 1132 (Cowan, March 2).

69   *Cong. Globe,* 39th Cong., 1st Sess. 2531 (Strouse, emphasis added, May 10).

70   *Cong. Globe,* 39th Cong., 1st Sess. 2079, 2080 (April 21). These representations of the original Constitution resemble the remembrances of Southern men at the time that the security of the Southern system began to erode. Men began to speak of the Union of 1787 as the "Old Union" and the "Union of Our Fathers." In 1861, the *New Orleans Picayune* opposed secession and called instead for "the reconstruction of the old Union." Quoted in David M. Potter, *The Impending Crisis* (New York: Harper and Row, 1976), 474.

71   *Cong. Globe,* 39th Cong., 1st Sess. 2538 (May 10).

72   *Cong. Globe,* 39th Cong., 1st Sess. 1121, 1123 (March 1).

73   *Cong. Globe,* 39th Cong., 1st Sess. 2081 (Nicholson, April 21). See also 1312 (Goodyear, March 10) ["the negro, as a race, has no aspirations for freedom . . ." "by nature far inferior to the white race, never accustomed to think or pro-

vide for themselves"]; and 2100 (Smith, April 21) [black unwillingness to work without being forced].

74 Quoted in Foner, *Reconstruction,* 279.
75 *Cong. Globe,* 39th Cong., 1st Sess. 1121 (March 1).
76 *Cong. Globe,* 39th Cong., 1st Sess. 2501 (May 9).
77 *Cong. Globe,* 39th Cong., 1st Sess. 2538 (May 10).
78 *Cong. Globe,* 39th Cong., 1st Sess. 2411 (Rogers, emphasis added, May 5).
79 Potter, *The Impending Crisis,* 173, 340–42.
80 Potter, *The Impending Crisis,* 342.
81 *Cong. Globe,* 39th Cong., 1st Sess. 2255, 2256 (Harding, April 28).
82 *Cong. Globe,* 39th Cong., 1st Sess. 2081, 2082 (April 21).
83 Hodes, *White Women, Black Men,* 9; see also that book's text and accompanying notes, 145, 167. Black men noted white male sexual access to black women as a longtime practice, 145, 168. After emancipation, Southern whites who sought to maintain racial hierarchy systematically began to invoke the idea that free black men would pursue sex and marriage with white women (145). See *Cong. Globe,* 38th Cong., 2nd Sess. 712 (Cox, Feb. 17, 1865).

3 Republican Slavery Criticism

1 Quoted in Hyman, *The Radical Republicans,* 39–40, 169.
2 *Cong. Globe,* 39th Cong., 1st Sess. 1011 (Feb. 24); 1015 (Feb. 24); 1072 (Feb. 28).
3 *Cong. Globe,* 39th Cong., 1st Sess. 2085 (April 21).
4 *Cong. Globe,* 39th Cong., 1st Sess. 39 (1865), quoted in VanderVelde, "The Labor Vision," 487.
5 *Cong. Globe,* 39th Cong., 1st Sess. 1159 (March 2).
6 Quoted in Hyman, *The Radical Republicans,* 304.
7 Appeals to "the brave soldiers of the North" and to "land made sacred by their noble deaths" appeared in almost every Republican speech on Reconstruction legislation. See, e.g., *Cong. Globe,* 39th Cong., 1st Sess. 2464 (Thayer), 2410 (Lawrence, May 5); 2509 (Spalding, May 9); 2511 (Eliot, May 9); 2534 (Eckley, May 10); 2691 (Morris, May 19); 2695 (Patterson, May 19).
8 Hyman, *The Radical Republicans,* 351.
9 Republicans frequently expressed disdain for Northern Democrats because "every traitor of the South and every sympathizer with treason in the North sustains the policy of the Democratic Party and the President." *Cong. Globe,* 39th Cong., 1st Sess. 2508 (Boutwell, May 9). See also 2401–2 (Ingersoll, May 5); 2409 (Lawrence, May 5). Eckley mocks Finck and the Northern Democrats, noting that they voted against "every measure necessary to sustain the Govt. and resist the rebellion. . . . To my colleague and the copperhead party," Eckley stated, "no credit [for the victory over slavery] is due," 2534 (May 10).
10 Hyman, *The Radical Republicans,* 349.
11 *Cong. Globe,* 39th Cong., 1st Sess. 1008, 1017 [Fessenden] (Feb. 24); 2534 [Eckley] (May 10).
12 *Cong. Globe,* 39th Cong., 1st Sess. 2247 (April 28).

13   *Cong. Globe,* 39th Cong., 1st Sess. 2535 [Eckley] (May 10).

14   *Cong. Globe,* 39th Cong., 1st Sess. 1016 (March 1) [no evidence that the South has had a change of heart]; 1307 (Orth, March 10) (war was like an "earthquake"; "reverberations" still remain); 1471–72 (Hill, March 17) ("old times seem to be coming back upon us," "crack of the slave drivers whip is distinctly perceptible," "each day's history [is] but developing some new phase of those problems [of restoration] and adding to them more complications and embarrassment"); 1619 (Myers, March 24) ("spirit of the rebellion is not all dead"); 1623 (Hart, March 24) ("I do not believe the southern heart can be changed in a day; perhaps not entirely in a generation"; [we] "must not forget with whom we have to deal"); 2084 (Perham, April 21) ("They are no better now, and we should be false to our high trust to allow these men to come back again to reenact the scenes of 1861"); 2085 (Perham, April 21) ("treason is still as deep . . ."); 2093 (Miller, March 24) ("the day of our peril is not yet passed"); 2468 (May 8) ("vanquished but unconverted rebels. . . . No consideration is more important than the animus of the masses of the Southern people"); 2535 (Eckley, May 10) ("rebels have not changed").

15   *Cong. Globe,* 39th Cong., 1st Sess. 2253 (Higby, April 28); 1113 (Wade, March 1).

16   Sen. James W. Nye (Nebraska) referred to the monopoly of wealth and political power of the planters and the "blighting influence and paralyzing effect on the industries of the [slave] states." *Cong. Globe,* 39th Cong., 1st Sess. 1071, 1073 (Feb. 28) . . . called the war "class upon class" (1074). Scofield stated: "The life habits of these people, their love of ease and domination, their pride, aristocracy, wealth and power were all the outgrowth of an institution" (2247, April 27). Miller referred back to the antebellum compromises with slavery: "it was 'policy' that induced compromise; it was 'policy' that induced the Missouri Compromise; it was 'policy' that induced the Fugitive slave law. I want no policy. I want principles" (2094, April 21).

17   *Cong. Globe,* 39th Cong., 1st Sess. 1622, 1623 (March 24).

18   Jeffrey K. Tulis, *The Rhetorical Presidency* (Princeton, N.J.: Princeton University Press, 1987), 13.

19   *Cong. Globe,* 39th Cong., 1st Sess. 1628 (Hart, March 24); 2084 (Perham, April 21).

20   *Cong. Globe,* 39th Cong., 1st Sess. 2403 (Ingersoll, May 5).

21   Quoted in Foner, *Reconstruction,* 260.

22   *Cong. Globe,* 39th Cong., 1st Sess. 2399 (May 5).

23   *Cong. Globe,* 39th Cong., 1st Sess. 2250 (April 28).

24   *Cong. Globe,* 39th Cong., 1st Sess. 2399 (Ingersoll, May 5). Many statements were made along these lines. See, e.g., 2464 (Thayer, May 8); 2459 (Stevens, May 8); 2468 (Kelley, May 8); 2511 (Eliot, May 9).

25   *Cong. Globe,* 39th Cong., 1st Sess. 2250 (Scofield, April 28).

26   This is supported by evidence in Hyman, *The Radical Republicans,* 92, 111, 127, 234, 264, 328.

27   *Cong. Globe,* 39th Cong., 1st Sess. 2506 (Schenck; Eldridge, May 9); 2510 (Mil-

ler, May 9); 2511 (Eliot, May 9); 2539 (Farnsworth, May 10); 2542 (Bingham, May 10).

28 *Cong. Globe,* 39th Cong., 1st Sess. 2399 (Ingersoll, May 5).

29 *Cong. Globe,* 39th Cong., 1st Sess. 2082 (Perham, April 21).

30 *Cong. Globe,* 39th Cong., 1st Sess. 1619 (Myers, March 24).

31 "Instead of having subdued the rebellion, you have but . . . transferred the conflict from the field to these halls, with fearful disadvantages to yourselves" (1471, March 17); cannot "lose by legislation all that is so gloriously achieved by its armies in the field" (1472, March 17); "How to secure the fruits of that victory and obtain a permanent peace is the question for solution. To admit such members of Congress as they would elect from the States lately in rebellion would secure neither, but lose us both, and we should permit them to gain everything through congressional action that they sought to accomplish by arms" (2535, May 10); "We have defeated them in arms, but in the proposition of the Democratic party, we invite them to the only field in which they have any chance of success in the contest in which they have been engaged" (2508, May 9).

32 Benedict, *A Compromise of Principle,* 125.

33 *Cong. Globe,* 39th Cong., 1st Sess. 2082 (Perham, April 21).

34 *Cong. Globe,* 38th Cong., 2nd Sess. 237 (Smith, Jan. 12, 1865); 39th Cong., 1st Sess. 1056 (Higby, Feb. 27); 1078 (Bingham, Feb. 28); 1117, 1119 (Wilson, March 1); 1123–24 (Cook, March 1); 1151 (Thayer, March 2); 1159 (Windom, March 2); 1291 (Bingham, March 9); 1293 (Shellabarger, March 9); 1305 (Orth, March 10); 1306–7 (Thayer, March 10); 1472 (Hill, March 17); 1478 (Anderson, March 17); 1617 (Moulton, March 24); 1621–22 (Myers, March 24); 1627 (Buckland, March 24); 1759 (Trumbull, April 4); 2082–83 (Perham, April 21); 2091–92 (Thomas, April 21); 2404 (Ingersoll, May 5). See also Foner's reference to "repeated tales of injustice" by "speaker after speaker," *Reconstruction,* 247.

35 *Cong. Globe,* 39th Cong., 1st Sess. 2399 (Ingersoll, May 5). See also 2536 (Eckley, May 10); 2410 (Lawrence, May 5).

36 *Cong. Globe,* 39th Cong., 1st Sess. 1757 (Trumbull, April 4). A. J. Rogers stated that all rights came under the designation "civil rights" (1122, March 1). See also 1157 (Thornton, March 2).

37 Foner, *Reconstruction,* 251, 257.

38 *Cong. Globe,* 39th Cong., 1st Sess. 1013–14 (Feb. 24); 1627 (Buckland, March 24).

39 Foner, *Reconstruction,* 258.

40 Sumner and Sen. Henry Wilson cited a "virtually identical" list of such rights. "We must see to it that the man made free by the Constitution . . . is a freeman indeed; that he can go where he pleases; work when and for whom he pleases; that he can sue and be sued; that he can lease and buy and sell and own property, real and personal; that he can go into the schools and educate himself and his children; that the rights and guarantees of the good old common law are his, and that he walks the earth, proud and erect in the conscious dignity

of a free man. . . ." Quoted in VanderVelde, "The Labor Vision," 476. See also Curtis, *No State Shall Abridge,* 48–52.

41   *Cong. Globe,* 39th Cong., 1st Sess. 2084 (Perham, April 21) (Emancipation "intended to carry with it the common rights of manhood"); 1759 (Trumbull, April 4) ("if the bill now before us [civil rights bill 1866], and which goes no further than to secure civil rights to the freedman, cannot be passed, then the constitutional amendment proclaiming freedom to all the inhabitants of the land is a cheat and a delusion"); 1151 (Thayer, March 2) (civil rights bill "gives practical effect" to the Thirteenth Amendment); 2510, 2511 (Miller, Eliot, March 9) (suggested that the civil rights bill applied the Bill of Rights to the states). The argument over whether the Thirteenth Amendment provided authority for the Civil Rights Bill of 1866 also provides clues about Republican understandings of formal emancipation/abolition. Wilson argued that the Thirteenth Amendment did provide authority for the Civil Rights Bill of 1866 (1118, March 1), but Bingham disagreed (1291, March 9). See also evidence gathered by Amar on Republican meanings of emancipation and the Thirteenth Amendment, "The Bill of Rights," 1217 n. 113. A. J. Rogers argued that Congress had no authority to pass the Civil Rights Bill (1120, March 1); Rogers: the privileges or immunities clause puts the whole terrain of rights under Federal supervision (2538, May 10).

42   *Reconstruction,* 251.

43   Foner discusses Thaddeus Stevens's views on confiscation and Reconstruction in *Politics and Ideology,* 128–49.

44   Quoted in Foner, *Reconstruction,* 242.

45   *Cong. Globe,* 39th Cong., 1st Sess. 222 (July 22, 1861).

46   Boyer was among several Democrats who quoted the joint resolution in its entirety in making the argument that Republican legislation was unconstitutional. *Cong. Globe,* 39th Cong., 1st Sess. 2467 (May 8). Cox also made extended use of the 1861 resolution. *Cong. Globe,* 38th Cong., 2nd Sess. 241 (Jan. 12, 1865).

47   *Cong. Globe,* 39th Cong., 1st Sess. 2408 (May 5).

48   *Cong. Globe,* 39th Cong., 1st Sess. 1008, 1012 [Fessenden] (Feb. 24); 1073, 1088 (Bingham, Feb. 28).

49   *Cong. Globe,* 39th Cong., 1st Sess. 1075 (Feb. 28).

50   *Cong. Globe,* 39th Cong., 1st Sess. 1619 (March 24).

51   See Cheever's speech, quoted in Hyman, *The Radical Republicans,* 341, in which he worries about "a reconstruction of white oligarchies" and a reduction of blacks to "serfdom."

52   *Cong. Globe,* 39th Cong., 1st Sess. 2540 (May 10).

53   *Cong. Globe,* 39th Cong., 1st Sess. 2092 (Thomas, April 21).

54   U.S. Constitution, amend. 14, sec. 2. "Representatives shall be apportioned among the several States according to their respective numbers, counting the whole number of persons in each State, excluding Indians not taxed. But when the right to vote at any election for the choice of electors for President and Vice-President of the United States, Representatives in Congress, the Executive and Judicial officers of a State, or the members of the Legislature thereof, is denied

to any of the male inhabitants of such State, being twenty-one years of age, and citizens of the United States, or in any way abridged, except for participation in rebellion, or other crime, the basis of representation therein shall be reduced in the proportion which the number of such male citizens shall bear to the whole number of male citizens twenty-one years of age in such State."

55 Fairman has pointed out a number of problems with the general language of sec. 2 (*Reconstruction and Reunion I*, 1265–69).

56 *Cong. Globe,* 39th Cong., 1st Sess. 2463 (Garfield, May 8); 2464 (Thayer, May 8); 2503 (Raymond, May 9); 2508 (Boutwell, May 9); 2510 (Miller, May 9); 2537 (Longyear, May 10).

57 *Cong. Globe,* 39th Cong., 1st Sess. 2690, 2691 (Morris, May 19).

58 *Cong. Globe,* 39th Cong., 1st Sess. 2410 (Lawrence, May 5).

59 *Cong. Globe,* 39th Cong., 1st Sess. 2533 (May 10).

60 *Cong. Globe,* 39th Cong., 1st Sess. 2252 (Higby); 1159 (Windom, May 28).

61 *Cong. Globe,* 39th Cong., 1st Sess. 1012, 1013 (Feb. 24).

62 *Cong. Globe,* 39th Cong., 1st Sess. 2084. In Hyman's collection of Radical Republican speeches and writings, statements to this effect are found consistently. *The Radical Republicans,* 258 (Boutwell); 266–67 (Grosvenor); 297 (Schurz); 324 (Stevens); 361 (Prentiss).

63 *A Compromise of Principle,* 40–41, 107.

64 For a general discussion of both Republican views on racial differences and Republican policies that demanded basic rights for blacks, see Foner, *Free Soil,* 261–300. Foner discusses Radical Reconstruction and civil rights policies in *Reconstruction,* 239–51.

65 *Cong. Globe,* 39th Cong., 1st Sess. 2404 (Ingersoll, May 5).

66 *Cong. Globe,* 39th Cong., 1st Sess. 2404.

67 *Cong. Globe,* 39th Cong., 1st Sess. 2773 (Eliot, May 23).

68 *Cong. Globe,* 39th Cong., 1st Sess. 2334–35 (Sumner, May 2).

69 *Cong. Globe,* 39th Cong., 1st Sess. 2774–78 (May 23).

70 Hyman, *The Radical Republicans,* 345–47.

71 See Amar, "The Bill of Rights," 1218–26; Richard L. Aynes, "On Misreading John Bingham and the Fourteenth Amendment," 103 *Yale Law Journal* 57 (1993), 66–74.

72 *Cong. Globe,* 39th Cong., 1st Sess. 2542 (May 10).

73 *Cong. Globe,* 39th Cong., 1st Sess. 2459 (May 8).

74 *Cong. Globe,* 39th Cong., 1st Sess. 2459, italics added (May 8). See also Hyman, *The Radical Republicans,* 40 [George Julian citing "error" in the original Constitution]. Charles Fairman asserted that Stevens's remarks give "no aid" (*Reconstruction and Reunion I*, 1284).

75 Hyman, *The Radical Republicans,* 248.

76 According to Lewis Coser, Halbwachs's work in the sociology of knowledge constitutes his most important contribution to sociological thought. Coser, "Introduction," *On Collective Memory,* ed. and trans. Lewis A. Coser (Chicago: University of Chicago Press, 1992), 1.

77 Halbwachs, *On Collective Memory,* 86.

78 Ackerman, *We the People,* 83.

79 Stephen Skorownek explains that Lincoln installed the repudiation-as-affirmation reconstructive trope. The repudiation of slavery was an affirmation of original polity principles. Of course, the exact definitions of both "original principles" and "slavery's repudiation" had been left open. *The Politics Presidents Make,* 208, 206–11, 220–21.

80 William H. Riker, *The Strategy of Rhetoric: Campaigning for the American Constitution* (New Haven, Conn.: Yale University Press, 1986), 9.

4   The Supreme Court's Official History

1   *Slaughter-House Cases,* 83 U.S. at 71. See also *United States v. Mosley* (the Fourteenth Amendment "was adopted with a view to the protection of the colored race . . .") 238 U.S. at 387; *Screws v. United States* ("Undoubtedly, the necessary protection of the new freedom was the most powerful impulse behind the Fourteenth Amendment") 325 U.S. at 140.

2   Robert H. Bork, *The Tempting of America: The Political Seduction of the Law* (New York: Free Press, 1990), 37, 166. See also, e.g., Michael Les Benedict, "Preserving Federalism: Reconstruction and the Waite Court," 1978 *Supreme Court Review* 39, 60 ("virtually eliminating the Privileges and Immunities Clause as a source of national power"); Walter F. Murphy, "*Slaughter-House,* Civil Rights, and Limits on Constitutional Change," 32 *American Journal of Jurisprudence* 1, 2 (1987) ("gutted the privileges or immunities clause"), Loren Beth, "The *Slaughter-House Cases* Revisited," 23 *Louisiana Law Review* 487 (1963); Howard Graham, "Our 'Declaratory' Fourteenth Amendment," in *Everyman's Constitution* (1968), 319–35.

3   See, esp. Benedict, "Preserving Federalism." Benedict emphasizes the Waite Court's recognition of congressional authority under the Thirteenth Amendment to protect rights when offenses are motivated by race.

4   109 U.S. 3 (1883). In *Civil Rights Cases,* the constitutionality of the Civil Rights Act of 1875 was at issue. The first section of this act provided, "That all persons within the jurisdiction of the United States shall be entitled to the full and equal enjoyment of the accommodations, advantages, facilities, and privileges of inns, public conveyances on land or water, theatres, and other places of amusement; subject only to the conditions and limitations established by law, and applicable alike to citizens of every race and color, regardless of any previous condition of servitude." The second section of the act made it a penal offense to deny any citizen of any race or color, regardless of previous servitude, any of the accommodations or privileges mentioned in the first section. The Court denied that Congress had the constitutional power to make this law.

5   Justice Joseph Bradley suggested, in dictum, that Congress might have power to prohibit racial discrimination in public accommodations under the commerce clause ["whether Congress, in the exercise of its power to regulate commerce amongst the several States, might or might not pass a law regulating rights in public conveyances passing from one State to another, is . . . a ques-

tion which is not now before us" 109 U.S. at 19]. In 1964 the Court sustained the public accommodation section of the 1964 Civil Rights Act on commerce clause grounds. *Heart of Atlanta Motel v. United States* 379 U.S. 241 (1964).

6   Beth argues that Miller's eloquent articulation of the "one pervading purpose" of the Reconstruction Amendments (to secure full liberty to blacks) was merely "a strategic obfuscation of the issues." "*Slaughter-House Cases* Revisited," 501.

7   See also *Ex parte Virginia*, 100 U.S. 339 (1880), where the Court upheld the indictment of a state officer (a judge) for explicitly disqualifying prospective jurors on racial grounds alone.

8   William Wiecek, *Liberty Under Law* (Baltimore: Johns Hopkins University Press, 1988), 103.

9   *Slaughter-House Cases,* 83 U.S. at 67–68.

10 *Slaughter-House Cases,* 83 U.S. at 71. See also *United States v. Mosley* [the Fourteenth Amendment "was adopted with a view to the protection of the colored race . . ."), 238 U.S. at 387; *Screws v. United States* ("Undoubtedly, the necessary protection of the new freedmen was the most powerful impulse behind the Fourteenth Amendment"), 325 U.S. at 140.

11 See, in general, Jonathan Glickstein, *Concepts of Free Labor in Antebellum America* (New Haven, Conn.: Yale University Press, 1991).

12 83 U.S. at 82; emphasis in text added.

13 83 U.S. at 68.

14 Republicans argued that the federal government had authority to prohibit slavery in the territories. Many Republicans, especially radical abolitionists, argued against federal authority over the rendition of fugitive slaves. They asserted that states had the authority or right to determine the status of their own residents and ensure peaceable rendition. Federal authority over rendition translated, in practical terms, into giving slave-catchers broad latitude to use violence and kidnapping.

15 83 U.S. at 72.

16 83 U.S. at 73.

17 83 U.S. at 73.

18 83 U.S. at 74.

19 83 U.S. at 75.

20 Legal historian Wiecek argues that in this respect the situation in the South was left much as it had been before the Civil War. In his words, "the foxes now effectively ruled over the chicken coops." *Liberty Under Law,* 97.

21 Foner, *Reconstruction,* 530. Foner stated that incorporation was "a virtually noncontroversial minimum Congressional interpretation of the Amendment's purposes." *Reconstruction,* 533. Foner presents evidence that Republicans aimed to nationalize a segment of "fundamental" citizenship rights, but not the entire body of them. *Reconstruction,* 228–80.

22 Karl Llewelyn argued that cases must be seen in terms of their "maximum" and "minimum" values, how little or how much they could be used. These values, he emphasized, were widely separate. *Bramble Bush* (New York: Oceana, 1930), 72–74.

23   83 U.S. at 78, 82. *Slaughter-House Cases* made the first declarations of this sort, stating that such changes in the "main features of the general system" were "unthinkable." Many cases repeated this declaration. *U.S. v. Cruikshank* 92 U.S. at 549–50. In *Maxwell v. Dow* the Court stated that the Fourteenth Amendment "did not radically change the whole theory of the relationship of the states and federal government to each other." 176 U.S. at 593. In 1945, Justice William Douglas repeated that the Fourteenth Amendment "did not alter the basic relations between the states and the national government" and cited the cases *U.S. v. Harris* 106 U.S. 629 and *In re Kemmler* 136 U.S. 436, 438. *Screws v. United States* 325 U.S. at 109. The dissenting opinion in *Screws* also denied that fundamental change in the state-national relation was wrought with the Fourteenth Amendment, 325 U.S. at 142–44.

24   83 U.S. at 78; emphasis added.

25   83 U.S. at 82; emphasis added.

26   83 U.S. at 96, Field, J., dissenting.

27   Justice Bradley suggested this as well. He, too, used the term "freeman" with frequency. 83 U.S. at 114, 116, 119.

28   Richard L. Aynes, "Constricting the Law of Freedom: Justice Miller, the Fourteenth Amendment, and the *Slaughter-House Cases*," 70 *Chicago-Kent Law Review* 627 (1994), 671 n. 190.

29   "The Bill of Rights," 1271.

30   83 U.S. at 112, Bradley, J., dissenting. See also Bradley's opinion in *U.S. v. Hall* 26, Fed. Cases 79 (No. 15, 282) C.C.S.D. Ala. (1871), 81. "By the original constitution citizenship in the United States was a consequence of citizenship in a state. By this [citizenship] clause, this order of things is reversed."

31   83 U.S. at 113.

32   Aynes offers a similar observation in "Constricting the Law of Freedom," 642. "In essence, Bradley argued that Miller had missed the purposes and result of the Union victory in the Civil War."

33   83 U.S. at 123.

34   83 U.S. at 116.

35   83 U.S. at 114.

36   83 U.S. at 121.

37   83 U.S. at 122.

38   In *Hall* a federal grand jury in Mobile, Alabama, found that during the election campaign in the autumn of 1870 the suspects, out of political and racial animosity, raided a political meeting of black Republicans. Two people were killed, and more than fifty others were injured. As a result of the grand jury's findings, the defendants were indicted and charged under the Enforcement Act of 1870, which was primarily aimed at securing the Fifteenth Amendment right of citizens to vote free from racially motivated interference by the state and by private individuals and groups. The Ku Klux Klan Act of 1871 was a more elaborate legislative attempt to ensure against violations by conspiratorial terrorist groups such as the Klan, of nationally enforceable political and civil rights of

U.S. citizens. Robert Kaczorowski argues that *Hall* accurately reflected legislative intent. Akhil Amar calls *Hall* "perhaps the most illuminating case arising under Congressional legislation [between 1868–73]." "The Bill of Rights," 1253–60. See Fairman on this case, *Reconstruction and Reunion II,* 188–93.

39   26 Fed. Cas. at 82.

40   25 Fed. Cases 707 (no. 14,897) (C.C.D.La. 1874), 714. Benedict, "Preserving Federalism," 73, notes that "Waite took the position which Bradley had developed in his Cruikshank circuit court opinion," but Benedict makes no mention of this quote from Bradley. Waite acknowledged that the right to assemble *for the purposes of petitioning Congress* was a right of national citizenship, but Waite expressly denied that the general assembly right was a right of national citizenship. "[T]he right of the people to assemble for lawful purposes . . . was originally placed [with the States], and it has never been surrendered to the United States." 92 U.S. at 552.

41   Bradley's views on the Fourteenth Amendment shifted. He started out with a relatively broad vision, but he later supported a narrower view. Fairman was an admirer of Justice Bradley, but only after Bradley's views of the Fourteenth Amendment shifted. Fairman attributes Bradley's shift to a continuing search for the truth. *Reconstruction and Reunion II,* 1379 n. 211, 1362. Hyman states that Bradley's shift "mirrored the national mood which wanted stability and national reconciliation." *A More Perfect Union,* 415–16.

42   83 U.S. at 128, 129.

43   83 U.S. at 125. See also Justice Noah Swayne's opinion in *Rhodes* 27 Fed. Cas. 785 (No. 16,151) C.C. KY (1867), 788 ["The thirteenth amendment . . . trenches directly upon the power of the states and of the people in the states"].

44   27 Fed. Cas. at 788. See Fairman's negative comment on *Rhodes* in *Reconstruction and Reunion I,* 1309.

45   27 Fed. Cas. at 793.

46   27 Fed. Cas. at 794.

47   27 Fed. Cas. at 788.

48   Aynes, "Constricting the Law of Freedom," 672–74.

49   *Maxwell v. Dow* 176 U.S. 581, 601–2 (1900).

50   Llewellyn, *The Bramble Bush,* 63.

51   In discussing the Supreme Court's view of postwar national authority, different kinds of situations are at issue, e.g., an increase in congressional authority to legislate on behalf of citizenship rights laws (*Cruikshank, Civil Rights Cases*) and an increase in federal judicial authority to strike down state laws (*Slaughter-House Cases, Strauder*). Two sorts of disputes are actually going on: federal-state and judicial-legislative. Federalism refers to the distribution of authority between the national/federal government and the states, and federal power usually means legislative power conferred upon the national Congress by the Constitution. Federal courts, such as the Supreme Court, exert national power, though judicial power is often addressed along the judicial-legislative axis. Of course, federal-state disputes and legislative-judicial dis-

putes cut across each other. This cross-matching renders references to "in-creased national power" imprecise with reference to national legislative power and/or national judicial power.

52   Llewellyn, *The Bramble Bush*, 63.

53   Robert Kaczorowski, *The Politics of Judicial Interpretation: The Federal Courts, the Department of Justice, and Civil Rights, 1866–1876* (New York: Oceana, 1985), 6–7. Congress established the circuit courts in 1869. The circuit judges were more committed to vigorous enforcement of federal laws, unlike eight of the eleven district judges who were Democrats or opposed to the administration's policy, or both.

54   21 *Northern Kentucky Law Review* 41, 115–16.

55   *U.S. v. Rhodes*, 27 Fed. Cases 785 (No. 16, 151) C. C. Ky. (1867).

56   *John Blyew and George Kennard v. United States* 13 Wall. 581 (1872).

57   The reasons that follow are adapted from Duncan Kennedy, "Freedom and Constraint."

58   Kennedy, "Freedom and Constraint," 518.

59   Kennedy, "Freedom and Constraint," 518.

60   Kennedy, "Freedom and Constraint," 518.

61   Kennedy, "Freedom and Constraint," 548.

62   Kennedy, "Freedom and Constraint," 550.

63   See Aynes, "Constricting the Law of Freedom," 655–65 (on Miller's hostility to the Republicans).

64   92 U.S. 542 (1875). This case involved a level of violence tantamount to a localized civil war in Louisiana. Following the state elections in 1872, both the Republicans and the Democrats claimed victory. Appointees from each party claimed to be the legitimate officeholders, and the Republicans succeeded in gaining possession of the parish courthouse. Led by the Democratic appoint-ees, a "veritable army" of "old time Ku Klux Klan" stormed the courthouse and, according to federal investigators, killed and mutilated at least sixty black citi-zens after they had surrendered. The investigators reported that the Democrats viewed the conflict over local political offices as a "test of white supremacy." The investigators concluded that the black Republicans had been massacred as a political vendetta motivated by racial hatred. The U.S. Attorney at New Orleans, James Beckwith, pleaded with Attorney General George H. Williams to authorize the most vigorous prosecution under the Enforcement Acts. Wil-liams's initial support for prosecution quickly diminished when he learned how much federal assistance would cost because of the magnitude of the violence. This description comes from Kaczorowski, *The Politics of Judicial Interpreta-tion*, 176–77.

65   92 U.S. at 549–50.

66   92 U.S. at 555, 556.

67   92 U.S. at 552.

68   25 Fed. Cases at 715 ("The fifth and eighth counts are open to the . . . objection of vagueness and generality").

69   92 U.S. at 559.

70   25 Fed. Cases 707, 714.

71   Benedict, "Preserving Federalism," 72–73.

72   See, e.g., *Mills v. Green*, 159 U.S. 651 (1895); *Giles v. Harris*, 189 U.S. 475 (1903). See also *Barney v. City of New York* 193 U.S. 430 (1904) (state officers' violation of state law did not constitute state action). Benedict, "Preserving Federalism," 77–79, argues that the Waite Court's construction of congressional power under the constitutional amendments "hardly subverted Republican intent." He lays responsibility at the feet of the Melville Fuller Court justices. Of course, the Waite Court's construction of the Fourteenth Amendment is a different question.

73   Kaczorowski, *The Politics of Judicial Interpretation*, 112.

74   Northern resolve to implement civil rights legislation eroded for many reasons. Foner emphasizes that it was only because of a slackening Northern desire to implement changes that the Southern planter class was permitted to reemerge as a political power. Though they had economic dominance in the region, the Southerners' national influence had weakened. Northern states, like Southern ones, felt their own local autonomy threatened by federal civil rights legislation. Northerners, especially the emergent industrial middle class, also did not like the rising taxes produced by the Civil War debt, pensions, and the postwar activist national state. The depression of the 1870s and the drop in the world market price for cotton only aggravated the situation and seeded greater resentment of higher taxes. And federal prosecutions under the Enforcement Acts meant that the cost of running the courts reached an unprecedented height. Furthermore, Democrats denied that the Klan even existed, calling reports of Klan violence Republican falsehoods. This denial encouraged Northern belief that increasing federal expenditures were unnecessary and wasteful.

75   Kaczorowski, *The Politics of Judicial Interpretation*, 206–7, discusses the administration's arguments in greater detail.

76   Foner, *Reconstruction*, 597.

77   This, in effect, buttressed the power of the industrial middle class, which wanted to reconcile political democracy with the unequal distribution of property. W. E. B. DuBois makes this same point in *Black Reconstruction in America*, namely, that had white and black labor joined forces, they might have been able to exert more control over factory conditions and wages.

78   A West Virginia grand jury indicted Strauder, a black man, for murder, and a jury convicted him of that crime. State law forbade blacks to serve on trial juries. Strauder's lawyer argued to the state court that this statutory exclusion denied his client equal protection of the laws. The state court rejected this argument. However, the Supreme Court, in a decision written by Justice William Strong, granted a writ of error, saying the state court had been wrong. This description of the case and the quoted text are found in Walter P. Murphy, James Fleming, and William F. Harris, *American Constitutional Interpretation* (New York: Foundation Press, 1986).

79   109 U.S. 3 (1883), 24–25.

80   109 U.S. at 33, Harlan, J., dissenting.

81   109 U.S. at 34.

82   109 U.S. at 35.

83   109 U.S. at 46.

84   Citizenship played a central role in a series of dissents written by the elder Justice Harlan between 1883 and 1908. See, e.g., *Civil Rights Cases* 109 U.S. 3, 26 (1883); *Hurtado v. California* 110 U.S. 516, 538 (1884); *Maxwell v. Dow* 176 U.S. 581, 605 (1900); and *Twining v. New Jersey* 211 U.S. 78 (1908). Harlan is known for his famous dissent in *Plessy v. Ferguson* 163 U.S. 537, 552 (1896), which, like his other dissenting opinions, relied on a substantive and expansive notion of citizenship. While conservative jurists laud his *Plessy* dissent, they ignore Harlan's emphasis on postwar citizenship.

85   *Hurtado v. California* 110 U.S. 516, 541; *Maxwell v. Dow* 176 U.S. at 587, 600, 614.

86   25 Fed. Cas. at 711–14. "The war of race, whether it assumes the dimensions of civil strife or domestic violence, whether carried on in a guerrilla or predatory form, or by private combinations, or even by private outrage or intimidation, is subject to the jurisdiction of the government of the United States; and when any atrocity is committed which may be assigned to this cause it may be punished by the laws and in the courts of the United States; but any outrages, atrocities or conspiracies, whether against the colored race or the white race, which do not flow from this cause, but spring from the ordinary felonious or criminal intent which prompts to such unlawful acts, are not within the jurisdiction of the United States, but within the sole jurisdiction of the states. . . . This fundamental principle, I think, applies to both the 13th and 15th amendments," 714.

87   With regard to the Southern Redeemers who gained political and cultural power during the 1870s, Foner explains that no single generalization sums them up. The people who actively resisted Republican legislation comprised secessionist Democrats, veterans of the Confederacy and new leaders, the reemergent planter class, and Union Whigs. What many of them shared was a commitment to dismantling Reconstruction, reducing if not eliminating the political power of blacks, and regaining control over the South's legal system. Planters, of course, wanted to restore their control over the labor force. Many white Southerners had no love lost for the elite planters, given the planters' economic and political strength (although they were not nearly as rich and powerful as before the war). This conflict does not mean that these whites allied themselves with Southern blacks, although some did. A Southern newspaper declared in 1875 that the Fourteenth and Fifteenth Amendments "may stand forever; but we intend to make them dead letters on the statute book." Quoted in Foner, *Reconstruction,* 590.

88   Quoted in Wiecek, *Liberty Under Law,* 102.

89   Foner, *Reconstruction,* 588.

90   See Kennedy's discussion on types of field configurations, "Freedom and Constraint," 538–44.

91   *Maxwell v. Dow* 176 U.S. 581, 591.

92   176 U.S. at 593.

93   *Maxwell v. Dow* 176 U.S. at 590.

94   Amar, "The Bill of Rights," 1276–78.

95   Jennifer Nedelsky, *Private Property and the Limits of American Constitutionalism* (Chicago: University of Chicago Press, 1990).

96   The Supreme Court's use of the Fourteenth Amendment to defend property rights in the late nineteenth century is well known and is regarded by many legal scholars as a perversion of the amendment. But these late nineteenth-century cases were, in a sense, a possible extension of the original Madisonian framework, since property rights in the original framework were central. The Republican provision of a new set of institutional directives to the federal courts—namely, pay attention to practices that enforce exclusion and second-class citizenship—is very different from the directives provided by the Founders. Of course, the kinds of property one owned in 1780 were vastly different from the property owned in 1890. The Founders' institutional directives were certainly stretched by the Court in its use of original notions of "liberty" contained in the due process clause (but not beyond recognition) in the late nineteenth century.

97   Categories and hierarchies of rights were part of the Founders' solution to the problem of balancing republican principles with protections for property. As Nedelsky explains, "Civil rights (which were defined narrowly as the right to property, the right to sue and the right to testify in court) were to be distinguished from political rights. Political rights, moreover, were conceived as a mere means to the true end of government, the protection of civil rights. In this view, political rights had no intrinsic value. By designating political rights as means, it was possible to treat them as purely instrumental and entirely contingent, and thus to make compromises of these rights appear not to involve compromise of principle." Nedelsky, *Private Property and the Limits of American Constitutionalism*, 5.

98   The idea that the Supreme Court should give extra scrutiny to the political process has been criticized by Robert Bork as illegitimate. Justice Harlan F. Stone's famous footnote 4 in *Carolene Products* 304 U.S. 144 (1938), in which Stone suggested that unusual scrutiny be given to political processes that could not ordinarily be assumed to protect "discrete and insular minorities," serves as a springboard for John Hart Ely's defense of judicial review as a representation-reinforcing task. See Ely, *Democracy and Distrust* (Cambridge, Mass.: Harvard University Press 1980). Bork criticizes both Ely's representation-reinforcing model and Justice Stone's "new" constitutional doctrine, calling them invitations to judicial activism and policy-making. What is being argued here is that Republicans opened political dialogue about what it meant to belong to "the people." Only justices in the minority (Bradley, Swayne, and Harlan) preserved this principle.

99   The statutory exclusion of black men from juries was unconstitutional. *Strauder v. West Virginia* 100 U.S. 303 (1880). The unequal application of a facially neutral statute was unconstitutional. *Yick Wo v. Hopkins* 118 U.S. 356 (1886).

100 176 U.S. at 601–2.

101 See, e.g., *Screws v. United States* 325 U.S. 91 (1944). This case involved a Georgia sheriff and two deputies who arrested a thirty-year-old black man under
questionable circumstances and then beat him to death after he had been
handcuffed. The sheriff challenged his conviction under sec. 20 of the Criminal Code (18 U.S.C. 52), which derived from sec. 2 of the Civil Rights Act of
1866 and contained language from the Ku Klux Klan Act of 1871. The justices
debated the history of sec. 20 as they considered the question of whether the
abuse of authorized power by state officials and agents infringing on rights
granted by the Constitution counted as "state action" under the Fourteenth
Amendment. A majority of justices (Douglas, Stone, Hugo Black, Stanley F.
Reed, Wiley B. Rutledge, and Frank Murphy) answered in the affirmative. Justices Felix Frankfurter, Robert Jackson, and Owen J. Roberts responded in the
negative. The dissenters' reference to the "familiar history that much of [Recon-
struction] legislation was born of that vengeful spirit which to no small degree
envenomed the Reconstruction era" testifies to the strength of Dunning School
history, which was itself rooted in Democratic portraits of the Republicans.

5   Dueling Histories: Fairman and Crosskey Reconstruct "Original Understanding"

1   U.S. Constitution, amend. 14, sec. 1. "All persons born or naturalized in the
United States, and subject to the jurisdiction thereof, are citizens of the United
States and of the State wherein they reside. No State shall make or enforce any
law which shall abridge the privileges or immunities of citizens of the United
States; nor shall any State deprive any person of life, liberty, or property, without due process of law; nor deny to any person within its jurisdiction the equal
protection of the laws."

2   William E. Nelson, "History and Neutrality in Constitutional Adjudication,"
72 *Virginia Law Review* 1237, 1253 (1986).

3   See, e.g., Amar, "The Bill of Rights," 1239. "Though [Fairman's] work has drawn
much praise, in my view Professor Fairman was a rather un-Fair-man in assessing the evidence for incorporation."

4   Between 1878 and 1928 a number of legal commentators, including William
Guthrie (1898) and Horace Flack (1908), argued that the Supreme Court's decisions were contrary to the intent of the Republican framers. See Richard Aynes,
"Constricting the Law of Freedom: Justice Miller, The Fourteenth Amendment,
and the *Slaughter-House Cases*," 70 *Chicago-Kent Law Review* 2 (1994), 681–85.
Even commentators who approved the Court's Reconstruction era decisions
thought the Court was wrong about "original intent." See, e.g., Charles Collins,
The Fourteenth Amendment and the States (1912), 15. These commentaries were
part of the context in which Fairman justified the Court's decisions.

5   See, e.g., Vicki Schultz, "Telling Stories About Women and Work," 103 *Harvard
Law Review* 1750 (1991).

6   See, e.g., Kimberle Crenshaw, "Demarginalizing the Intersection of Race and

Sex," *University of Chicago Legal Forum* (1988); Martha Mahoney, "Whiteness and Women, in Practice and Theory," 5 *Yale Journal of Law and Feminism* 2 (1991); Angela P. Harris, "Race and Essentialism in Feminist Legal Theory," 42 *Stanford Law Review* 581 (1992).

7   Cass Sunstein, "On Analogical Reasoning," 106 *Harvard Law Review* 741 (1993), 773.

8   Catharine MacKinnon's critique (1987, 1989) of liberal legalism is implicitly a critique of a collection of symbolic elements. MacKinnon, however, does not offer a step-by-step analysis of how the various conceptual elements that make up liberal legalism interact to produce legal decisions that miss, for example, the harm of pornography and hate speech.

9   Felix Cohen, "Transcendental Nonsense and the Functional Approach," 35 *Columbia Law Review* 6 (1935), 846.

10   Scheppele takes up the question, When does a story begin? She discusses how the boundaries of legal narratives are shaped by "legal habits." The traditional legal strategy looks (narrowly) to when "the trouble" began, i.e., the set of events that gave rise to the question at hand. "Foreword: Telling Stories," 87 *Michigan Law Review* 8 (1989), 2094–97.

11   Stanley Fish makes the point that "within a set of interpretive assumptions, to know what you can do is, ipso facto, to know what you can't do; indeed, you can't know one without the other; they come together in a diacritical package, indissolubly wed." *Is There a Text in This Class?* (Cambridge, Mass.: Harvard University Press, 1980), 356.

12   See Paul Brest, "The Misconceived Quest for Original Understanding," 60 *Boston University Law Review* 204 (1980).

13   Fish conceptualizes interpretation as a structure of constraints and discusses how interpreters supply "predetermined contexts." It is against these contexts that "utterances" are made meaningful. *Is There a Text in This Class,* 303–21.

14   See the dissenting opinions of Justices Frank Murphy and Wiley Rutledge in *Adamson,* 332 U.S. 46, 123–25. Amar articulates a different view, arguing that the privileges or immunities clause includes "both more and less than Amendments I–VIII," "The Bill of Rights," 1228. Amar terms this a "refined incorporation" position and identifies it as closest to Ely's view, *Democracy and Distrust,* 22–30.

15   Goffman's study of frames made no claims to be talking about core matters of sociology—social organization and social structure. "Those matters," he said "have been and can continue to be quite nicely studied without reference to frame at all" (*Frame Analysis,* 13). Kenneth Burke, a literary critic (but claimed by a University of Chicago book series to belong to the "heritage of sociology"), goes further than Goffman in linking the study of frames to the study of social structure. For an introduction to Burke's writings on symbols and social relations and a discussion of his influence on sociologists, including Goffman, see Joseph R. Gusfield, ed., *On Symbols and Society* (Chicago: University of Chicago Press, 1989), 1–49.

16   Woolgar, *Science: The Very Idea,* 67–82. See also Bruno Latour's discussion, "Writing Texts That Withstand the Assaults of a Hostile Environment," *Science in Action* (Cambridge, Mass.: Harvard University Press, 1987), 45–62.

17   *United States v. Classic* 313 U.S. 299 (1942); *United States v. Screws* 325 U.S. 91 (1944). From 1936 until 1947 the Supreme Court handed down a series of cases that required states to guarantee sections of the First and Sixth Amendments.

18   *Adamson v. California* 332 U.S. 46, 68–123 (1947). See also *Betts v. Brady* 316 U.S. 455, 474 (1942) (Black, J., dissenting) and *Duncan v. Louisiana* 391 U.S. 45, 162–71 (1968) (Black, J., dissenting).

19   Technically, the question of incorporation and questions of the federal-state relation are not synonymous. But the two ideas intersect at the point of national citizenship rights. Generally speaking, the incorporation view is associated with greater national protection for citizenship.

20   *Adamson v. California,* 332 U.S. at 71 (1947).

21   *Palko v. Connecticut* 302 U.S. 319 (1937).

22   332 U.S. 46, 59–68 (Frankfurter, J., concurring).

23   Crosskey's book, *Politics and the Constitution* (Chicago: University of Chicago Press, 1953), 1171, 1381, n. 11, contained his first response to Fairman's 1949 article. Crosskey's 1954 article was a more elaborate and detailed response.

24   Harold M. Hyman, "Federalism: Legal Fiction and Historical Artifact?" 1987 *Brigham Young University Law Review* 905, 924.

25   Curtis discusses the influence of Fairman on scholarship in *No State Shall Abridge,* 110–13. Richard L. Aynes also discusses the Fairman-Crosskey conflict in "Charles Fairman, Felix Frankfurter, and the Fourteenth Amendment," 70 *Chicago-Kent Law Review* 3 (1995), 1243–56.

26   "The Most-Cited Law Review Articles," *California Law Review.*

27   *Bartkus v. Illinois* U.S. 121, 124 (1959).

28   Alexander Bickel, "The Original Understanding and the Segregation Cases," 69 *Harvard Law Review* 1 (1955), 102. Fairman was Frankfurter's student, and Bickel was Frankfurter's clerk. For a discussion of the Harvard connection among the three of them, see Aynes, "Fairman, Frankfurter, and the Fourteenth Amendment," 1199–1209.

29   Justice Harlan cited Fairman's article in his concurring opinion to *Griswold v. Connecticut* 381 U.S. at 479 (1965). Harlan also cited the article in a dissenting opinion, *Duncan v. Louisiana* 391 U.S. at 174, 188 (1968).

30   Michael Perry, "Interpretivism, Freedom of Expression, and Equal Protection," 42 *Ohio State Law Journal* 261 (1981), 286.

31   Michael Kammen, *A Machine That Would Go of Itself: The Constitution in American Culture* (New York: Knopf, 1986), 345.

32   Aynes cites John P. Frank, Robert Munro, and John Harrison as some of the scholars who articulated a negative view of Bingham. On the other side, he lines up David Donald, Howard Graham, and Stanley Kutler as supporters of Crosskey's more positive assessment of Bingham. "On Misreading John Bingham," 59.

33 Curtis, *No State Shall Abridge,* 3.

34 Raoul Berger, *Government by Judiciary* (Norman: University of Oklahoma Press, 1977), 413.

35 Simmel observed years ago that conflict socializes its participants. For a discussion on how participation in scientific debate reflects and reproduces commitments to certain paths of action and thought, see Susan Leigh Star's introduction to a special issue of *Social Problems* 35:3 (1989), 94–95, 121.

36 Fish, *Is There a Text in This Class?,* 309.

37 See, e.g., Horwitz's argument "Foreword" that originalism is unable to cope with the crisis of legitimacy, which has followed the modernist insight that meanings are fluid and historically changing. Horwitz associates "modernism" with legal realism, Peter Berger and Thomas Luckmann's *The Social Construction of Reality* (New York: Anchor Books, 1967) and Thomas Kuhn's *The Structure of Scientific Revolutions* (Chicago: University of Chicago Press, 1970). While the dominant metaphor for constitutional thinking, Newtonian mechanics, has been condemned as "static" since the 1890s by those who view the Constitution "as organism not a mechanism" (Kammen, *A Machine That Would Go of Itself,* 16–22), Horwitz argues that the tension between modernism and the desire for fundamentality has reached a crisis point where the Court evades its legitimacy dilemma by taking refuge in highly technical formulae and reified concepts (Horwitz, "Foreword," 116–17).

38 For a discussion of how the imposition of context and the making of sense occur simultaneously, see Fish, *Is There a Text in This Class?,* 313.

39 While Fairman's Fourteenth Amendment history defended state autonomy on matters of citizenship, Fairman was a nationalist on matters involving business and labor regulation. He sought to justify the expansion of federal regulation of commerce. For a discussion on the nationalist strand of Fairman's thought, see Aynes, "Charles Fairman, Felix Frankfurter, and the Fourteenth Amendment," 1203–4.

40 Fairman, *Mr. Justice Miller and the Supreme Court, 1862–1890* (Cambridge, Mass.: Harvard University Press, 1939).

41 Fairman, "The Supreme Court and the Constitutional Limitations on State Governmental Authority," 21 *University of Chicago Law Review* 40 (1953).

42 Fairman, "A Reply to Professor Crosskey," 22 *University of Chicago Law Review* 144 (1954).

43 Fairman, *Reconstruction and Reunion I* (1971), in vol. 6 of *History of the Supreme Court of the United States,* ed. Paul A. Freund (New York: Macmillan, 1971); Charles Fairman, *Reconstruction and Reunion II* (1987), in vol. 7 of *History of the Supreme Court of the United States,* ed. Paul A. Freund and Stanley Katz (New York: Macmillan, 1987).

44 *Politics and the Constitution,* 1056. "The decision of the Court [in *Barron*] and the doctrine for which it stands constitute one of the most extensive and indefensible of all the various failures of the Court to enforce the Constitution against the states as the document was written." *Politics and the Constitution,*

1081. See Amar, "The Bill of Rights and the Fourteenth Amendment," 1200 nn. 29, 30, for a succinct critique of Crosskey's claim about incorporation in the original Constitution.

45 *Politics and the Constitution,* 1381.

46 See Amar, "The Bill of Rights," 1197 (referring to Justice Frankfurter's "utter disregard of the language and history of the privileges or immunities clause").

47 83 U.S. (7 Pet.) 243 (1833).

48 Of course, both catholics and protestants approach the text interpretively, with imaginations informed by taken-for-granted assumptions. The distinction between catholics and protestants is useful for mapping the different ways by which interpreters ascribe authority to their counterparts, that is, how they locate sources of authority and meaning. Fairman and Crosskey used different strategies for locating sources of interpretive authority. It is important to emphasize, however, that interpreters are rarely if ever catholic or protestant on all questions. Catholic and protestant views on constitutional meaning are situational. While Fairman's approach to constitutional meaning was catholic on the question of incorporation, his approach turned protestant when he considered post–New Deal Court decisions. Crosskey took a protestant approach to the meaning of the original Constitution and the Fourteenth Amendment, but he was less disposed to reject Court cases in the 1940s that expanded national power. It was Fairman's and Crosskey's framing assumptions that shaped their "religiousity" on particular questions.

49 Amar, "The Bill of Rights," 1203–12.

50 Fairman, "The Supreme Court and the Constitutional Limitations on State Governmental Authority," 44–77. Fairman cited Madison, events of the First Congress in which the Bill of Rights was proposed in 1789, records of state conventions in which the Constitution was ratified, and case law affirming the *Barron* decision.

51 Fairman, "Does the Fourteenth Amendment Incorporate the Bill of Rights?" 36; *Reconstruction and Reunion I,* 1124, 1275, 1301.

52 *Prigg v. Pennsylvania* (1842) complicates this even further, for it provided the one exception to this general rule. The fugitive slave clause was contained in art. 4, sec. 2, in addition to the privileges and immunities clause. In *Prigg,* the Court offered a federal remedy when states infringed on the right to the return of fugitive slaves. (The Pennsylvania legislature had provided jury trials for accused fugitives; the Court exercised national judicial authority in striking down this state legislation.) Thus, the right to the return of fugitive slaves was the first fundamental right ever to receive the protection of the national judiciary. A federal remedy for violations of slave property rights lies under art. 4, sec. 2. The nonenforcement doctrine of art. 4, sec. 2, would have extended to the fugitive slave issue. Fairman has regarded Prigg as debunking the antislavery theory on which incorporation rested (the nonenforcement doctrine of art. 4, sec. 2, wherein no federal enforcement authority was provided for state violations of rights.)

53 Numerous scholars since the mid-1980s have presented evidence of antebellum and postbellum Republican criticisms of slavery, namely, that slavery led to denials of Bill of Rights guarantees. See, e.g., Curtis, *No State Shall Abridge,* 36; Hyman and Wiecek, *Equal Justice Under Law,* 15; Amar, "The Bill of Rights," 1275 ("Slavery led to state repudiation of virtually every one of the Bill's rights and freedoms, most definitely including the Bill's 'inestimable privilege' of juries — grand, petit and civil — in cases involving liberty"). See also Jacobus ten Broek, *Antislavery Origins of the Fourteenth Amendment* (Berkeley: University of California Press, 1951), 38–39, 125–26. Amar, "The Bill of Rights," 1276, notes that Republican congressmen invoked Southern violations of Bill of Rights guarantees many times in many contexts.

54 Fairman, *Reconstruction and Reunion I,* 1301; emphasis in the text added.

55 A key speech took place on February 28, 1866, in which Bingham referred to *Barron* twelve times. *Cong. Globe,* 39th Cong., 1st Sess., 1088–94. During a later speech, Bingham referred to *Barron* six times. *Cong. Globe,* 39th Cong., 1st Sess., 1291–93.

56 *Cong. Globe,* 39th Cong., 1st Sess., 1089–90. Quoted in Fairman, "Does the Fourteenth Amendment Incorporate the Bill of Rights?" 34. Justice Black cited this same passage in the appendix he attached to his decision, stating, "With full knowledge of the import of the *Barron* decision, the framers and backers of the Fourteenth Amendment proclaimed its purpose to be to overturn the rule the case had announced." *Adamson v. California* 332 U.S. at 95–96.

57 Fairman, "Fourteenth Amendment," 34. Bingham was in "deep error" regarding *Barron,* according to Fairman, *Reconstruction and Reunion I,* 1289.

58 Fairman, "Fourteenth Amendment," 26. Fairman later implied that the Republicans were incompetent framers and displayed low levels of understanding of the law, *Reconstruction and Reunion I,* 1274, 1276.

59 In his 1971 history of Reconstruction, Fairman referred to the "unschooled jurisprudence of the abolitionists." *Reconstruction and Reunion I,* 1136. Fairman labeled Bingham's mode of thought as "peculiar." *Reconstruction and Reunion I,* 1270, 1288, n. 5). See Aynes, "On Misreading John Bingham," 66, n. 54 (a summary of sources documenting praise for Bingham's intellectual abilities).

60 Fairman, "Fourteenth Amendment," 51.

61 Fairman, "Fourteenth Amendment," 53.

62 Fairman called Bingham's speech (39th Cong., 1st Sess., 2541) a "confused discourse." *Reconstruction and Reunion I,* 1287. Fairman called Bingham's speech (39th Cong., 1st Sess., 1034) a "jumbled exposition," *Reconstruction and Reunion I,* 1275.

63 *Reconstruction and Reunion I* at 1164–65, 1167.

64 *Reconstruction and Reunion I* at 96, 1161, 1160.

65 Aynes, "Fairman, Frankfurter, and the Fourteenth Amendment," 1204.

66 Four legal writers published constitutional law treatises in 1867–68. Three of the treatises support the incorporation thesis. Farrar also believed that the original Constitution forbade slavery (a widely rejected view), and Fairman

used this negative response to delegitimate Farrar's support for the incorporation thesis. He referred to Farrar's incorporation thesis as "an example of what
can be practiced through a zeal to redress injustice." *Reconstruction and Reunion I*, 1129. Fairman said nothing about Paschal and Pomeroy's support for
incorporation. See Aynes, "On Misreading John Bingham," 83–91.

67 Hyman and Wiecek, *Equal Justice Under Law,* 409; Curtis, *No State Shall
Abridge,* 172–73; Kaczorowski, *The Politics of Judicial Interpretation,* 863, 932.

68 *Wisconsin Law Review* 479, 493.

69 Wiecek, *Antislavery Constitutionalism,* 7.

70 Presenting the Fourteenth Amendment to the Senate, Jacob Howard discussed
the "privileges and immunities" of citizens. After quoting a passage in *Corfield
v. Coryell* (1823), Howard stated, "To these privileges and immunities . . . should
be added the personal rights guarantied and secured by the first eight amendments of the Constitution." *Cong. Globe,* 39th Cong., 1st Sess., 2765 (1866).

71 *Politics and the Constitution,* 1084, 1090, 1096, 1126, 1133.

72 *Politics and the Constitution,* 1076. Crosskey called *Barron* "one of the most extensive and indefensible of all the various failures of the Court to enforce the
Constitution against the states as the document was written" (1081).

73 Crosskey's dedication in *Politics and the Constitution* reads: "To the Congress of
the United States in the hope that it may be led to claim and exercise for the
common good of the country the powers justly belonging to it under the Constitution." Crosskey's central idea was that congressional power fell short of
what the original Constitution intended. The Court's illegitimate expansion of
states' rights had resulted in "cluttering" the powers of Congress "with a mass
of technicalities that make their exercise difficult, expensive and in no small
degree ineffectual." *Politics and the Constitution,* 1082.

74 Irving Brant, a biographer of James Madison and one of Crosskey's critics,
stated that "in spite of appalling misrepresentations, there is a vast amount of
sound reasoning in Mr. Crosskey's work." ("Mr. Crosskey and Mr. Madison,"
450). Perhaps the most "appalling misrepresentation" for which Crosskey was
criticized was his portrayal of Madison. In brief, Crosskey argued that Madison falsified his notes of the Constitutional Convention. If Crosskey's charges
were true, Brant observed (447), "Madison would be rated as one of the most
accomplished forgers in world's history. . . . To falsify the record, it would have
been necessary for Madison either to (1) Foresee in 1787 the issues raised in
1819 by the Missouri Compromise, and forestall them by misquoting a dozen
men in his original notes or (2) Replace four pages of the original manuscript
with fictitious notes written after 1819 on a black sheet of paper with the same
watermark as that used in 1787 and duplicate at about the age of 70 a youth-
ful handwriting which had disappeared from all his other writings." In spite of
Crosskey's portrayal of Madison, Brant hoped that the good in his work would
not be thrown away with the bad.

75 See Aynes, "Fairman, Frankfurter, and the Fourteenth Amendment," 1255,
n. 384, for an alternative view of how Crosskey could build a plausible view

of the Fourteenth Amendment and a less plausible view of the original Constitution. Aynes argues that Crosskey came closer to the truth in his Fourteenth Amendment history because he used traditional methods of interpretation that relied on "plain meaning."

76 Holmes, "The Path of the Law," address delivered at Boston University School of Law, January 8, 1897, Collected Papers, 1920, 173.

77 Crosskey, "Charles Fairman, Legislative History," 4–5.

78 Amar calls attention to this. "The Bill of Rights," 1223. See also Chester James Antieau, *The Original Understanding of the Fourteenth Amendment,* 38. Curtis also has researched language use, *No State Shall Abridge,* 64–65. Curtis argues that the words "rights," "liberties," and "privileges and immunities" were used interchangeably.

79 Curtis, some thirty years after Crosskey, offered similar instructions for "recovering" original intent. He stated that the meaning of the Fourteenth Amendment "should be sought in the abuses that produced it and in the political and legal philosophy of those who proposed it. The congressional debates are a further guide to meaning. In evaluating the debates, one should look primarily to those who supported the amendments and not primarily to statements of opponents. The remarks of leading proponents are entitled to great weight. And the greatest weight of all should be given to the statements of members of the committee that reported the amendment to Congress." *No State Shall Abridge,* 12–13. Curtis asserts, like Crosskey, that Fairman misread the evidence. "The major fault with Professor Fairman's effort to understand the Fourteenth Amendment is that it overlooked the antislavery origins of the amendment." *No State Shall Abridge,* 100.

80 See, e.g., Stevens's speech that identified "a defect" in the Constitution, which was that the Constitution did not limit the states with regard to matters of personal rights. Stevens represented the Civil War as springing from "the vicious principles incorporated into the institutions of our country." *Cong. Globe,* 39th Cong., 1st Sess., 2459.

81 Curtis relabeled Republican legal theories as "unorthodox." *No State Shall Abridge,* 46.

82 Crosskey, "Charles Fairman, Legislative History," 70.

83 Crosskey, "Charles Fairman, Legislative History," 11.

84 Crosskey, "Charles Fairman, Legislative History," 25.

85 Art. 4, sec. 2, contains the privileges and immunities clause of the original Constitution. Crosskey attributed to Republicans the belief that art. 4, sec. 2, guaranteed to each individual in every state the *full* body of rights that inhered in national citizenship. The Republican view of art. 4, sec. 2, according to Crosskey, was that it required states to guarantee the Bill of Rights. In 1940 the accepted view of art. 4, sec. 2, was that it *only* guaranteed to individuals the minimum rights which each state chose to grant its own residents; it did not grant a full body of national rights.

86 Crosskey attributed to Republicans the belief that the Fifth Amendment's due

process clause had always applied to the states. In 1940 the accepted view of the antebellum Fifth Amendment was that it did not bind the states. As evidence, Crosskey reprints Henry Wilson's speech on the Fifth Amendment which suggests that the Republicans intended to apply Fifth Amendment guarantees to the states.

87 Crosskey, "Charles Fairman, Legislative History," 8.

88 Quoted in Crosskey, "Charles Fairman, Legislative History," 29.

89 Crosskey, "Charles Fairman, Legislative History," 29–30.

90 Crosskey, "Charles Fairman, Legislative History," 81.

91 These assumptions still operated in 1971. See Fairman, *Reconstruction and Reunion I,* 1357–58.

92 Quoted in Crosskey, "Charles Fairman, Legislative History," 80.

93 Crosskey, "Charles Fairman, Legislative History," 80.

94 Crosskey, "Charles Fairman, Legislative History," 80.

95 The Court in *Adamson v. California* took a similar view. The Court emphasized the "contemporaneous knowledge" of the judges in *Slaughter-House.* Frankfurter stated that incorporation of the Bill of Rights "was rejected by judges who were themselves witnesses of the process" and were "duly regardful of the scope of the authority that was left to the states even after the Civil War." *Adamson v. California* 332 U.S. at 62.

96 Fairman, "Does the Fourteenth Amendment," 82–83.

97 Some commentators call this Fairman's "most credible argument." Aynes, "On Misreading John Bingham," 62, 94.

98 The term is Bourdieu's, *Outline of a Theory of Practice* (Cambridge: Cambridge University Press, 1977), 73.

99 Fairman, "Fourteenth Amendment," 137.

100 *Adamson v. California* 332 U.S. at 61–62, 64. Frankfurter said that the use of the due process clause would have been an "extraordinarily strange way of requiring grand juries."

101 See Amar, "The Bill of Rights," 1250 (reference to Fairman's "workhorse assumptions").

102 See, e.g., *Cong. Globe,* 39th Cong., 1st Sess., 988–91, 1056, 1064–65, 1152–55, 1262–72. Republicans were concerned about the abuse of official authority and expressed great skepticism about the trustworthiness of Southern authorities. Amar refers to Fairman's "anachronistic hostility to grand juries." "The Bill of Rights," 1247.

103 Frankfurter viewed the durability of precedent as a clear indicator of its acceptability. He emphasized the "unquestioned prestige the case *Twining v. New Jersey* (1908) had enjoyed for 40 years." The case rejected the claim that the Fourteenth Amendment applied the Fifth Amendment to the states. *Twining* stated that the privileges and immunities clause of the Fourteenth Amendment "did not forbid states to abridge the personal rights enumerated in the first eight amendments." *Twining v. New Jersey* 211 U.S. 78, 99.

104 Crosskey, "Charles Fairman, Legislative History," 71.

105 Crosskey, "Charles Fairman, Legislative History," 114.

106 In the standard legal debate over "original understanding," participants have typically drawn on either the state-centered or the nation-centered elements of Republican thought. Battle lines have been marked either/or. Harold M. Hyman and William E. Nelson stand out because they attempt to bridge the divide between both camps. Nelson argues that judges should heed the dual Republican "command to protect rights and to leave legislatures unfettered to adopt laws for the public good" (*The Fourteenth Amendment*, 11). But even with equality defined as a "master concept that best gives effect to both individual rights and to legislative freedom," Nelson does not confront historiographical and hermeneutic puzzles inherent in applying this two-sided command.

107 See Fish's discussion of institutional systems of intelligibility. The term "interpretive communities" refers to the sources of systems of intelligibility that enable and delimit the operations (thinking, seeing, reading) of extending agents. *Is There a Text in This Class?*, 320, 331–35.

6   Recipes for "Acceptable" History

1 Fairman, "Fourteenth Amendment," 153, 154.
2 Fairman, "Fourteenth Amendment," 43.
3 "The question to raise," states Steve Woolgar (drawing on Garfinkel's exercises in breaching social norms), "is when and why an attack that crosses someone else's path is possible, one that generates, at the intersection, the whole gamut of accusations of irrationality." *Science: The Very Idea*, 206.
4 *Maxwell v. Dow* 176 U.S. 581, 601–2. Fairman deemphasized the significance of Howard's speech in his 1949 article by attempting to show that other Republicans did not share Howard's views. In *Adamson*, Justice Felix Frankfurter also dismissed Howard's statement: "Remarks of a particular proponent of the Amendment [i.e., Howard] no matter how influential, are not to be deemed part of the Amendment. What was submitted for ratification was his proposal, not his speech." *Adamson v. California* 332 U.S., at 64. Crosskey, of course, attempted to demonstrate that Howard's speech was "part of" the amendment.
5 Bickel, "The Original Understanding and the Segregation Decisions," 69 *Harvard Law Review* 1 (1955), 5, n. 13. "Fairman demonstrated that the argument [for incorporation] was based on a misreading and an incomplete reading of the original understanding."
6 See e.g., *Erie* (1938), which overruled a 96-year-old precedent.
7 While Fairman entrusted the control of citizenship rights to the states, and while his Fourteenth Amendment history was a defense of state autonomy *on matters of citizenship,* he sought to justify the expansion of federal regulation of *commerce.* He supported New Deal efforts to use the commerce clause to sustain the regulation of business and labor (see Aynes, "Fairman, Felix Frankfurter, and the Fourteenth Amendment," 1203–4), but he remained a defender of states' rights on matters of citizenship.
8 "To act at a distance," as Woolgar puts it, is to successfully claim that representations emanate from the object itself, and that the production of the repre-

sentation did not interfere with the "pre-existing character" of the object. "The
scientist/observer has to be the trusted teller of the tale and yet his involve-
ment in the representation must not be seen as impinging upon the object's
character, i.e., his representation is not just a distortion or partial reflection of
what was actually the case." *Science: The Very Idea,* 78–79.

9   On the "Freedom National" platforms of the Republican Party, see Foner, *Free
Soil,* 73–102.

10   Madison argued in *The Federalist,* no. 10, and in the 1st Congress that states
were likely to tyrannize minorities. See Amar, "The Bill of Rights as a Constitution," 100 *Yale Law Journal* 1131, 1146–49 (1991).

11   See, e.g., Julius Goebel, "Ex Parte Clio," 54 *Columbia Law Review* 450 (1954);
Henry M. Hart, "Book Review: *Politics and the Constitution,*" 67 *Harvard Law
Review* 1439 (1954); and Irving Brant, "Mr. Crosskey and Mr. Madison," 54
Columbia Law Review 443 (1954). The reasons why Crosskey's book was subjected to vigorous and harsh attack are subject to investigation along the lines
indicated here. Crosskey's Congress-centered view of the original Constitution,
and the damage to his reputation that this view earned him, are features of my
story about the contest to construct "credible" Fourteenth Amendment history.

12   Henry Hart, who wrote a vigorous and damaging attack on Crosskey's 1953
book, and Justice Frankfurter, who condemned the incorporation thesis when
it was put forward by Justice Hugo Black in 1947, both had ties to Harvard.
This, perhaps, makes one wonder about the extent to which there was a "Harvard take" on constitutional analysis during this period, or a Harvard influence
on questions about incorporation. Fairman was professor of law and political science at Stanford University when he wrote his history, but he had ties
to Harvard and Frankfurter (Aynes, "Fairman, Frankfurter, and the Fourteenth
Amendment," 1205–8). The widespread rejection of Crosskey's histories of the
original Constitution and the Fourteenth Amendment, however, suggests that
the Hart-Frankfurter perspective was not limited, or peculiar, to Harvard. Indeed, Crosskey's reputation as a constitutional historian would not have been
so damaged by Hart had many others not shared his set of assumptions. The
extent to which the Hart-Frankfurter take on constitutional history originated
or was first developed at Harvard remains a question. Addressing it would require that many institutional locales (and many communications among those
associated with these locales) be studied, and such an investigation would require comparisons that exceed the central concern of this book. Even if communications between Frankfurter and Fairman were uncovered, they would
not establish that the Hart-Frankfurter take on constitutional analysis was developed at Harvard. That is, the finding of such communications would not
rule out the possibility that other institutional actors in other regions were
elaborating the same views at the time. Widespread and contemporaneous rejection of Crosskey's work gives weight to this likelihood. It is conceivable
that the Harvard associations of Hart and Frankfurter increased the value and
credibility of their work, but gauging that "prestige factor" would be exceedingly difficult. The widespread use of the Hart-Frankfurter perspective would

make it difficult to isolate any "extra" authorization for this perspective (on top of the authorization it enjoyed, anyway) that resulted from a Harvard association. For a view of the significance of their Harvard connection, see Aynes, "Fairman, Frankfurter and the Fourteenth Amendment."

13   Brant, "Mr. Crosskey and Mr. Madison," 446.

14   Star, "Introduction," *Social Problems*, 17.

15   Star investigates the practices of nineteenth-century British neurophysiologists who debated localization theory, i.e. whether functions of the brain were localized in identifiable areas or diffused. See *Regions of the Mind: Brain Research and the Quest for Scientific Certainty* (Stanford, Calif.: Stanford University Press, 1989).

16   Star, *Regions of the Mind*, 20.

17   Star, *Regions of the Mind*, 94–95.

18   Star, *Regions of the Mind*, 94.

19   Star, *Regions of the Mind*, 121.

20   Star, *Regions of the Mind*, 21, 27.

21   Michael Schudson, "How Culture Works: Perspectives from Media Studies on the Efficacy of Symbols," *Theory and Society* 18 (1989), 153–80.

22   Schudson, "How Culture Works," 167.

23   The foolhardiness (and illegitimacy) of federal intervention in state matters was generally taken as the "lesson" of *Lochner v. New York* (1905). To "Lochnerize" has become a pejorative term, referring to judges' reading their personal preferences into the Constitution. This "memory" of the case was institutionalized in legal training, and knowledge of this memory was widespread and easily accessible. It was a powerful institutional symbol shaping ethics of proper judicial action.

24   See Cass Sunstein, "Lochner's Legacy," 87 *Columbia Law Review* 873 (1987), 882–83.

25   Morton Horwitz shows how common law distributions were the product of state choices in *The Transformation in American Law, 1780–1860* (Cambridge, Mass.: Harvard University Press, 1977).

26   *Smith v. Texas* 308 U.S. 122, 130 (1940).

27   Nonlegal evidence supports the view that the 1940s marked a change in U.S. culture. Analyzing the racial and gendered meanings of the exhibits at the American Museum of Natural History, anthropologist Donna Haraway notes that it was in the 1940s that exhibits in the museum's African hall were first labeled racist. Donna Haraway, "Teddy Bear Patriarchy: Taxidermy in the Garden of Eden," *Primate Visions* (New York: Routledge, 1989).

28   Robert M. Cover, "The Origins of Judicial Activism in the Protection of Minorities," 91 *Yale Law Journal* 1287 (1982).

29   See, e.g., Ely, *Democracy and Distrust;* Bruce A. Ackerman, "Beyond Carolene Products," 98 *Harvard Law Review* 713 (1985); Paul Brest, "The Fundamental Rights Controversy: The Essential Contradictions of Normative Constitutional Scholarship," 90 *Yale Law Journal* 1063 (1981).

30   While Frankfurter at first praised Harlan Stone for his footnote, he later repudi-

ated the view that legislation touching the First Amendment was presumptively invalid. All legislation, Frankfurter insisted, carried presumptive validity.

31 The available model for women's citizenship took the form of caretaker and mother. See Gwendolyn Mink, "The Lady and the Tramp: Gender, Race and the Origins of the American Welfare State," in *Women, the State, and Welfare,* ed. Linda Gordon (Madison: University of Wisconsin Press, 1990).

32 See, e.g., *Missouri ex. rel Gaines v. Canada* 305 U.S. 580 (1938).

33 Richard Kluger, *Simple Justice* (New York: Vintage, 1975); Mark Tushnet, *The NAACP's Legal Strategy Against Segregated Education* (Chapel Hill: University of North Carolina Press, 1987).

34 Sewell, "A Theory of Structure: Duality, Agency, and Transformation," *American Journal of Sociology* 98:1 (1992).

35 Martin Jay, *Force Fields: Between Intellectual History and Cultural Critique* (New York: Routledge, 1993), 105.

36 Jay, *Force Fields,* 105.

7 *History as an Institutional Resource: Warren Court Debates over Legislative Apportionment*

1 Bork, *The Tempting of America,* 83.

2 Celeste Michele Condit examines this dynamic as it occurs in a different context, namely, the development of the American abortion debate. See *Decoding Abortion Rhetoric* (Urbana: University of Illinois Press, 1990).

3 *Colegrove v. Green* 328 U.S. 549 (1946).

4 *Adamson v. California* at 59 (Frankfurter, J., concurring).

5 Alabama, Tennessee, and Oklahoma did not reapportion, even though their constitutions specifically required it and established formulas for its accomplishment. See David O. Walter, "Reapportionment and Urban Representation," *Annals of the American Academy of Political and Social Science* 195 (January 1938), 13, cited in Royce Hanson, *The Political Thicket: Reapportionment and Constitutional Democracy* (Englewood Cliffs, N.J.: Prentice-Hall, 1966), 15.

6 In 1920 the urban population of the United States exceeded the rural population for the first time. By 1960 a second population transformation was clear. The suburban population began to equal, and in many states to exceed, that of the central cities. For a discussion of this trend and its impact on apportionment politics, see Hanson, *The Political Thicket,* 18–28.

7 For a more complete discussion of the Dirksen amendment, see Hanson, *The Political Thicket,* 92–101.

8 *Colegrove v. Green* 328 U.S. at 552–54, 556.

9 *Wesberry v. Sanders* 371 U.S. 1, 29–30, 33, 34, 41 (Harlan, J., dissenting).

10 U.S. Constitution, amend. 14, sec. 2. "Representatives shall be apportioned among the several States according to their respective numbers, counting the whole number of persons in each State, excluding Indians not taxed. But when the right to vote at any election for the choice of electors for President and Vice

President of the United States, Representatives in Congress, the Executive and Judicial officers of a State, or the members of the Legislature thereof, is denied to any of the male inhabitants of such State, being twenty-one years of age, and citizens of the United States, or in any way abridged, except for participation in rebellion, or other crime, the basis of representation therein shall be reduced in the proportion which the number of male citizens shall bear to the whole number of male citizens twenty-one years of age in such State."

11   *Wesberry v. Sanders* 371 U.S. at 42, 48.

12   Harlan's dissenting opinion in *Reynolds v. Sims* covered thirty-six pages and contained a seven-page appendix citing twenty statements of congressmen in the 39th Congress on sec. 2 of the Fourteenth Amendment. The opinion devoted roughly three pages to "The Language of the Fourteenth Amendment"; fourteen pages to a "Proposal and Ratification of the Amendment"; four pages to a review of state apportionment practices, "After 1868"; and about eight pages to a review of Court precedent holding that legislative apportionment did not fall under Court jurisdiction.

13   *Reynolds v. Sims* 377 U.S. 533, 590–91.

14   *Cong. Globe,* 39th Cong., 1st Sess., 2459. Quoted in *Reynolds v. Sims* 377 U.S. at 596.

15   *Cong. Globe,* 39th Cong., 1st Sess., 2542. Quoted in *Reynolds v. Sims* 377 U.S. at 598–99.

16   *Cong. Globe,* 39th Cong., 1st Sess., 2766. Quoted in *Reynolds v. Sims* 377 U.S. at 600.

17   *Reynolds v. Sims* 377 U.S. at 599.

18   Harlan included the citations to the *Cong. Globe,* 39th Cong., 1st Sess., 2463, 2464, 2467, 2468, 2469, 2498, 2502, 2508, 2510, 2511.

19   *Reynolds v. Sims* 377 U.S. 598, 608.

20   *Reynolds v. Sims* 377 U.S. at 535, 579.

21   *Reynolds v. Sims* 377 U.S. at 555.

22   The majority in *Reynolds* quoted this statement from an earlier case, *Gray v. Sanders* 372 U.S. 379, 381 (1963).

23   *Colegrove v. Green* 328 U.S. 549, 552–56 (1945).

24   *Colegrove v. Green* 328 U.S. at 554.

25   Harlan and Frankfurter portrayed the "political thicket" of apportionment as eternal. But certain dimensions of apportionment fights do not fit that term. The growing public rejection of racial doctrines that necessitated Republican concessions is one example.

26   See Robert Cover, "Origins of Judicial Activism in the Protection of Minorities," 91 *Yale Law Journal* 1287 (1982).

27   *Baker v. Carr* 369 U.S. at 327.

28   *Reynolds v. Sims* 377 U.S. at 565, 567.

29   *Reynolds v. Sims* 377 U.S. at 555, 562.

30   *Reynolds v. Sims* 377 U.S. at 565, 566.

31   The term is Duncan Kennedy's. Judges face a "perceived obviousness gap when

they want a case to come out the way their sense of justice or rightness tells
them it ought to in spite of what seems at first like the immediate resistance of
'the law.'" Kennedy, "Freedom and Constraint," 526.

32   Kennedy, "Freedom and Constraint," 545.

33   Kennedy, "Freedom and Constraint," 559.

34   The dissenters in *Baker, Wesberry,* and *Reynolds* cited the facts that most states
at the time of the adoption of the Fourteenth Amendment had nonpopulation-
based apportionments and that in 1961 all but eleven states continued nonpopulation-based methods. They also cited the fact that from 1947 through
1954, four cases raising precisely the same issues as those decided in Reynolds
were all dismissed. See, e.g., *Reynolds v. Sims* 377 U.S. at 614.

35   Kennedy, "Freedom and Constraint," 546.

36   Kennedy, "Freedom and Constraint," 557.

37   Kennedy, "Freedom and Constraint," 551.

38   C. Vann Woodward, *The Strange Career of Jim Crow* (New York: Oxford University Press, 1974), 74–83.

39   Jim Crow transportation laws were first enacted in this yearly progression:
Florida (1887), Mississippi (1888), Texas (1889), Louisiana (1890), Alabama
(1891), Arkansas (1891), Tennessee (1891), Georgia (1891), Kentucky (1892).
Lofgren, *The Plessy Case* (New York: Oxford University Press, 1987), 22.

40   *Reynolds v. Sims* 377 U.S. at 574. Similar discussions of the federal analogy
occur in the earlier apportionment cases *Gray v. Sanders* 372 U.S. at 378 and
Wesberry v. Sanders 376 U.S. at 9–14.

41   *Reynolds v. Sims* 377 U.S. at 564–65.

42   *Reynolds v. Sims* 377 U.S. at 576.

43   *Reynolds v. Sims* 377 U.S. at 545, 547, 549, 552, 565, 570, 576.

44   William J. Brennan, "The Constitution of the United States: Contemporary
Ratification," in Sanford Levinson and Steven Mailloux, eds., *Interpreting Law
and Literature* (Evanston, Ill.: Northwestern University Press, 1988), 14.

45   For example, the idea of a federal ban on the extension of slavery in the territories in 1865 produced a civil war. Desegregation orders in *Brown* were effectively ignored for more than ten years.

46   I borrow this phrase from Bruno Latour and Michael Callon, who borrow
it from Marx. "Don't Throw the Baby Out with the Bath School: A Reply to
Collins and Yearley," in Andrew Pickering, ed., *Science as Practice and Culture*
(Chicago: University of Chicago Press, 1992).

*8   Constitutional Law as a "Culture of Argument": Toward a Sociology
of Constitutional Law*

1   The analogy of ships in bottles comes from H. M. Collins, "The Seven Sexes: A
Study in the Sociology of a Phenomenon, or the Replication of Experiments in
Physics," *Sociology* 9:205 (1975). He expands the metaphor in *Changing Order.*

2   Scheppele, "Foreword," 2088.

3   Sewell, "A Theory of Structure," 23.

4   Nancy Fraser, "Pragmatism, Feminism, and the Linguistic Turn," in *Feminist Contentions* (New York: Routledge, 1995), 157.

5   The discussion that follows draws on Fraser's views of the "most fruitful way" for feminists to make the linguistic turn. "Pragmatism, Feminism and the Linguistic Turn," 158–68.

6   Stuart Hall, "Cultural Studies: Two Paradigms," in Nicholas B. Dirks, Geoff Eley, and Sherry B. Ortner, eds., *Culture, Power, History* (Princeton, N.J.: Princeton University Press, 1994).

7   Culture is neither an imposed program nor a purely voluntaristic "toolkit." See, e.g., Ann Swidler, "Culture in Action: Symbols and Strategies," *American Sociological Review* 51 (1986).

8   "The word black box is used by cyberneticians whenever a piece of machinery or a set of commands is too complex. In its place they draw a little box about which they need to know nothing but its input and output." Bruno Latour, *Science in Action* (Cambridge, Mass.: Harvard University Press, 1987), 2.

9   Sewell, "A Theory of Structure," 16.

10   See, e.g., Cass Sunstein, *After the Rights Revolution: Reconceiving the Regulatory State* (Cambridge, Mass.: Harvard University Press, 1990).

11   See, e.g., Elijah Anderson, *Streetwise: Race, Class, and Change in an Urban Community* (Chicago: University of Chicago Press, 1990); Felix Padilla, *The Gang as an American Enterprise* (New Brunswick, N.J.: Rutgers University Press, 1992).

12   See, e.g., Stanley Aronowitz, *The Politics of Identity: Class, Culture, and Social Movements* (New York: Routledge, 1993).

13   See, e.g., Becky Thompson and Sangeeta Tyagi, eds., *Beyond a Dream Deferred: Multicultural Education and the Politics of Excellence* (Minneapolis: University of Minnesota Press, 1993); Pierre Bourdieu and Jean-Claude Passeron, *Reproduction in Education, Society, and Culture* (London: Sage, 1977).

14   See, e.g., Arlie Hochschild, *The Second Shift* (New York: Avon Books, 1989).

15   See, generally, Barbara Smith, "Introduction," *Home Girls: A Black Feminist Anthology* (Boston: Kitchen Table, Women of Color Press, 1983); Deborah King, "Multiple Jeopardy, Multiple Consciousness," 7 *Signs* (1988); Patricia Hill-Collins, *Black Feminist Thought* (1990).

16   Berger and Luckmann, *The Social Construction of Reality.*

17   Bourdieu states his aim to extend economic calculation to all the goods, material and symbolic without distinction, that present themselves as rare and worthy of being sought after. *Outline of a Theory of Practice,* 178.

18   Robert Post discusses law as a "relatively autonomous" system in his introduction to *Law and the Order of Culture* (Berkeley: University of California Press, 1991). Mark Tushnet also uses the phrase "relative autonomy" in connection with law. "A Marxist Analysis of American Law," 1 *Marxist Perspectives* 96 (1978).

19   Lynn Hunt discusses the fragmented nature of culture in *The New Cultural History* (Berkeley: University of California Press, 1989). Jean Comaroff and John Comaroff define culture "not as an overdetermining closed system of signs but as a set of polyvalent practices, texts, and images that may at any time be

contested." Comaroff and Comaroff, *Of Revelation and Revolution: Christianity, Colonialism, and Consciousness in South Africa* (Chicago: University of Chicago Press, 1991), 17.

20   Hall, "Cultural Studies: Two Paradigms," 520.

21   This notion of institutional power diverges from Dennis Wrong's definition of power as the "capacity of some persons to produce intended and foreseen effects on others." Wrong, *Power: Its Forms, Bases, and Uses* (New York: Harper and Row, 1979), 2. My notion moves away from Wrong's and Robert Dahl's emphasis on conscious intention. In keeping with Bertrand Russell's analysis of power, institutional power is but one *form* of it. As Russell states, "No one [of these forms of power] can be regarded as subordinate to any other, and there is no form from which the others are derivable." Russell, *Power: A New Social Analysis* (London: George Allen and Unwin, 1938), 10–11. This does not mean that it is a simple matter to study the power of the Supreme Court.

22   James Boyd White, *Justice as Translation: An Essay in Cultural and Legal Criticism* (Chicago: University of Chicago Press, 1990), xiii.

23   White's reference is to Ronald Dworkin, who argues that rules are activated, in a sense, by principles. Principles shape the direction of rule application.

24   See Kenneth Burke, *A Grammar of Motives* (Berkeley: University of California Press, 1969); Erving Goffman, *Frame Analysis* (New York: Harper and Row, 1974).

25   This is Stephen Toulmin's model of argumentation. *The Uses of Argument* (Cambridge: Cambridge University Press, 1958).

26   Goffman's study of frames made no claims to be talking about core matters of sociology—social organization and social structure. "Those matters," he said "have been and can continue to be quite nicely studied without reference to frame at all." Goffman, *Frame Analysis*, 13.

27   Gusfield, "Introduction," *On Symbols and Society*, 23.

28   See, e.g., Pierre Bourdieu, *Outline of a Theory of Practice* (Cambridge: Cambridge University Press, 1977), and *The Logic of Practice* (Stanford, Calif.: Stanford University Press, 1990 [1980]).

29   See, e.g., MacKinnon, *Toward a Feminist Theory of the State;* Kimberle Williams Crenshaw, "Race, Reform, and Retrenchment: Transformation and Legitimation in Antidiscrimination Law," 101 *Harvard Law Review* 1331 (1988); Patricia J. Williams, "*Metro Broadcasting, Inc. v. FCC:* Regrouping in Singular Times," 104 *Harvard Law Review* 525 (1990).

30   See, e.g., Martha Fineman, "Images of Mothers in Poverty Discourses" 1991 *Duke Law Journal* 274 (1991); Martha Minow, *Making All the Difference: Inclusion, Exclusion, and American Law* (Ithaca, N.Y.: Cornell University Press, 1990); Patricia J. Williams, *The Alchemy of Race and Rights* (Cambridge, Mass.: Harvard University Press, 1991); Scheppele, "Foreword," 2073. Linguistic anthropologists and sociolinguists have developed what Elizabeth Mertz calls "the new anthropological vision of socially grounded linguistic creativity," a vision particularly suited to the study of law. See Mertz, "Language, Law, and Social

Meanings: Linguistic/Anthropological Contributions to the Study of Law" 26 *Law & Society Review* 413 (1992).

31 Bourdieu, *Outline of a Theory of Practice,* 73.

32 Quoted in Calhoun, "Habitus, Field and Capital," in *Bourdieu: Critical Perspectives,* 71.

33 Duncan Kennedy defines legal fields as collections of precedent, rules, policies, historic images, and social stereotypes. He first analogizes legal fields to a physical medium, bricks, which might be manipulated by judges. The analogy is meant to convey that both freedom and constraint characterize judicial work. Kennedy then rejects the brick analogy. Legal fields, he states, are more like messages from the "ancients" that guide ethically serious people about how they ought to proceed in particular instances.

34 The famous "switch in time" in 1937 is one example. After the Court had invalidated New Deal legislation in a series of 5–4 decisions, FDR threatened to increase the number of Court justices from nine to fifteen (in order to get his legislation held constitutional). After this proposal, Justice Owen Roberts frequently switched from voting with the conservative justices. The Court then proceeded to uphold New Deal legislation. This incident clearly revealed the historical and political dimensions of Court decision-making.

35 *Griswold v. Connecticut* 381 U.S. at 479.

9   Conclusion

1 David King, *The Commissar Vanishes: The Falsification of Photographs and Art in Stalin's Russia* (New York: Holt, 1997).

2 Walter Benjamin, "Theses on the Philosophy of History," *Illuminations: Essays and Reflections,* ed. Hannah Arendt (New York: Schocken Books, 1969), 261, 255.

3 Benjamin, *Illuminations,* 255.

4 See, e.g., Margery Austin Turner, Michael Fix, and Raymond J. Struyk, *Opportunities Denied, Opportunities Diminished: Racial Discrimination in Hiring* (Washington, D.C.: Urban Institute Press, 1991); Joe Feagin and Melvin Sikes, *Living With Racism: The Black Middle-Class Experience* (Boston: Beacon Press, 1991).

Bibliography

Ackerman, Bruce A. "Beyond Carolene Products." 98 *Harvard Law Review* 713 (1985).
———. *We the People.* Cambridge, Mass.: Harvard University Press, 1991.
Amar, Akhil Reed. "The Bill of Rights and the Fourteenth Amendment." 101 *Yale Law Journal* 1193 (1992).
Anderson, Elijah. *Streetwise: Race, Class, and Change in an Urban Community.* Chicago: University of Chicago Press, 1990.
Ankersmit, F. R. "Historiography and Postmodernism." *History and Theory* 28:2 (1989).
Aronowitz, Stanley. *The Politics of Identity: Class, Culture, and Social Movements.* New York: Routledge, 1983.
Aynes, Richard L. "Charles Fairman, Felix Frankfurter, and the Fourteenth Amendment." 70 *Chicago-Kent Law Review* 1197 (1995).
———. "Constricting the Law of Freedom: Justice Miller, the Fourteenth Amendment, and the Slaughter-House Cases." 70 *Chicago-Kent Law Review* 627 (1994).
———. "On Misreading John Bingham and the Fourteenth Amendment." 103 *Yale Law Journal* 57 (1993).
Ball, Milner. "Stories of Origin and Constitutional Possibilities." 87 *Michigan Law Review* 2280 (1989).
Bartlett, Katharine. "Feminist Legal Methods." 103 *Harvard Law Review* 829 (1990).
Bell, Derrick. *And We Are Not Saved: The Elusive Quest for Racial Justice.* New York: Basic Books, 1987.
———. "Learning the Three 'I's' of America's Slave Heritage." 68 *Chicago-Kent Law Review* 1037 (1993).
Belz, Herman, "The Civil War Amendments to the Constitution." 5 *Constitutional Commentary* 115 (1988).
Bender, Thomas, ed. *The Antislavery Debate: Capitalism and Abolition as a Problem in Historical Interpretation.* Berkeley: University of California Press, 1992.
Benedict, Michael. *A Compromise of Principle: Congressional Republicans and Reconstruction.* New York: Norton, 1974.
———. "Preserving Federalism: Reconstruction and the Waite Court." 1978 *Supreme Court Review* 39 (1978).

Benjamin, Walter. "Theses on the Philosophy of History." *Illuminations.* New York: Schocken Books, 1969.

Berger, Peter, and Thomas Luckmann. *The Social Construction of Reality.* New York: Anchor Books, 1967.

Berger, Raoul. *Government by Judiciary.* Norman: University of Oklahoma Press, 1977.

Berlin, Ira. *Slaves Without Masters: The Free Negro in the Antebellum South.* New York: Pantheon, 1974.

Bestor, Arthur. "The American Civil War as a Constitutional Crisis." 69 *American Historical Review* 327 (1964).

Beth, Loren. "The *Slaughter-House Cases* Revisited." 23 *Louisiana Law Review* 487 (1963).

Bickel, Alexander. *The Least Dangerous Branch.* New Haven, Conn.: Yale University Press, 1962.

———. "The Original Understanding and the Segregation Decisions." 69 *Harvard Law Review* 1 (1955).

Bork, Robert. *The Tempting of America: The Political Seduction of the Law.* New York: Free Press, 1990.

Bourdieu, Pierre. *Language and Symbolic Power.* Cambridge, Mass.: Harvard University Press, 1991.

———. *The Logic of Practice.* Stanford, Calif.: Stanford University Press, 1980.

———. *Outline of a Theory of Practice.* Cambridge: Cambridge University Press, 1977.

Bowers, Claude. *The Tragic Era.* Cambridge, Mass.: Harvard University Press, 1929.

Brandon, Mark E. *Free in the World: American Slavery and Constitutional Failure.* Princeton, N.J.: Princeton University Press, 1998.

Brant, Irving. "Mr. Crosskey and Mr. Madison." 54 *Columbia Law Review* 443 (1954).

Brennan, William J. "The Constitution of the United States: Contemporary Ratification." In *Interpreting Law and Literature,* ed. Sanford Levinson and Steven Mailloux. Evanston, Ill.: Northwestern University Press, 1988.

Brest, Paul. "The Fundamental Rights Controversy." 90 *Yale Law Journal* 1063 (1981).

———. "The Misconceived Quest for Original Understanding." 60 *Boston University Law Review* 204 (1980).

Burke, Kenneth. *A Grammar of Motives.* Berkeley: University of California Press, 1969.

———. *On Symbols and Society.* Chicago: University of Chicago Press, 1989.

Cohen, Felix. "Transcendental Nonsense and the Functional Approach." 35 *Columbia Law Review* 6 (1935).

Collins, H. M. *Changing Order: Replication and Induction in Scientific Practice.* London: Sage, 1985.

———. "The Seven Sexes: A Study in the Sociology of a Phenomenon, or the Replication of Experiments in Physics." *Sociology* 9:205 (1975).

Comaroff, Jean, and John Comaroff. *Of Revelation and Revolution: Christianity, Colonialism, and Consciousness in South Africa.* Chicago: University of Chicago Press, 1991.

Condit, Michele Celeste. *Decoding Abortion Rhetoric.* Baltimore: Johns Hopkins University Press, 1989.

Cover, Robert M. "Foreword: Nomos and Narrative." 97 *Harvard Law Review* 4 (1983).
———. "The Origins of Judicial Activism in the Protection of Minorities." 91 *Yale Law Journal* 1287 (1982).
Crenshaw, Kimberle. "Demarginalizing the Intersection of Race and Sex." *University of Chicago Legal Forum* (1989).
———. "Race, Reform, and Retrenchment: Transformation and Legitimation in Anti-discrimination Law." 101 *Harvard Law Review* 1331 (1988).
Crosskey, William W. "Charles Fairman, 'Legislative History,' and the Constitutional Limitations on State Authority." 22 *University of Chicago Law Review* 1 (1954).
———. *Politics and the Constitution in the History of the United States.* Chicago: University of Chicago Press, 1953.
Curtis, Michael Kent. "The 1859 Crisis Over Hinton Helper's Book, *The Impending Crisis:* Free Speech, Slavery, and Some Light on the Meaning of the First Section of the Fourteenth Amendment." 68 *Chicago-Kent Law Review* 3 (1993).
———. "The 1837 Killing of Elijah Lovejoy by an Anti-Abolition Mob: Free Speech, Mobs, Republican Government, and the Privileges of American Citizens." 44 *UCLA Law Review* 4 (1997).
———. *No State Shall Abridge.* Durham, N.C.: Duke University Press, 1986.
———. "Resurrecting the Privileges or Immunities Clause and Revising the *Slaughter-House Cases* Without Exhuming *Lochner:* Individual Rights and the Fourteenth Amendment." 38 *Boston College Law Review* 1 (1996).
Davis, David Brion. "Slavery and the American Mind." In *Perspectives and Irony in American Slavery,* ed. Harry P. Owens. Jackson: University Press of Mississippi, 1976.
Davis, Angela. *Women, Race, and Class.* New York: Vintage, 1974.
Dewey, John. "Logical Method and Law." *Cornell Law Quarterly* 10, no. 1 (1924).
DuBois, W. E. B. *Black Reconstruction in America, 1860–1880.* New York: Atheneum 1962 (1935).
Dunning, William A. *Reconstruction: Political and Economic, 1865–1877.* 1935. New York: Harper and Row, 1968.
Ely, John Hart. *Democracy and Distrust.* Cambridge, Mass.: Harvard University Press, 1980.
Fairman, Charles. "Does the Fourteenth Amendment Incorporate the Bill of Rights?" 2 *Stanford Law Review* 5 (1949).
———. *Mr. Justice Miller and the Supreme Court.* Cambridge, Mass.: Harvard University Press, 1939.
———. *Reconstruction and Reunion I.* In *History of the Supreme Court of the United States.* Vol. 6. Ed. Paul A. Freund. New York: Macmillan, 1971.
———. *Reconstruction and Reunion II.* In *History of the Supreme Court of the United States.* Vol. 7. Ed. Paul A. Freund and Stanley Katz. New York: Macmillan, 1987.
———. "A Reply to Professor Crosskey." 22 *University of Chicago Law Review* 144 (1954).
Fehrenbacher, Don. *Prelude to Greatness: Lincoln in the 1850s.* Stanford, Calif.: Stanford University Press, 1962.

Fineman, Martha. "Images of Mothers in Poverty Discourses." 1991 *Duke Law Journal* 274 (1991).

Finley, M. I. *Ancient Slavery and Modern Ideology*. New York: Viking Press, 1980.

Fish, Stanley. *Doing What Comes Naturally*. Durham, N.C.: Duke University Press, 1989.

———. *Is There a Text in This Class?* Cambridge, Mass.: Harvard University Press, 1980.

———. "The Young and the Restless." In *The New Historicism*, ed. Aram Veeser. New York: Routledge, 1989.

Fleming, Walter. *The Sequel of Appomattox*. New Haven, Conn.: Yale University Press, 1919.

Foner, Eric. *Free Soil, Free Labor, Free Men: The Ideology of the Republican Party Before the Civil War*. London: Oxford University Press, 1970.

———. *Reconstruction: America's Unfinished Revolution, 1863–1877*. New York: Harper and Row, 1988.

———. *Politics and Ideology in the Age of the Civil War*. Oxford: Oxford University Press, 1980.

Foucault, Michel. *The Archaeology of Knowledge*. New York: Pantheon, 1972.

Franklin, John Hope. *The Free Negro in North Carolina, 1790–1860*. Chapel Hill: University of North Carolina Press, 1969.

Fraser, Nancy. "Pragmatism, Feminism, and the Linguistic Turn." In *Feminist Contentions*, ed. Linda Nicholson. New York: Routledge, 1995.

Fredrickson, George M. *The Black Image in the White Mind*. New York: Harper and Row, 1971.

———. *The Inner Civil War: Northern Intellectuals and the Crisis of the Union*. Urbana: University of Illinois Press, 1993 (1965).

Freehling, William W. *The Road to Disunion: Secessionists at Bay, 1776–1854*. New York: Oxford University Press, 1990.

———. "The Founding Fathers and Slavery." 77 *American Historical Review* 81–93 (1972).

Friedlander, Saul, ed. *Probing the Limits of Representation*. Cambridge, Mass.: Harvard University Press, 1992.

Geertz, Clifford. "The Impact of the Concept of Culture on the Concept of Man." In *The Interpretation of Cultures*. New York: Basic Books, 1973.

Gienapp, William E. *The Origins of the Republican Party, 1852–1856*. Oxford: Oxford University Press, 1987.

Glickstein, Jonathan. *Concepts of Free Labor in Antebellum America*. New Haven, Conn.: Yale University Press, 1991.

Goebel, Julius. "Ex Parte Clio." 54 *Columbia Law Review* 450 (1954).

Goffman, Erving. *Frame Analysis*. New York: Harper and Row, 1974.

Graham, Howard Jay. *Everyman's Constitution: Historical Essays on the Fourteenth Amendment*. Madison: State Historical Society of Wisconsin, 1968.

Grey, Thomas. "Do We Have an Unwritten Constitution?" 27 *Stanford Law Review* 703 (1975).

Gusfield, Joseph, ed. *On Symbols and Society*. Chicago: University of Chicago Press, 1989.

Halbwachs, Maurice. *On Collective Memory*. Ed. and trans. Lewis A. Coser. Chicago: University of Chicago Press, 1992.

Hall, Jacquelyn Dowd. "The Mind That Burns in Each Body: Women, Rape, and Racial Violence." In *Powers of Desire: The Politics of Sexuality*, ed. Ann Snitow. New York: Monthly Review Press, 1983.

Hall, Stuart. "Cultural Studies: Two Paradigms." In *Culture, Power, History*, ed. Nicholas B. Dirks, Geoff Eley, and Sherry B. Ortner. Princeton, N.J.: Princeton University Press, 1994.

Hanson, Royce. *The Political Thicket: Reapportionment and Constitutional Democracy*. Englewood Cliffs, N.J.: Prentice-Hall, 1966.

Haraway, Donna J. *Primate Visions: Race and Gender in the World of Modern Science*. New York: Routledge, 1989.

———. "Situated Knowledges: The Science Question in Feminism and the Privilege of Partial Perspective." In *Simians, Cyborgs, and Women: The Reinvention of Nature*. New York: Routledge, 1989.

Harris, Angela P. "Race and Essentialism in Feminist Legal Theory." 42 *Stanford Law Review* 581 (1992).

Hart, Henry M. Book Review: *Politics and the Constitution*. 67 *Harvard Law Review* 1439 (1954).

Hodes, Martha. *White Women, Black Men: Illicit Sex in the Nineteenth Century*. New Haven, Conn.: Yale University Press, 1997.

Holmes, Oliver Wendell. "The Path of the Law." Address delivered at Boston University School of Law, January 8, 1897. *Collected Legal Papers*, 1920.

Horwitz, Morton J. "Foreword: The Constitution of Legal Change: Legal Fundamentality Without Fundamentalism." 107 *Harvard Law Review* 30 (1993).

———. *The Transformation of American Law, 1780–1860*. Cambridge, Mass.: Harvard University Press, 1977.

Hunt, Alan. *Explorations in Law and Society: Toward a Constitutive Theory of Law*. New York: Routledge, 1993.

Hunt, Lynn. *The New Cultural History*. Berkeley: University of California Press, 1989.

Hyman, Harold M. *A More Perfect Union*. Boston: Houghton Mifflin, 1975.

———. *The Radical Republicans and Reconstruction*. Indianapolis: Bobbs-Merrill, 1967.

Hyman, Harold, and William Wiecek. *Equal Justice Under the Law: Constitutional Development, 1835–1875*. New York: Harper and Row, 1974.

Jay, Martin. *Force Fields: Between Intellectual History and Cultural Critique*. New York: Routledge, 1993.

———. "Of Plots, Witnesses, and Judgments." In *Probing the Limits of Representation*, ed. Saul Friedlander. Cambridge, Mass.: Harvard University Press, 1992.

Jones, Jacqueline. *The Dispossessed*. New York: Basic Books, 1990.

Kaczorowski, Robert. *The Politics of Judicial Interpretation: The Federal Courts, the Department of Justice, and Civil Rights*. New York: Oceana Press, 1985.

Kammen, Michael. *A Machine That Would Go of Itself: The Constitution in American Culture.* New York: Knopf, 1986.

Kennedy, Duncan. "Freedom and Constraint in Adjudication: A Critical Phenomenology." 36 *Journal of Legal Education* 518 (1986).

Kenyon, Cecelia. "Introduction." *The Antifederalists.* Indianapolis: Bobbs-Merrill, 1966.

King, David. *The Commissar Vanishes: The Falsification of Photographs and Art in Stalin's Russia.* New York: Holt, 1997.

King, Deborah. "Multiple Jeopardy, Multiple Consciousness." *Signs* 14, no. 1 (1988).

Kluger, Richard. *Simple Justice.* New York: Vintage, 1975.

Kuhn, Thomas. *The Structure of Scientific Revolutions.* Chicago: University of Chicago Press, 1970.

Latour, Bruno. *Science in Action.* Cambridge, Mass.: Harvard University Press, 1987.

Latour, Bruno, and Steve Woolgar. *Laboratory Life.* Beverly Hills, Calif.: Sage, 1979.

Lawrence, Charles. "If He Hollers, Let Him Go." In *Words That Wound,* ed. Mari Matsuda et al. Boulder, Colo.: Westview Press, 1993.

Levinson, Sanford. *Constitutional Faith.* Princeton, N.J.: Princeton University Press, 1988.

———. "Slavery in the Canon of Constitutional Law." 68 *Chicago-Kent Law Review* 1087 (1993).

Levy, Leonard. "The Fourteenth Amendment and the Bill of Rights." In *Seasoned Judgments.* Oxford: Oxford University Press, 1972.

Llewellyn, Karl. *Bramble Bush.* New York: Oceana Press, 1930.

Litwack, Leon F. *North of Slavery.* Chicago: University of Chicago Press, 1961.

Lofgren, Charles. *The Plessy Case: A Legal-Historical Interpretation.* New York: Oxford University Press, 1987.

MacKenzie, Donald A. *Statistics in Britain, 1865–1930: The Social Construction of Scientific Knowledge.* Edinburgh: Edinburgh University Press, 1981.

MacKinnon, Catharine A. *Feminism Unmodified: Discourses on Life and Law.* Cambridge, Mass.: Harvard University Press, 1987.

———. *Toward a Feminist Theory of the State.* Cambridge, Mass.: Harvard University Press, 1989.

Mahoney, Martha. "Whiteness and Women, in Practice and Theory." 5 *Yale Journal of Law and Feminism* 2 (1991).

Maltz, Earl M. "The Fourteenth Amendment as a Political Compromise." 45 *Ohio State Law Journal* 1 (1984).

Matsuda, Mari. "Public Response to Racist Speech." In *Words That Wound,* ed. Mari Matsuda et al. Boulder, Colo.: Westview, 1993.

Mertz, Elizabeth. "Language, Law, and Social Meanings: Linguistic/Anthropological Contributions to the Study of Law." 26 *Law & Society Review* 413 (1992).

Miller, Charles A. *The Supreme Court and the Uses of History.* Chicago: University of Chicago Press, 1969.

Mink, Gwendolyn. "The Lady and the Tramp: Gender, Race, and the Origins of the American Welfare State." In *Women, the State, and Welfare,* ed. Linda Gordon. Madison: University of Wisconsin Press, 1990.

Minow, Martha. *Making All the Difference: Inclusion, Exclusion, and American Law.* Ithaca, N.Y.: Cornell University Press, 1990.

Morrison, Stanley. "Does the Fourteenth Amendment Incorporate the Bill of Rights?" 2 *Stanford Law Review* 137 (1949).

Murphy, Walter P. "*Slaughter-House,* Civil Rights, and Limits on Constitutional Change." 32 *American Journal of Jurisprudence* 1 (1987).

————. *The Triumph of Nationalism: State Sovereignty, the Founding Fathers, and the Making of the Constitution.* Chicago: University of Chicago Press, 1967.

Murphy, Walter P., James Fleming, and William F. Harris. *American Constitutional Interpretation.* New York: Foundation Press, 1986.

Nedelsky, Jennifer. *Private Property and the Limits of American Constitutionalism.* Chicago: University of Chicago Press, 1990.

Nelson, William E. *The Fourteenth Amendment: From Political Principle to Judicial Doctrine.* Cambridge, Mass.: Harvard University Press, 1988.

————. "History and Neutrality in Constitutional Adjudication." 72 *Virginia Law Review* 1237 (1986).

O'Brien, Patricia. "Michel Foucault's History of Culture." In *The New Cultural History,* ed. Lynn Hunt. Berkeley: University of California Press, 1989.

Omi, Michael, and Howard Winant. *Racial Formation in the United States.* New York: Routledge, 1994.

Paludan, Phillip. *A People's Contest: The Union and the Civil War, 1861–1865.* Lawrence: University Press of Kansas, 1988.

Patterson, Orlando. *Slavery and Social Death: A Comparative Study.* Cambridge, Mass.: Harvard University Press, 1982.

Perry, Michael. "Interpretivism, Freedom of Expression, and Equal Protection." 42 *Ohio State Law Journal* 261 (1981).

Post, Robert, ed. *Law and the Order of Culture.* Berkeley: University of California Press, 1991.

Potter, David M. *The Impending Crisis.* New York: Harper and Row, 1976.

Richards, David A. J. *Conscience and the Constitution: History, Theory, and Law of the Reconstruction Amendments.* Princeton, N.J.: Princeton University Press, 1993.

Riker, William H. *The Strategy of Rhetoric: Campaigning for the American Constitution.* New Haven, Conn.: Yale University Press, 1986.

Rossiter, Clinton, ed. *The Federalist Papers.* New York: New American Library, 1961.

Russell, Bertrand. *Power: A New Social Analysis.* London: George Allen and Unwin, 1938.

Scalia, Antonin. "Originalism: The Lesser Evil." 57 *University of Cincinnati Law Review* 849 (1989).

Scheiber, Harry N. "Federalism and the Constitution: The Original Understanding." In *American Law and the Constitutional Order,* ed. Lawrence Friedman and Harry Scheiber. Cambridge, Mass.: Harvard University Press, 1978.

Scheppele, Kim Lane. "Foreword: Telling Stories." 87 *Michigan Law Review* 8 (1989).

————. *Legal Secrets: Equality and Efficiency in the Common Law.* Chicago: University of Chicago Press, 1988.

————. "The Re-vision of Rape Law." 54 *University of Chicago Law Review* 1095 (1987).

Schudson, Michael. "How Culture Works: Perspectives from Media Studies on the Efficacy of Symbols." 18 *Theory and Society* (1989).

Schultz, Vicki. "Telling Stories About Women and Work." 103 *Harvard Law Review* 1750 (1991).

Sewell, William H. "A Theory of Structure: Duality, Agency, and Transformation." *American Journal of Sociology* 98:1 (1992).

Shamir, Ronen. *Managing Legal Uncertainty: Elite Lawyers in the New Deal*. Durham, N.C.: Duke University Press, 1995.

Skowronek, Stephen. *The Politics Presidents Make: Leadership from John Adams to George Bush*. Cambridge, Mass.: Belknap Press, 1993.

Smith, Barbara. "Introduction." *Home Girls: A Black Feminist Anthology*. Boston: Kitchen Table, 1983.

Smith, Dorothy E. *The Conceptual Practices of Power: A Feminist Sociology of Knowledge*. Boston: Northeastern University Press, 1990.

Soifer, Aviam. "Protecting Civil Rights: A Critique of Raoul Berger's History." 54 *New York University Law Review* 651 (1979).

Star, Susan Leigh. Introduction to special issue of *Social Problems* 35:3 (1988).

————. *Regions of the Mind: Brain Research and the Quest for Scientific Certainty*. Stanford, Calif.: Stanford University Press, 1989.

Stinchcombe, Arthur L. *Theoretical Methods in Social History*. Orlando, Fla.: Academic Press, 1978.

————. *Constructing Social Theories*. Chicago: University of Chicago Press, 1968.

Sunstein, Cass R. "On Analogical Reasoning." 106 *Harvard Law Review* 741 (1993).

————. "Lochner's Legacy." 87 *Columbia Law Review* 873 (1987).

Swidler, Ann. "Culture in Action: Symbols and Strategies." *American Sociological Review* 51 (1986).

ten Broek, Jacobus. *The Antislavery Origins of the Fourteenth Amendment*. Berkeley: University of California Press, 1951.

Thompson, Becky, and Sangeeta Tyagi, eds. *Beyond a Dream Deferred: Multicultural Education and the Politics of Excellence*. Minneapolis: University of Minnesota Press, 1983.

Toulmin, Stephen. *The Uses of Argument*. Cambridge: Cambridge University Press, 1958.

Tulis, Jeffrey K. *The Rhetorical Presidency*. Princeton, N.J.: Princeton University Press, 1987.

Tushnet, Mark. "Following the Rules Laid Down." 96 *Harvard Law Review* 781 (1983).

————. *The NAACP's Legal Strategy Against Segregated Education, 1925–1950*. Chapel Hill: University of North Carolina Press, 1987.

VanderVelde, Lea S. "The Labor Vision of the Fourteenth Amendment." 138 *University of Pennsylvania Law Review* 437 (1989).

Wells, Ida B. "How to Stop Lynching." In *Black Women in White America*, ed. Gerda Lerner. New York: Vintage, 1972.

White, Hayden. *The Content of the Form: Narrative Discourse and Historical Representation.* Baltimore: Johns Hopkins University Press, 1987.

White, James Boyd. *Justice as Translation.* Chicago: University of Chicago Press, 1990.

Wiecek, William. *Liberty Under Law.* Baltimore: Johns Hopkins University Press, 1988.

———. *The Origins of Antislavery Constitutionalism in America, 1760–1848.* Ithaca, N.Y.: Cornell University Press, 1977.

Williams, Patricia J. *The Alchemy of Race and Rights.* Cambridge, Mass.: Harvard University Press, 1991.

———. "*Metro Broadcasting, Inc. v. FCC:* Regrouping in Singular Times." 104 *Harvard Law Review* 525 (1990).

Wood, Gordon S. *Creation of the American Republic.* Chapel Hill: University of North Carolina Press, 1969.

Woodward, C. Vann. *The Strange Career of Jim Crow.* New York: Oxford University Press, 1974.

Woolgar, Steve. *Science: The Very Idea.* London: Tavistock, 1981.

Wrong, Dennis. *Power: Its Forms and Uses.* New York: Harper and Row, 1979.

Index

Ackerman, Bruce, 4, 59, 217 n.8
Adamson v. California, 14, 102, 126, 154, 157
Akerman, Amos, 82
Amar, Akhil Reed, 4, 14, 69, 100, 116, 223 n.35
American Civil War, 1, 2, 15, 19, 24, 28–34, 46, 47, 56, 63–74, 106–19, 140, 145, 156, 157, 164–75, 184, 187. *See also* Northern Democrats; Republicans; Supreme Court: on Civil War
American Revolution, 12, 135, 147
Antislavery, multiple meanings of, 24–28
Apportionment, 15, 51; racial dimensions of, 158, 159, 165. See also *Reynolds v. Sims*
Article 4, section 2, 70, 109, 111, 122, 245 n.85
Aynes, Richard L., 14, 69, 100, 115, 116, 244 n.75

Baker v. Carr, 157, 158, 168, 169, 174
Barnburners, 27
Barron v. Baltimore, 36, 49, 56–60, 66, 79, 102, 106–24, 133. *See also* Bill of Rights
Banks, Nathaniel P., 52
Bell, Derrick, 11

Benedict, Michael, 47, 53, 61, 79, 233 n.40
Benjamin, Walter, 209
Berger, Raoul, 104
Bestor, Arthur, 8, 110
Bickel, Alexander, 104, 133, 134
Bill of Rights, 5–7, 14, 27, 36, 48, 49, 55–60, 66, 67, 71, 79, 81, 87–93. *See also* Crosskey, William; Fairman, Charles
Bingham, John A., 50, 55, 56, 70, 104, 110–20, 123, 132, 160–63
Birth of a Nation, 13
Black, Hugo, 14, 102–4, 133, 136, 152, 154, 175, 206, 210
Black codes, 10, 29, 30, 39, 44, 47, 48, 53–55, 62, 86, 92, 129, 141, 212, 213
Blacks, 9–12, 30–33, 38, 39, 62, 84, 88, 117, 129, 135, 136, 140, 145, 151, 152, 161–67, 176, 177, 183, 211, 218 n.14, 236 n.87. *See also* Northern Democrats: on blacks; Republicans: on blacks
Bork, Robert, 16, 156, 237 n.98
Bourdieu, Pierre, 187, 196, 202–4
Bradley, Joseph P., 12, 13, 56, 68–71, 76, 80, 82, 86, 90, 91, 145, 233 n.41
Brown v. Board of Education, 76, 141, 165, 171
Buckland, Ralph P., 47

Burke, Kenneth, 200, 201, 239 n.15

Calhoun, John C., 62
Cardozo, Benjamin, 103, 134
Chase, Salmon P., 25, 68
Citizenship, rights of, 65, 91–95, 104,
    110, 122–29, 138, 143, 144, 150, 152,
    157, 169–74, 178–83, 193, 199, 205,
    206, 210, 247 n.7. *See also* Fourteenth
    Amendment
Citizenship clause, 11, 38, 41, 66
Civil rights: as distinct from political
    rights, 47, 237 n.97
Civil Rights Act of 1866, 24, 76, 77, 126,
    228 n.41, 238 n.101
Civil Rights Act of 1875, 86, 87, 230
    nn.4, 5
Civil Rights Cases, 62, 71, 86, 87
Civil War. *See* American Civil War
Cohen, Felix, 99
Color-blind standard, 54, 211–14. *See
    also* Black codes; Republicans: on
    rights
Constitution of 1787, 9, 11, 31, 106–
    14, 137, 159, 204. See also *Barron v.
    Baltimore;* Northern Democrats: on
    original Constitution; Republicans:
    on original Constitution
Cover, Robert, 149
Cowan, Edgar, 35
Cox, Samuel S., 31, 34, 36
Crittenden Resolution of 1861, 50, 123
Crosskey, William, 2, 4, 14, 15, 19, 21,
    22, 49, 93, 96–108, 117–24, 127–40,
    143, 144, 152, 154, 175, 184, 208, 210,
    242 n.4
Curtis, Michael Kent, 4, 14, 100, 104,
    116, 245 n.79

Dana, Richard Henry, 46
Declaration of Independence, 6, 38, 56,
    109, 164
Declaratory theory of rights, 30, 49
Democrats. *See* Northern Democrats;
    Southern Democrats

Dirksen amendment, 158
Douglas, Stephen, 27, 29, 40, 43, 76,
    182, 222 n.33
Douglass, Frederick, 23, 24, 49, 90
Dred Scott v. Sanford, 66, 67, 118, 119
DuBois, W. E. B., 1, 13, 115, 116, 152, 235
    n.77
Dunning school history, 13, 106, 115,
    116, 127, 152

Eckley, Ephraim R., 43
Eliot, Thomas D., 53, 54
Emancipation. *See* Formal emancipa-
    tion
Enforcement Acts of 1870–71, 48, 54,
    79, 82, 129, 158, 212, 232 n.38, 234
    n.64, 235 n.74
Epistemology, 21, 22
Equal protection clause, 172. See also
    Reynolds v. Sims

Fairman, Charles, 2–5, 11, 14, 15, 20–22,
    49, 55, 74, 85, 96–116, 120–28, 132–
    48, 152–57, 184, 206–10, 241 n.39,
    242 n.48, 247 n.7, 248 n.12
Farnsworth, John F., 51
Farrar, Timothy, 115
Federalist No. 45, 78
Federalist No. 51, 90
Federal system, 5, 6, 23, 36, 49, 57, 58,
    64–67, 75, 126–30, 136–38, 146, 149,
    198, 199, 205, 233 n.51, 240 n.19. See
    also *Reynolds v. Sims; Slaughter-House
    Cases*
Fessenden, William P., 43, 47, 50, 52
Field, Stephen J., 68, 69, 90
Fifteenth Amendment, 12, 80, 81, 158,
    164, 167
Finck, William E., 34
First Amendment, 79, 137, 147, 149
Fish, Stanley, 21, 22, 220 nn.39, 40
Fletcher v. Peck, 170–71
Foner, Eric, 11, 24–26, 47–49, 65–74,
    84, 152, 216 n.5, 235 n.74, 236 n.87

Formal emancipation, 2, 9, 10, 25, 28, 29, 34, 53, 54, 140, 212
Fourteenth Amendment, 2–7, 12–16, 24, 30–37, 56, 63, 68–74, 78, 82–95, 197. *See also* Crosskey, William; Fairman, Charles; Harlan, John M. (elder); *Reynolds v. Sims; Slaughter-House Cases;* Waite Court; Warren Court
Frames. *See* Interpretive frameworks
Frankfurter, Felix, 14, 22, 74, 103, 112, 115, 126, 127, 133, 134, 154, 157–59, 168–71, 182, 248 n.12, 249 n.30
Fraser, Nancy, 190
Freedmen's bureau, 35, 39, 54
Free labor, 7, 25–28, 47, 118
Free soil, 10, 25, 26
Fuller Court, 13, 81, 82

Gag rule, 23, 36, 64
Garrison, William Lloyd, 23, 24
Gibbons v. Ogden, 79
Goffman, Erving, 96, 98, 200, 239 n.15
Graham, Howard, 4, 110, 115
Grant administration, 82–84
Grosvenor, William M., 29, 46

Habermas, Jürgen, 153, 190
Halbwachs, Maurice, 58, 59
Hall, Stuart, 191
Hammond, Henry, 23, 36
Harding, Aaron, 31
Harlan, John M. (elder), 13, 87, 88, 91, 102, 171, 175, 213
Harlan, John M., 104, 112, 159–64, 166
Hart, Roswell, 45
Harvard University, 136, 248 n.12
Helper, Hinton, 23, 36
Henderson, John, 122, 123
Hendricks, Thomas A., 39
Higby, William, 28, 44, 119
Holmes, Oliver Wendell, 91, 118, 149, 150
Hopwood v. Texas, 212
Howard, Jacob M., 122, 123, 133, 160, 161, 163

Hurtado v. California, 87, 91
Hyman, Harold M., 9, 57, 104, 217 n.7, 219 n.23

Incorporation debate, 2–6. *See also* Crosskey, William; Fairman, Charles
Ingersoll, Ebon C., 45, 53
Interpretive frameworks, 14–15, 96–102, 105–8, 147, 148, 182, 183, 192–202, 205, 209, 239 n.15

Jay, Martin, 153
Johnson, Andrew, 34, 36, 43, 50
Joint Committee of Fifteen. *See* Joint Committee on Reconstruction
Joint Committee on Reconstruction, 28, 35, 36, 37, 111, 115
Julian, George W., 42
Juries, 125, 126, 147, 148, 180, 246 nn.100, 102

Kaczorowski, Robert, 116
Kammen, Michael, 104
Kelley, William D., 119, 121
Kennedy, Duncan, 11, 18, 77, 78, 82, 173–75, 187
Kluger, Richard, 151
Ku Klux Klan, 13, 30, 61–63, 79, 82, 129, 234 n.64, 235 n.74, 238 n.101
Ku Klux Klan Act of 1871. *See* Enforcement Acts of 1870–71

Lawrence, William, 52
Legal fields, 77–82, 183, 187, 192, 204, 255 n.33
Levinson, Sanford, 11, 106, 108
Levy, Leonard, 155
Liberty, conceptions of, 12, 30, 56, 60, 64, 67, 68, 89–91, 116, 147
Lincoln, Abraham, 9, 10, 23, 27–29, 41, 45, 59, 69, 222 n.33
Llewellyn, Karl, 75, 76
Lochner v. New York, 91, 144–47, 184
Lofgren, Charles, 177
Lovejoy, Elijah, 23, 26, 36

Madison, James, 78, 90, 135
Majoritarianism. *See* Popular sovereignty
Malapportionment. *See* Apportionment
Maxwell v. Dow, 87, 89, 91, 94, 133
Miller, Samuel F., 11, 12, 38, 61, 72–81, 89, 93, 94, 103, 106, 141, 156, 183, 206; on Civil War, 63–69, 74; on Fourteenth Amendment, 66–68, 78–81, 87, 143; on liberty, 12, 64, 90
Miscegenation, 27, 40, 41
Moderate Republicans, 5, 6, 27, 28, 38, 42, 47–49, 83, 167, 210, 214, 216 n.5
Morrison, Stanley, 127
Myers, Leonard, 44, 46, 50

NAACP, 19, 151, 184
Nelson, William E., 30, 44, 247 n.106
New Deal, 96, 97, 112, 134–37, 140, 148–52, 206
Newtonian model of law, 15, 16, 140, 141, 152, 176, 219 n.27
Nicholson, John A., 37, 39
Northern Democrats, 3, 4, 10, 11, 29, 30–37, 49, 50, 57, 59, 62, 82, 84, 94, 114, 128, 134, 135, 140–43, 156, 167, 169, 182, 183, 187, 206–12; on blacks, 27, 38–41, 53, 81; on emancipation, 34, 35, 40, 48; on ex-Confederates, 30–35, 43, 46; on original Constitution, 36–39; on Republicans, 35, 36, 40; on slavery, 1, 2, 10–12, 26, 27, 31–38; on Southern Democrats, 31–33, 38

Original understanding, 2–5, 14–17, 88, 100, 212, 219 n.29. *See also* Crosskey, William; Fairman, Charles

Palko v. Connecticut, 103, 134
Paschal, George, 115
Peckham, Rufus, 89
Perham, Sidney, 42, 45, 46, 52, 53
Perry, Michael, 104
Phelps, Charles E., 31, 34

Plessy v. Ferguson, 86, 91, 171, 177, 213
Poland, Luke, 121
Politics and the Constitution, 101, 106, 117, 136, 137
Pomeroy, John N., 115
Popular sovereignty, 2, 27–41, 89–91, 145
Positivism, 22, 138
Potter, David M., 40
Prejudice. *See* Blacks; Race
Privileges or immunities clause, 11, 38, 41, 61, 66

Race, 10, 11, 27–30, 97, 129, 140, 141, 146, 165, 178, 182, 188, 195, 197, 211–14. *See also* Blacks; Northern Democrats: on blacks; Republicans: on blacks; White supremacy
Radical Republicans, 4, 6, 24, 42, 53, 65, 83, 167, 210, 214, 216 n.5
Randall, Samuel J., 33, 35, 50
Reconstruction Act of 1867, 167, 170, 171
Reconstruction amendments, 12, 18, 61–65. *See also* Fifteenth Amendment; Fourteenth Amendment; Thirteenth Amendment
Rehnquist Court, 7, 8, 211–14
Republicans, 4–7, 11, 13, 26, 27, 30, 46, 51, 55, 56, 59, 65, 76, 83, 106–24, 128–39, 147, 152, 158, 164–72, 179, 182, 208–13; on blacks, 27, 44, 45, 51–56; on emancipation, 48, 53; on ex-Confederates, 30, 43–46, 51, 52; on liberty, 67, 89, 90; on Northern Democrats, 30, 46; on original Constitution, 6, 7, 55–57; on political violence, 47, 48, 51, 54; on rights, 12, 47–49, 54, 57; on slavery, 2, 6, 7, 10–12, 26–56, 110, 123, 145, 166, 170, 180; shift to party of business, 83–85; on states' rights, 38, 48–50, 85, 112, 135, 145. *See also* Moderate Republicans; Radical Republicans
Reynolds v. Sims, 156–84, 186
Richards, David A. J., 4, 217 n.9

Rights, 1, 2, 5–8, 12, 23, 27–37, 48, 110, 116, 202. *See also* Bill of Rights; Citizenship, rights of

Riker, William, 60

Ritter, Burwell C., 34

Rogers, Andrew Jackson, 28, 31, 32, 33, 34, 37, 38, 40

Scalia, Antonin, 8, 16, 212

Schudson, Michael, 143

Schurz, Carl, 43

Scofield, Glenni W., 43, 45

Screws v. United States, 238 n.101

Secession, 31–34, 38, 42, 64, 65, 71

Section 2, of Fourteenth Amendment, 51, 156, 159–63, 166, 167

Sewell, William, 151, 189, 190, 194

Shanklin, George S., 31, 35, 39, 40

Shaw v. Reno, 211

Skorownek, Stephen, 218 n.12

Slaughter-House Cases, 11, 38, 56, 61–81, 89, 90, 91, 93, 106, 119, 138–45, 175

Slave power, 6, 26, 35, 44, 49, 124, 216 n.5

Slavery, 1, 8–11, 13, 14, 19, 23–29, 53, 65, 109, 110, 114–16, 135, 140, 188, 221 n.9. *See also* American Civil War; Northern Democrats: on slavery; Republicans: on slavery; Supreme Court: on Civil War

Sociology of knowledge, 18–20, 185–211

Southern Democrats, 31–33, 38, 125, 183

Star, Susan Leigh, 20, 142, 143

States' rights, 105, 112, 117, 121, 137, 145–47

Stevens, Thaddeus, 46, 56, 115, 119, 160, 163

Stone, Harlan, 149, 150

Strauder v. West Virginia, 54, 69, 85, 141, 235 n.78

Strouse, Myer, 37

Sumner, Charles, 42, 48, 53

Sunstein, Cass, 99, 146

Supreme Court, 2–8, 11, 12–14, 19, 20, 30, 49, 97, 98, 103–9, 117, 119, 124–27, 133–36, 140–43, 150, 187, 205, 210; on Civil War, 61–95. *See also* Fuller Court; Rehnquist Court; Waite Court; Warren Court

Swayne, Noah H., 12, 13, 56, 68, 71–76, · 80, 90, 91, 145

Taney, Roger B., 119

ten Broek, Jacobus, 4, 110, 115

Thirteenth Amendment, 9–12, 23, 24, 28, 32, 33, 42, 45, 72, 73, 76, 80, 83, 87, 92, 94, 114, 218 n.12, 228 n.41

Trumbull, Lyman, 47

Tulis, Jeffrey, 44

Tushnet, Mark, 151

United States v. Blyew, 77

United States v. Cruikshank, 78–80, 82, 83, 92, 106

United States v. Hall, 71, 76, 232 n.38

United States v. Rhodes, 72, 77

VanderVelde, Lea S., 4, 24, 116

Voting rights, 24–28, 47, 197. See also *Reynolds v. Sims;* Fifteenth Amendment

Waite Court, 12, 13, 78–81, 89, 130

Warren Court, 2–7, 11–20, 62, 63, 91, 93, 97, 104, 136, 140, 148, 152, 155–84, 197, 205, 208, 211

Weber, Max, 20

Wesberry v. Sanders, 158, 159

White, G. Edward, 76

White, Hayden, 209

White, James Boyd, 185, 200

White supremacy, 38–41, 53, 148, 166, 171, 213, 214. *See also* Apportionment: racial dimensions of; Northern Democrats: on blacks; Republicans: on blacks

Wiecek, William M., 4, 63, 115

Williams, George H., 82

Williams, Patricia J., 218 n.14

Wilson, Henry, 42
Wilson, James F., 33
Windom, William, 43

Woods, William, 71, 82
Woolgar, Steve, 101
Wright v. Rockefeller, 178

Pamela Brandwein is Assistant Professor of Sociology and
Political Economy in the School of Social Sciences at the
University of Texas at Dallas.

Library of Congress Cataloging-in-Publication Data
Brandwein, Pamela.
Reconstructing reconstruction : the Supreme Court and the
production of historical truth / Pamela Brandwein.
p.   cm.
Includes bibliographical references and index.
ISBN 0-8223-2284-6 (cloth : alk. paper). — ISBN 0-8223-2316-8
(pbk. : alk. paper)
1. Constitutional history—United States.   2. Reconstruction.
3. Slavery—United States—History.   4. Election law—United
States—History.   5. Civil rights—United States—History.
I. Title.
KF4541.B688   1999
342.73'029—dc21   98-35155   CIP